Happiness and Virtue Ethics in Business

Research on happiness has steadily increased over the last decade, with different streams of inquiry converging into what has come to be known as "Modern Happiness Studies" (MHS). In this book, Alejo José G. Sison draws on the latest research in economics and psychology as well as Aristotelian virtue ethics to show why happiness is the ultimate value proposition for business. Using non-technical language and a number of illustrative vignettes, he proposes ways for businesses to cultivate the virtues, providing advice on production and service enhancement, customer satisfaction, employee well-being and overall organizational wellness. This book will appeal to a wide readership, including graduate students and researchers in business ethics, moral philosophy, and positive psychology.

ALEJO JOSÉ G. SISON is Professor in the Philosophy Department, University of Navarre, where his research deals with issues at the juncture of ethics, economics, and politics. He was President of the European Business Ethics Network (EBEN) from 2009 to 2012.

Happiness and Virtue Ethics in Business

The Ultimate Value Proposition

ALEJO JOSÉ G. SISON

CAMBRIDGE
UNIVERSITY PRESS

CAMBRIDGE
UNIVERSITY PRESS

University Printing House, Cambridge CB2 8BS, United Kingdom

Cambridge University Press is part of the University of Cambridge.

It furthers the University's mission by disseminating knowledge in the pursuit of education, learning and research at the highest international levels of excellence.

www.cambridge.org
Information on this title: www.cambridge.org/9781107044630

© Alejo José G. Sison 2015

First published 2015

A catalogue record for this publication is available from the British Library

ISBN 978-1-107-04463-0 Hardback

Para ken ni Mamang ko,
Karagsakan ti biag.

Contents

Figure

Foreword

This is a beautifully written book, rich in information, useful even to a wide audience, and easy to read. Sison's essay fulfills two main functions. On the one hand, it brings new and persuasive arguments to bear on the "happiness paradox," first introduced by Richard Easterlin in 1974. On the other hand, the book suggests how to overcome the paradox, relying on recent advances in neurosciences, particularly in neuroeconomics, and in biotechnology regarding memory and mood. All in all, Sison speaks in favor of a decisive resumption of virtue ethics in order "to learn to be happy."

Recent well-known developments in happiness and economics mark a strong revival of reciprocal interest between economists and managerial scientists, on one side, and moral philosophers, on the other. Happiness is back in economics, although it is not a new concept in the tradition of economics. We find it at the very beginning of modern economic science, when it was clear to everyone that the common good is not simply the unintended result of individual search for private interest. Indeed, self-interest can be transformed into public happiness not spontaneously, but only within the norms and institutions of civil life. The history of economic thought informs us that it is with the advent of the marginalistic revolution that the category of utility completely superseded that of happiness within economics. And since then, it has tended to be referred to as the "dismal science."

Mainstream economics has been characterized, up to now, by an anthropology based on solipsism and instrumental rationality, which leaves no room for understanding the issue of happiness that, ontologically, depends on non-instrumental interpersonal relationships. Twentieth-century economics has become a science which studies instrumental interactions among individuals. The interpersonal dimension enters into play only when and if it affects individual utility. Today, as Sison clearly shows, no one believes any longer that this choice of anthropological reductionism is of any help in allowing the discipline to grasp the new and big problems afflicting our societies. The fact is that within the utilitarian perspective, one sees the "other" as a mere instrument for the attainment of utilitarian goals. But it is common knowledge that happiness postulates the existence of the "other" as an end in itself. It takes two to be happy – Aristotle used to say – whereas one can maximize his or her utility alone.

Another important message derives from this book. In a rightly famous essay, Romano Guardini writes: "The human person cannot understand himself as if closed within himself, because he exists in the form of a relation. Although the person is not born from an encounter, it is certain that he becomes real only in the encounter" (Guardini 1964: 90). If human beings discover themselves in interpersonal relationships, and fulfill themselves in their relations with others, it follows that their fundamental need is one of relationality. If we think about it, the demand for a better quality of life goes well beyond the simple demand for goods "made well." Rather, it is a demand for care, for participation – in other words, for relationality. The quality we increasingly hear about today does not just involve consumer products, but also (and perhaps above all) human relations. If it is true, as I believe it is, that the quality of life is measured along the axis of freedom, perceived as the possibility of self-realization, whereas increases in per capita income only point to individuals' greater spending power, then it is equally true that interpersonal relationships are real goods, and as such cannot be excluded from economic discourse.

What is characteristic of the human person is relationality – the fact that the other becomes a *you*. If my being in relation to another can only be justified in terms of opportunity – the opportunity to obtain consensus or to resolve conflicts, as the neo-contractualist school of thought would have it – I shall never be able to escape from the "unsociable sociability" Kant spoke of. In this case, I shall of course be free in the sense of self-determination, but certainly not in the much weightier sense of self-realization, since freedom as self-realization requires relating to others as a value in itself. If it is true that today no one is any longer prepared to dissolve his or her "I" into any kind of "we," it is equally true that the alternative cannot be the social atom, so dear to individualist thinking, but an "I-person" who does not accept dissolving into any kind of mechanism, even if it is an efficient one like the market.

It follows that the full realization of personal identity cannot be limited to mere respect for the freedom of others, as liberal–individualistic philosophy, for which living together is an option, would have it. We know, in fact, that for each of us this is just not the case. The choice is never between living in solitude and living in society, but between living in a society according to one set of rules or another. The radical perception of freedom claims that it is simply not enough to think of individuality by leaving out relationships with others. If it is true that personal identity derives from our relationships with others, then reducing happiness to utility would prevent us from gaining a proper understanding of a fundamental element of personal wellbeing.

What is the ultimate foundation of interpersonal relationships? The principle of self-preservation. My fundamental aim, that I be preserved in time, cannot be achieved if I isolate myself from others. I need other human beings to judge whether I am worth preserving. Do they have grounds for doing so? They certainly do, since they themselves need to be recognized by me as worth preserving. In needing the same form of recognition, I act as a mirror. Preservation of the self is the outcome of this interaction. The original resource a human being can offer to another is the capacity to recognize the worth of the other to exist, a resource that can only be produced if it is shared. In this way, recognizing other human beings as ends in themselves, and recognizing the same human beings as means to the end of preserving oneself, are united. The good of self-preservation is achieved. The fact that recognizing others brings about the reciprocal recognition that oneself needs, does not make this attitude merely instrumental. Oneself is constituted by the recognition thereof by the other. A person's capacity to calculate the means needed to achieve a given end depends on the achievement of reciprocal recognition. This is why one can say that mutual recognition is basically antecedent to self-interest. Before becoming a possible means for individual ends, the interaction with others appears as an end in itself. Individual ends themselves emerge because such interaction is possible. Recognition of the other person's reality and the possibility of putting yourself in his or her place is of essential importance. Another person's interests are someone's interests as much as yours are.

Sison's well-written, jargon-free book will capture the attention of anyone seriously interested in the future of our market systems. There is nothing to marvel at here. When one acknowledges the looming crisis of our civilization, one is practically obliged to abandon any dystopic attitude and dare to seek out new paths of thought.

Stefano Zamagni
Professor of Economics, University of Bologna
Adjunct Professor of International Economics,
Johns Hopkins University, SAIS Europe

REFERENCE

Guardini, R. 1964. *Scritti filosofici*, vol. II. Milan: Vita e Pensiero.

Preface

– Are you happy? And why?

– Absolutely, absolutely. I'm happy! And it's a tranquil happiness because at this age one no longer has the same happiness of a young person, there's a difference. There's a certain interior peace, a strong sense of peace, of happiness, that comes with age. But it's a road that has always had problems. Even now there are problems but this happiness doesn't go away because of the problems. No, it sees the problems, suffers because of them and then goes forward, it does something to resolve them and goes ahead. But in the depth of my heart there is this peace and happiness. It's truly a grace from God, for me. It's a grace and it's not through my own merit.

Pope Francis
March 31, 2014

A sure-fire way of boosting happiness, we are told, is by writing gratitude letters. So perhaps there's no better way to start than by heeding this piece of advice.

First of all, I'd like to thank my parents, Angel (+) and Asuncion; my siblings, their spouses, my nieces and nephews, Jay, Baby, and David; Maripi, Art, Michelle, and Peej; Josephine; Pio (+), Connie, Benjel, Francis, Joey, and Princess; Eric, Libby, JV, Kim, Cholo, Miko, Maricris, Lizelle, France, and EJ; Mai (+); Lung; Corito; Boyet, Cherry, Egon, Peter, and Joseph; Felix, Josie, Angeli, Monica, Felicia, and Karlene; and of course, Chet.

My mentor, Rafael Alvira.

My friends and colleagues, for their generous ear and steady encouragement while this project was taking shape, and in particular, Antonio Argandoña and Arps de Vera, for their unwavering support.

My students in Pamplona, Barcelona, Manila, and Guatemala.

My editors, Paula Parish and Claire Wood.

And most especially, Bishop Álvaro del Portillo (+), from whose fatherly care I benefited during so many years.

Alejo José G. Sison
Madrid
September 27, 2014

Introduction

The ultimate value proposition

Crises can be healthy and sobering. In the midst of what some now call the "Great Recession," the Harvard Business School graduating class of 2010, fully aware of the dreadful employment possibilities and greatly reduced earning capacities from which perhaps they would never recover, asked professor Clayton Christensen (2010) to address them on how to apply management principles and techniques to their lives. Surprisingly, he focused not on any grand business or management idea, but on happiness and meaning as the measure of one's life. In characteristic business school fashion, he articulated his response in three simple steps.

The first consists in asking oneself, "How can I be happy in my career?" This entails a serious inquiry on the meaning of happiness and on what one's most powerful motivation in work and in life really is. It usually doesn't take long for people to realize that it is not so much about stellar performance, exceptional financial gain, or outstanding business success. Rather, it's more about taking responsibility to help others learn and grow, and reveling in those shared achievements. A very poor and even mistaken idea is to think of management simply as "making money" by "doing deals," buying and selling companies when the opportunity arises. The short-term rewards this provides pales in comparison to the deep and lasting satisfaction that building up people bestows. It seems, then, that happiness has to do more with one's end-goal or purpose in life, than with any immediate business objective.

The second question deals with how family and social relationships, including one's faith, can somehow be transformed into enduring sources of happiness. This step touches on strategy. With the first question, one defines the objective, albeit in broad strokes. Now one engages in a series of investment decisions regarding the different resources at his disposal, such as time, energy, talent, and of course, money. Certainly, resource allocation has to reflect one's set of priorities, with ends taking precedence over means, and higher-order goals over lower-order ones. Christensen (2010) himself speaks of his struggles to maintain coherence in the face of competing demands from his wife, children, church, community, career, company, and so forth. When called upon to take on leadership roles, one needs to rely on "tools of cooperation" which help align goals and interventions among the different participants or members of the organization. These refer to a variety of "instruments of persuasion," from threats of punishment to empathy, which the leader deftly employs depending on the people, times, and places he encounters, in order to build up consensus within the group (Sison 2003). Through reinforcement and repetition, this consensus becomes, in due course, the foundation for an organizational or corporate culture. This describes a distinctive way of doing things which gently nudges people's behavior almost effortlessly toward the desired direction. At the same time, however, Christensen (2010) warns of the temptation of "instant gratification" or the tendency to pursue only what produces immediate results, probably as proof of one's effectiveness and efficiency. For indeed, highly driven people find it difficult to see beyond quarterly objectives – they think, "close the sale now and get the hefty bonus soon after," for instance – while they systematically underinvest in projects that may take years to bear fruit, if ever, such as raising a child properly. The first one gives them a surge and an ego-boost, while the second forces them to face their own limitations and grapple with a part of reality they can't control.

Lastly comes the issue of how to live a life of integrity, or at the very least, how to keep oneself out of jail. After all, among Christensen's classmates at Harvard Business School was Jeffrey Skilling, former Enron CEO, convicted of nineteen counts of conspiracy, securities fraud, insider trading, and lying to auditors, for which he received a 24-year sentence. Christensen (2010) suggests forgetting what one has learned in finance and microeconomics, about basing decisions on the marginal costs and marginal revenues of alternative lines of action. Telling oneself, "I know this is wrong in general, but in this particular case, the marginal cost of doing it just once seems negligible" could end up justifying the most horrendous acts of dishonesty and unfaithfulness to commitments in the long run. We are definitely not in want of examples for this. People change through their actions, and without them even noticing, they could very easily fall down to the very bottom of the slippery slope. Hence it is best, and actually even easier, to stick to one's guns and uphold the principles one wishes to live by 100 percent of the time, rather than just aiming for 98 percent compliance. In the business of managing one's life, marginal thinking brings ruin, for in the end, one always pays a full cost that one may have never even imagined at first.

Christensen's experience furnishes some compelling reasons on the need for a book on happiness directed mainly, though not exclusively, to business people. For business, just like any other economic activity for that matter, does not take place in a vacuum, nor even in that useful abstraction customarily referred to as the "market." Rather, building up a business actually only makes sense within the context of a life and a dense web of social roles and relations, including one's family, community, professional group, church, school, civil society, country, and so forth. So one first needs to see and, in fact, never lose sight of this wider picture, even before setting the standards with which success, both in business and in life, is to be measured.

Providing goods and services that satisfy society's needs and wants would almost certainly figure in any textbook account of an entrepreneur's function. But why anyone should, in the final analysis, want to take on the risks and challenges it involves, with the enormous amount of work it implies, is something on which all manuals fall silent. A similar thing happens regarding the importance of satisfying people's desires, an issue which most authors simply prefer to take for granted. Is any and every desire equally worth satisfying? Then what are we to do in the face of conflicts and limited resources? In a market-oriented society such as ours, it should be fairly easy to know what needs and wants are, as well as the specific kinds of products that cater to them. However, why do consumers choose some particular brands or items instead of others? What is it that makes those goods so appealing and likeable? Surely, there ought to be something, too, in consumers' psychological makeup that could, at least partly, explain their preferences and choices. How do these instances of desire and motivation work? What influence do the different demographic and cultural markers exert? Are institutional constraints of any significance?

Underlying the above-mentioned queries is the topic of happiness. Happiness is truly the ultimate business proposition. It is the end-goal of all wants and desires, and the object of all promises. All economic operations and transactions are merely intermediate steps which hopefully will lead in the end to happiness.

Besides the entrepreneur, there's another business type called the "manager." He is the one entrusted with the task of ensuring that production goes on smoothly, in order to deliver the highest returns to the firm's owners and investors, we are often told. But is that all? Should profits be sought single-mindedly, regardless of the welfare of workers, clients or consumers, the environment, and society at large? Probably not. At this stage, almost everyone acknowledges the manager's responsibility for the safety and quality of his company's products, the conditions in which these goods are manufactured, and their overall impact on the planet. There is also a growing consciousness that managerial duties are not directed to the providers of capital alone, but to other stakeholders as well, such as workers, suppliers, consumers, competitors, local communities, government, the environment, and so forth. In fact, "stakeholder happiness enhancement" (Jones and Felps 2013) has even been proposed as an objective for the modern corporation.

Again, implicit in all these considerations is the concern for happiness. Particularly, in the case of workers, a manager would like to know the key factors that contribute to job satisfaction insofar as it is linked to productivity, for instance. Such knowledge could then serve as a guide in implementing the right policies in recruitment, compensation, training, and governance (Sison 2008). Happiness is what makes people working in a company thrive.

Be it as entrepreneurs or as managers, business people are above all human beings who as such have an inexorable interest in happiness. Our purpose is to guide them in their search, presenting the best results of modern happiness studies, complemented with the enduring intuitions of Aristotelian virtue ethics. Just like Christensen, we'd like to accompany the reader along three main steps. The first lies in discerning what happiness means and how it can be measured (Chapter 1); the second, in designing resource allocation strategies for different contributory factors, such as income, psychological pleasures and satisfactions, work and leisure, and institutions (Chapters 2–6); and finally, the third, in discovering the integrative power of virtue that goes beyond merely "having" and "doing" to "becoming" truly happy (Chapter 7 and the conclusion).

PLAN OF THE BOOK

Here's the book plan at a glance:

Chapter 1 Modern happiness studies and "individual subjective wellbeing": you only get what you measure. This introductory chapter deals with the distinctive features of modern happiness studies and its object, individual subjective wellbeing. Unlike "classical" studies on happiness, this novel approach distinguishes itself in being truly "scientific": that is, empirical and quantitative. The methodological controversies between welfare economists and hedonic psychologists regarding wellbeing and its measurement are discussed, as well as the possible ways of overcoming them through narrative.

Chapter 2 Happiness and income: how much happiness can money buy? This chapter starts off with an exposition of the Easterlin Paradox – "An increase in income does not necessarily entail an increase in individual subjective wellbeing" – set against the dominant neoclassical economic background. It then continues with a detailed critique, explaining the limits in which income, whether absolute or relative, affects subjective wellbeing of the individual and the group. The field thus opens up to other social sciences, such as sociology and political science, insofar as these employ empirical and quantitative methods. As a point of contrast, references are made to a multidimensional account of poverty and inequality, as well as their consequences for happiness.

Chapter 3 Choice, desire, and pleasure: is happiness getting what you want or wanting what you get? The impact of different consumption models on happiness is presented. Above a fairly low threshold of income, it is no longer how much money one has, but how one spends it that matters. Stories of how scaled-down lifestyles result in greater subjective wellbeing are included. This chapter deals with Scitovsky's observation that the market economy often fails to deliver happiness and wellbeing, despite abundant resources and a wide range of choices. At the root of this failure are certain psychological mechanisms involving choices, desires, and pleasures that are usually ignored. Explanations are offered of how early education within the family and character-building exercises influence the transformation of desires.

Chapter 4 The biotechnology of happiness: not just a "quick fix." Inputs from cutting-edge research in the fields of decision theory, neuroscience, neuroeconomics, and biotechnology, regarding memory and mood, are discussed. The key to properly managing these challenges lies, above all, in education, particularly in appropriate habit-formation.

Chapter 5 Working on happiness. Work is a two-faced Janus that detracts from and contributes to happiness at the same time. We discover how the loss of work exerts a strong downward pressure not only on the happiness of individuals, but also on the other members of society who may even continue working. This may be attributed to two kinds of causes, some psychological or individual, and others, social. We look into how these causes affect people differently, depending on demographic factors such as sex, age, education and so forth. We also examine the importance of job satisfaction for general wellbeing. Although favorable work conditions are essential to happiness, they are not a substitute for the sense of autonomy, mastery, and purpose that individuals experience while working. In other words, intrinsic motivation outweighs extrinsic motivation in workplace satisfaction. Empirical studies reveal that, while extrinsic motivation may be sufficient for purely mechanical or routine work, this isn't so for creative, intellectual work, which requires intrinsic motivation. Under certain conditions, extrinsic motivation may even expel intrinsic motivation. The links between happiness and leisure, a lot more complex than normally imagined, will similarly be studied. The chapter ends with a description of how inflation affects happiness in a manner not foreseen by neoclassical economics.

Chapter 6 Happiness, politics, and religion: now and at the hour of our death. Despite widespread belief to the contrary, happiness is never achieved by an individual in isolation. Much of it depends on the quality of social institutions which mediate between individuals and their environment. Differences in institutions – the way societies are organized, their rules and customs – account for major variations in levels of happiness. This chapter focuses on how liberal democracies and free market regimes generally boost the wellbeing of citizens, while autocratic or state-controlled governments suppress it. Similarly, adherents of "open market" faiths report higher levels of satisfaction than followers of "monopolistic" creeds. Explanations could often be traced to varying levels of voluntary participation, which are linked to autonomy and an internal locus of control.

Chapter 7 Aristotelian virtue ethics: the forgotten philosophical tradition on happiness. A recap is proffered of the major gains of modern happiness studies in our understanding of individual subjective wellbeing, together with its deficiencies. We detect a lack of integration of what would otherwise be valid inputs from economics, psychology, sociology, political science, and so forth. This signals the need for a philosophical approach widely construed; one that looks into the radical principles or causes of human flourishing. This moves us to revisit Aristotle's indications of what constitutes happiness (*eudaimonia*) for human beings. We shall integrate data regarding income, pleasure, work, consumption, institutions, and so forth into the different kinds of lifestyles that Aristotle considers in the *Nicomachean Ethics*. Thus, we discover the pre-eminent role assigned to virtue, in its capacity to weave external and material factors into a life conceived as a meaningful whole. This chapter constitutes a defense of virtue in attaining happiness.

Conclusion: learning to be happy. This final chapter revisits the business types of the entrepreneur and the manager. It examines lessons on how modern happiness studies combined with Aristotelian virtue ethics contribute to their flourishing as professionals and human beings.

One last note before reading on. Whoever expects to find in this book a unique, newfangled, and extensive treatment of Aristotle's theory on happiness and the virtues may be in for a disappointment. In fact, such topics are not dealt with in earnest until the penultimate chapter, when the book is about to come to a close. No matter how meritorious such an effort may be, it is not this volume's actual purpose. Rather, the objective it seeks to achieve is far more modest, and consists in calling attention to the gaping hole that exists in modern happiness studies insofar as it neglects or chooses to ignore virtue ethics.

Although most happiness researchers nowadays acknowledge Aristotle's pioneering work and even mention his idea of flourishing or *eudaimonia* in passing, hardly anyone stops to seriously consider the crucial role that virtue plays in attaining it. This is to some extent understandable, given that the majority of these investigators have been trained, after all, either as welfare economists or as experimental psychologists, and not as philosophers. But we believe there is much value to be gained by bringing virtue once again to the discussion table when happiness is at stake, the undeniable gains of empirical and quantitative methods of research notwithstanding. We believe virtue ethics has so much to offer in clarifying, if not in outrightly solving many of the difficulties that modern happiness studies currently encounters. Only after exploring, to the best of our knowledge, the limits which modern happiness studies has reached, do we then, with a certain degree of confidence, introduce the ways in which we think Aristotelian virtue ethics may amend and complement it. The time has come for Aristotelian virtue ethics to come to the aid of modern happiness studies, so to speak, and to remedy its crippling amnesia. We should all be a lot better off for it.

REFERENCES

Christensen, C. 2010. "How will you measure your life?," *Harvard Business Review*, July (http://hbr.org/2010/07/how-will-you-measure-your-life/ accessed March 4, 2014).

Jones, T. M. and Felps, W. 2013. "Stakeholder happiness enhancement: A neo-utilitarian objective for the modern corporation," *Business Ethics Quarterly*, 23 (3): 349–379.

Sison, A. J. G. 2003. *The moral capital of leaders: Why virtue matters*. Cheltenham, UK/Northampton, MA: Edward Elgar.

Corporate governance and ethics: An Aristotelian perspective. Cheltenham, UK/Northampton, MA: Edward Elgar.

I Modern happiness studies and "individual subjective wellbeing"

You only get what you measure

Seldom is one able to pinpoint the birth of a new branch of knowledge or scientific discipline. But that, precisely, is what occurred in 1974 with "modern happiness studies," as it has come to be known, when Richard Easterlin published his essay "Does economic growth improve the human lot? Some empirical evidence" (Easterlin 1974). This article was Easterlin's contribution to the *Festschrift* in honor of Moses Abramovitz. In his research, Abramovitz had challenged the neoclassical orthodoxy in economics regarding a positive correlation between output, on the one hand, and welfare or wellbeing, on the other. Even before that, however, Arthur Pigou had already set the stage for the discussion. Although Pigou acknowledged that "happiness," understood as social welfare, was a much broader concept than economic welfare, normally measured in terms of "gross national product" (GNP), he nevertheless suggested that both indicators moved in tandem, if not by the same intervals, at least always in the same direction. Abramovitz was probably the first to raise a voice of dissent. He suspected that an increase in output could very well trigger higher expectations among economic agents, thereby cancelling out foreseeable improvements in welfare, but he never managed to confirm the hypothesis. This task was left for Easterlin to carry out.

What exactly was "modern" or new with the discipline that Easterlin had inaugurated? Obviously, it could not have been the topic itself, since happiness, in a broad sense, and our yearning for it, had always been present in the human mind. It had to be, then, the approach or method, at once empirical and quantitative, with which happiness was examined. As a result of this novel, typically scientific mode of inquiry, several characteristics or features were introduced into the subject matter under discussion. Happiness had morphed into what we now call "individual subjective wellbeing."

Easterlin, the "Father of Modern Happiness Studies," gathered data based on "self-reports" – statements or responses that individuals make about themselves, their frame of mind, mood, outlook, feelings, and so forth. He depended on two sources, Gallup polls and surveys using Cantril's (1965) "self-anchoring striving scales." In the Gallup polls, respondents were first primed with the question, "In your own words, what does 'happiness' mean to you?" Afterwards, they were queried, "In general, how happy would you say that you are – very happy, fairly happy or not very happy?" Using the Cantril scales is a tad more complicated. Initially, individuals are asked to describe, according to their own views, the two extremes or "anchors" of the range of happiness, where "ten" represents maximum or absolute happiness and "zero" the complete lack of happiness. Immediately after, people are requested to give a number from "zero" to "ten" which best captures their state. Clearly, both forms of inquiry comply with the requirements for positive scientific knowledge: that is, they are based on experience and linked to numerical values.

In succeeding years, these techniques have given rise to a variety of similar methods of inquiry regarding individual subjective wellbeing. They have been included in the US General Social Surveys (Davis, Smith, and Marsden 2001), the Eurobarometer Surveys, and the World Values Survey (Inglehardt et al. 2000), among others.

Probably the biggest advantage of Easterlin's chosen method for determining happiness, however crude, is that it avoids getting mired in an unending philosophical discussion about what happiness really means or should mean. Happiness is whatever the subject takes it to be: "individual subjective wellbeing" understood more as a descriptive term a person may use for himself than as the name or label of any thing or object that others necessarily recognize as such. After all, happiness could only exist insofar as it is experienced individually and subjectively, never in the abstract as a detached reality.

Therefore, it makes sense to acknowledge that people themselves are the best judges of their overall state or position with regard to happiness, given a frame of reference. They should have the final word. Of course, numerous objections can be raised, from doubts on the ability of individuals to "correctly" assess their own states (they may be "wrong") to the chance that they may be intentionally misleading the interviewer (they may be lying). Respondents may inadvertently mistake happiness for what is, in truth, something else, such as a fleeting or "false" pleasure. Or they may erroneously calibrate the degree or intensity of the experience, giving it an "eight" when it should be a "five," in fact. Also, in interpersonal comparisons, it may occur that two individuals assign the same numerical value to completely different mental states, or on the contrary, assign different numerical values to equivalent mental states. Similarly, the very possibility that happiness has a collective or social dimension, and that countries and traditions have a role in determining the happiness one experiences, seems to be ignored. It is assumed, rather, that under the guise of individual subjective wellbeing, happiness belongs to each person alone and in particular, beyond the reach of anyone else's influence.

This tension between the objective and the subjective view of happiness had been at the background of Easterlin's work from the very beginning. By overly insisting on objective and external indicators, such as GNP and income, that could be verified by any third-party observer, he thought that welfare economists like himself ran a serious risk of becoming irrelevant in the study of subjective wellbeing or happiness. Even GNP itself was much criticized as an indicator, and it was viewed by many as a mere excuse for greater state intervention, insofar as it served as basis for tax collection (Johns and Ormerod 2007). No one, least of all welfare economists, could afford to be entirely dismissive of what people believe, think, or say regarding their own happiness. Poised to take over the field while coming from the opposite end of the spectrum were the "hedonic psychologists," those who specialize in the study of the experience of pleasure or wellbeing (or, indeed, their opposites, pain and misery). They take as data exactly what welfare economists leave out: that is, the things people say about their own feelings and behaviors. Oftentimes, this information is interpreted in light of identifiable personality traits, such as extraversion or neuroticism, for which heredity and heritability are determining factors. If they are considered at all, objective economic conditions, such as GNP and per capita income, are only taken into account in a manner secondary to subjective elements, such as psychological makeup and genetics. For hedonic psychologists, therefore, happiness or subjective wellbeing was a matter to be decided within the limits of one's own skin, whereas for welfare economists, it was an issue to be settled, above all, by data coming from without.

In expressing his fears, Easterlin was prescient, to a large extent, on the diminishing impact of purely objective or economic measures on happiness or wellbeing. The inadequacy of income per capita in dealing with distributional issues, differences in prices and purchasing power, and availability of basic goods and services is well known. Indeed, income per capita in a country would remain unchanged, even if all the money were in the hands of just one person and a functioning market were completely absent. A second indicator of welfare, the so-called of a socioeconomic class in a given area, represents a marked improvement, therefore, insofar as it complements income per capita with other bits of information regarding health, education, employment, housing, and so forth. Moreover, this measure of material comfort or wellbeing could be further enriched with data on the civil rights and political liberties enjoyed by a given population through the "quality of life" index. The "quality of life" index, in turn, may also be enhanced through an analysis of "capabilities" and "functionings," the worthwhile activities in which individuals may freely engage and which they integrate into their lives in the quest to achieve fulfillment or flourishing (Nussbaum and Sen 1993). Despite attempts to broaden the definition of "quality of life" to include people's perceptions, thoughts, and feelings, nonetheless, it normally refers only to the external components or conditions that make life desirable.

Indeed, there are several possible objective metrics of happiness, and the choice among them is not at all a value-free one. Rather, it reflects what a society truly values, and sets the standard by which its general performance is to be measured. For instance, a country that has opted to focus on GNP, stock indices, and trade data sends the signal that it has the interests of businesses and financial institutions at the forefront, while leaving other at least equally valid concerns, such as equity and social mobility, to occupy much lower ranks among its priorities (Graham 2011).

Several reasons prodded Easterlin to go against the welfare economic orthodoxy of his time, regarding the futility of drawing scientific conclusions based on statements made by individuals or groups about their subjective wellbeing or happiness (Easterlin 2002: ix–x). Some proceed from economic studies and others from findings made by psychologists. Among the observations of economists were positive correlations, at a given point in time, between levels of subjective wellbeing and income, and through a given period or longitudinally, between subjective wellbeing and educational levels, for instance. Similarly, negative correlations were detected between levels of subjective wellbeing, on the one hand, and unemployment and inflation rates, on the other, for a given population. If self-reports on subjective wellbeing were entirely "unscientific," in the sense of being arbitrary or without a solid base, then it would be very difficult to account for consistent correlations with hard, economic facts. Self-reports on subjective wellbeing, therefore, seem to be congruent with possible predictions based on objective economic data such as income, educational levels, and rates of unemployment and inflation, to name a few.

As for the arguments coming from psychology, it was discovered that self-reports on happiness largely concurred with reports and evaluations made by professional psychologists, peers, friends, and relatives of individuals. Also, positive self-reports on happiness correlate with better health and lower incidences of depression or suicide. Again, none of this would happen if what was contained or expressed by self-reports were completely opaque to anyone else, aside from the individuals themselves. Contrary to what appears at first glance, there may be something objectively scientific even in subjective self-reports on happiness. The hard, objective, and externally observable data favored by economists and the soft, subjective self-reports used by psychologists, despite the disparity of their methods, seem to converge on the same thing. Moreover, properly utilizing the two basic approaches together, rather than just one or the other, could prove to be advantageous for the progress or development of the nascent field. And this is what Easterlin was to accomplish with his ground-breaking work on income and happiness, which we will analyze in due course.

But first, let us have a closer look at the different ways of measuring happiness, initially, as individual subjective wellbeing, and the difficulties they entail.

MEASURING HAPPINESS

So far we have outlined the two major approaches in measuring happiness, intuitively understood as "individual subjective wellbeing," in early modern happiness studies. One is objective, taking happiness to be a function of externally observable economic data or indicators such as GNP, income, unemployment, inflation, and so forth. The other is subjective, diagnosing happiness through self-reports or statements regarding an individual's psychological or mental state. We have also seen how both approaches lend themselves to spot checks on happiness on a single occasion, or longitudinal observations of happiness through a given period of time.

Modern happiness studies distances itself from mainstream economics by choosing to examine individual subjective wellbeing rather than objective conditions such as income, standard of living, quality of life, and so forth. Although happiness, indeed, has several meanings, both in ordinary speech and in scholarly literature, positive emotions, pleasant feelings, and good moods seem essential. They form the core of individual subjective wellbeing, the umbrella concept that covers the positive evaluations people make of their lives (with negative evaluations accounting for "illbeing"). In fact, subjective wellbeing may be thought of as the level of positive affect minus the level of negative affect experienced at a given moment by individuals, as indicated by the PANAS scales (Watson, Clark, and Tellegen 1988), for instance. Examples of positive affect – pleasant moods, emotions, or reactions – are joy and affection. Through varying degrees of intensity or arousal, they signify that life proceeds in a desirable way, just as one wishes. Anger and sadness, on the other hand, represent examples of negative affect. Their occurrence in different intensities shows that life for the individual is not going on as desired or planned. As we have seen earlier, individual subjective wellbeing manifests itself in several ways, through both verbal and non-verbal behaviors.

We shall now consider the wide variety of measurement strategies linked to an idea of happiness as pleasant feelings, emotions, or moods. A first group consists of global or overall assessments of life as a whole. A "life satisfaction" survey, for instance, reveals either an individual's appraisal of all the different areas or domains of life at a given moment, or an integrative evaluation of his life from the time of birth to the present. A second group is composed of domain-specific or episodic assessments of one's life. Among major life domains usually included in surveys are physical and mental health, work, leisure, social relationships, and family. Episodic assessments refer to evaluations of particular activities, together with the time, place, and context in which such activities occur.

In line with the global or overall assessments are, among others, the "Satisfaction with Life Scale," the "Flourishing Scale," the "Approaches to Happiness Questionnaire," the "Authentic Happiness Inventory," the "Fordyce Emotions Questionnaire," and the "General Happiness Questionnaire." And more akin to the domain-specific or episodic assessments are, among others, the "Experience Sampling Method" also known as "Ecological Momentary Assessment," the "Day Reconstruction Method," and other diary methods that aim to assess people's experiences online in specific activities and situations. Let us go through them briefly.

Among the first techniques essayed is the "Satisfaction with Life Scale," devised by Diener and associates, which seeks to measure "global cognitive judgments of satisfaction with one's life" (Diener et al. 1985). This instrument is composed of five statements – "In most ways, my life is close to ideal," "The conditions of my life are excellent," "I am completely satisfied with my life," "So far I have gotten the most important things I want in life," and "If I could live my life over, I would change nothing" – to which an individual is supposed to indicate his agreement in accordance with a scale from "1 – Strongly disagree" to "7 – Strongly agree." The final score is then tallied, such that the uppermost range, 31–35, corresponds to "Extremely satisfied" and the lowermost range, 5–9, corresponds to "Extremely dissatisfied." The designers of this scale admit that there is no single key to life satisfaction, and that it results, rather, from several factors: social relationships; performance at work, school, or in some other important role; and personal satisfaction. People with high life satisfaction scores tend to have close and supportive relationships with family and friends, and excellent performance in their professional life and roles, making the activities in which they engage more enjoyable. They also tend to be content with themselves, their religious or spiritual life, their learning, growth, and leisure. Life satisfaction, though, can change with time, effort, and some external circumstances. The loss of a family member or a close friend can cause dissatisfaction with life, although with time, usually, people recover. Likewise, those who are dissatisfied with life and suffer from poor performance at work could, at a given moment, switch to a job which better fits their strengths or one more aligned with their goals and values.

A later alternative, also elaborated by Diener and colleagues, is the "Flourishing Scale" (Diener et al. 2010). Through a procedure similar to the "Satisfaction with Life Scale," the respondent is asked to rate eight statements covering areas such as relationships, self-esteem, purpose, engagement, competence, and optimism. Once added up, the final score is supposed to reflect the individual's psychological wellbeing (that's why it was formerly known as the "Psychological Wellbeing Scale"). The higher the number, the greater the subject's psychological strengths and resources, as well as his self-perceived success. For some, this goes beyond "psychological wellbeing" narrowly defined: that is, wellbeing concentrated on positive hedonic experience or positive affect.

Crafted by Peterson (2003), the "Approaches to Happiness Questionnaire" contains eighteen propositions such as "My life serves a higher purpose" or "What I do matters to society" that many people find positive and desirable. These are divided into three categories representing possible approaches to happiness: engagement (strength of relationships in work, love, friendship, leisure, and parenting), meaning (belief and service to something larger than oneself), and pleasure (quantity and intensity of pleasant experiences). The respondent is then asked to reflect on the extent to which such statements actually describe the way he lives his life, with options ranging from "5 – Very much like me" to "1 – Not like me at all." Results are afterwards compared with each of the three approaches or categories. In interpreting the scores, we are told that higher values in engagement and meaning have been shown to lead to greater life satisfaction; while, contrary to what many are wont to think, higher values in pleasure do not seem to increase life satisfaction.

Another instrument also created by Peterson (2005) is the "Authentic Happiness Inventory Questionnaire." It purports to measure "overall happiness" in terms of "positive emotions" such as peace, gratitude, satisfactions, pleasure, and so forth. Presented are twenty-four groups of statements in which the respondent is supposed to select, from among five options, the one with which he feels most closely identified. For example, group one offers the following choices:

I feel like a failure.
I do not feel like a winner.
I feel like I have succeeded more than most people.
As I look back on life, all I see are victories.
I feel I am extraordinarily successful.

Surprisingly, however, no claims are made in the end regarding the final score one obtains and its relation to happiness, except how one fares in comparison to other people who have taken the test, classified in terms of sex, age, and so forth.

Similarly focusing on the positive emotion component is the "Fordyce Emotions Questionnaire," which measures "current happiness" (Fordyce 1988). It consists of two questions. The first measures perceived happiness or unhappiness through an eleven-point scale, ranging from (0) "extremely unhappy" to (10) "extremely happy." The second estimates the percentage of time the individual feels happy, unhappy, or neutral (neither happy nor unhappy), from a total of 100 percent. Thus, it indicates not only the quality or intensity but also the frequency or duration of current happiness.

Again centering on emotions as indicative of "enduring happiness" is the "General Happiness Questionnaire," also known as the "Subjective Happiness Scale" (Lyubomirsky and Lepper 1999). By means of a four-item test about how happy one considers himself in general, compared to his peers, compared to very happy people, and compared to not very happy people in a seven-point scale, we obtain a measure of "global happiness" or "global subjective wellbeing." Unlike the "Satisfaction with Life Scales," which only looks into the cognitive component, or the "Fordyce Emotions Questionnaire," which investigates the affective component alone, this instrument claims to integrate both in a more comprehensive view of psychological wellbeing.

Practically all of these global methods of assessing happiness as individual subjective wellbeing could be accommodated within the context of Seligman's (2011) PERMA theory – an acronym for "Positive Emotion," "Engagement," "Relationships," "Meaning," and "Accomplishment/Achievement" – within the "positive psychology" movement. Building on an earlier work (Seligman 2002), which identified "positive emotions" (feeling good), "engagement" (being absorbed in activities or "flow"), and "meaning" (leading a purposeful life) as the building blocks of happiness, Seligman expands the model by adding two more elements, "relationships" (being authentically connected to others) and "accomplishment/achievement" (having a sense of fulfillment or success in one's endeavors).

Although the emphasis in the above-mentioned global assessments is on affect, nevertheless, they always contain cognitive elements as well. "Affect" refers to people's longer-lasting moods and more fleeting emotions or feelings, insofar as they capture instantaneous evaluations of events and situations. In general terms, affect may either be "positive" – that is, desirable or pleasant – or "negative," as something which we instinctively reject. The "Authentic Happiness Inventory" and the "Fordyce Emotions Questionnaire" center on affect. The cognitive elements allude to judgments as the more rational or intellectual aspect of individual subjective wellbeing. These could be of "satisfaction," when life is overall perceived as favorable, or of "dissatisfaction," when it is perceived to be contrary to our wishes for the most part (Veenhoven 1993). The "Satisfaction with Life Scale," the "Flourishing Scale," and the "Approaches to Happiness Questionnaire" are instruments that address cognitive elements. Some research techniques endeavor to distinguish each of these components – positive affect, negative affect, and (dis-)satisfaction – in the global or overall measure of individual subjective wellbeing (Lucas, Diener, and Suh 1996). The "General Happiness Questionnaire," for instance, seeks to take into account both affect and the cognitive element of individual subjective wellbeing.

Let us now have a look at the domain-specific or episodic methods of inquiry into happiness. Although individuals themselves continue to be the judges of their own thoughts, feelings, and mental states, these are recorded in real time and wherever those individuals happen to be. Thus, possible distortions arising from the memory of those experiences, which are a common feature of global assessments through subjective methods, are mostly avoided (Stone, Shiffman, and DeVries 1999).

The "Experience Sampling Method" (ESM) inquires into an individual's thoughts and affective states at the exact time and place in which an activity is carried out (Larson and Csikszentmihalyi 1983; Hektner, Schmidt, and Csikszentmihalyi 2006). This is done through the sending of signals by means of stopwatches, beepers, or smartphones, at which moment participants are asked, for instance, to note down what they are doing, with whom, whether they are enjoying it, and how much. This could yield interesting information on the activities, company, and times of the day that individuals find most or least satisfying. For example, individuals generally register high levels of wellbeing after meals. This instrument is also known as the "Ecological Momentary Assessment Method" (Stone, Shiffman, and DeVries 1999).

In the observation that ESM is costly, disruptive, and provides little information about uncommon or brief events which may, nonetheless, prove significant, Kahneman et al. (2004) invented the "Day Reconstruction Method" (DRM). This combined experience sampling with time-budget studies to assess how people spend their time and how they experience various activities and settings within the context of a full day, rather than as disconnected moments or episodes. The population sample was composed of more than 900 working women from Texas, with an average age of 38 years and an average household income of $54,700. First, participants were asked to write a diary consisting of a sequence of episodes or events. Next, they were supposed to describe each event and situation, together with the associated feelings experienced. Among the activities registering highest mean ratings of positive affect were intimate relations, to which around 15 minutes a day were dedicated, socializing, and relaxing, in which around 2 hours and 20 minutes a day were spent, and praying or meditating, for which around 25 minutes a day were allotted. On the other hand, lowest mean ratings of positive affect were associated with commuting, which took more than an hour and a half on the reference day, working, which lasted for about 7 hours, and housework, which occupied a little more than an hour. Data obtained from this method also revealed a V-shaped diurnal pattern for tiredness, with the lowest point at around 12 o'clock noon. Similarly, negative affect tended to fall most of the day from its highest point early in the morning.

These techniques of measuring happiness or individual subjective wellbeing are "objective" inasmuch as they conform to the ideal of hedonics as a "physics of happiness." For Kahneman, Diener and Schwartz (1999: 3–10) the building-blocks or "atoms" of happiness understood as pleasure are called "instant utilities," borrowing a phrase from Bentham. These are slices of an individual's purely subjective experience, located on a horizontal axis of pleasure and pain (the good/bad dimension) and on a vertical axis of intensity of the experience (the arousal/lethargy dimension). Apart from purely physical experiences, the "pleasures of the mind" or anticipations of pleasure, together with episodes of "flow" and the influences of mood and focus, have all to be taken into account in the evaluation. An "instant utility" may very well then stand for the strength of disposition to continue or to interrupt the current experience. Units of "instant utilities" are subjected to all sorts of mathematical operations to yield measures of objective happiness over a period of time within a domain of life.

Standard economic theory, however, remains unimpressed and skeptical of most of these developments coming from hedonic psychology and positive psychology in the measurement of happiness as individual subjective wellbeing. It continues to be stubbornly attached to an "objectivist" view (Frey 2008: 15), where happiness is primarily a utility function, deriving from the possession and enjoyment of tangible goods and services: above all, leisure. Certainly "enjoyment" refers to subjective experiences, but these do not fulfill the requirements of objective scientific data observable to neutral third parties. Although subjective experiences cannot be denied, for the sake of good scientific practice, nevertheless, they should be ignored in favor of consumption behaviors. Thus, positive subjective experiences or wellbeing could only be inferred from consumption behaviors or actual choices, which manifest or reveal individual preferences. By themselves, externally observable consumption behaviors, inasmuch as they declare individual choices, are supposed to provide all the necessary information concerning the subject's utilities, both real and expected, to the investigator. These utilities, therefore, are the objective measure of individual subjective wellbeing for mainstream economic thinking.

Such an "objectivist" position has the advantage of avoiding the difficulties encountered by previous theories. Foremost is that of establishing the cardinal utility of different goods and services, thus providing a basis for interpersonal comparison among individual utility functions (Frey 2008: 15). So far, all attempts toward this end have proven futile. However, the stance has also generated problems of its own. Firstly, it presupposes that individuals know exactly what they want and what is best for them. Because of this, they should be able to accurately predict their utilities from the available options. Secondly, it likewise presupposes that individuals unfailingly behave in a rational manner in pursuing their goals. But research findings have all but disproved these two claims in various ways, as we shall see later.

Not only have there been serious inconsistencies detected in preferences, but also all sorts of anomalies in decision making, leaving in doubt that utility can be gleaned from observed choices (Frey 2008: 15–16). Human beings are subject to biases such that their imagined or remembered utility differs significantly from the one they actually experience (Kahneman, Wakker, and Sarin 1997). It then becomes extremely difficult, if not impossible, to properly maximize or optimize one's utility function, as strict rationality would seem to demand. Moreover, apart from the projected outcome utility, the procedural utility, which is of a different sort, likewise needs to be considered. Utility derives or may be expected not only from the results or consequences of choices, but also from the process or act of choosing itself. For instance, the difference between procedural utility and outcome utility partly explains why many people participate in lotteries, despite their very slim chances of winning. The hope and thrill of perhaps winning a prize (procedural utility) makes up for the more than probable loss (outcome utility). There seems to be no other way forward, then, than for standard or mainstream economics to admit its own limitations and to welcome, albeit begrudgingly, inputs from psychology.

Many of the findings of psychology prove complementary, rather than contradictory, to those of economics. Statistical analyses have yielded important correlations among constructs, as well as reliability and consistency in the different findings (Frey 2008: 19–22). Particularly valuable in the reconciliation between "objectivist" economic approaches and "subjectivist" psychological approaches to happiness are the inputs from physiology. For instance, changes in brain electrical activity and heart rate go hand in hand with negative affect reports. And brain scans using functional magnetic resonance imaging (fMRI) techniques show that in people with high levels of subjective wellbeing, the left prefrontal cortex registers greater activity than the right side. Likewise, studies combining brain imaging and biochemical sampling allow us to detect the concentration of neurotransmitters and hormones such as dopamine, serotonin, oxytocin, cortisol, and prolactin, among others, in the blood, as individuals experience good and bad feelings (Ryff, Singer, and Love 2004; Urry et al. 2004).

ISSUES OF MEASUREMENT

It should be crystal clear at this point that attempts at measuring happiness or individual subjective wellbeing are not at all problem-free. The majority of the difficulties encountered are re-editions of those that eighteenth-century utilitarians such as Bentham and Stuart Mill faced. It is certainly not fortuitous that Kahneman, Wakker, and Sarin's very influential 1997 article was entitled "Back to Bentham? Explorations of experienced utility" (Kahneman, Wakker, and Sarin 1997).

For Bentham, happiness boiled down to pleasure, and the objective of his "An introduction to the principles of morals and legislation" (2000) was to present a precise, analytical, and scientific method with which to calculate "utils," the units of pleasure or happiness that a course of action brings. The calculation of "utils" was supposed to serve as a guide for individual and collective decision making among alternative bundles of goods in order to achieve the goal of "the greatest happiness of the greatest number." It was as if our minds were equipped with "hedonometers" or pleasure-calculating machines. Subsequently, this approach was to employ mathematics more extensively – in particular, as a consequence of the "marginalist revolution" – thus paving the way for the transformation of the discipline from "political economy" into "economics." What else is the pervasive recourse in modern economics to cost–benefit analysis as the tool of choice in decision making and the obsession with cost-effectiveness in business, but remnants of Benthamite util-calculation?

However, no amount of mathematical progress, not even the contributions of late nineteenth-century German experimental psychologists, was able to solve the quandary of cardinalism. No agreement could be reached on the cardinal number or "objective value" attached to goods. No matter how hard we try, we do not count "utils" all in the same way because they are not natural units. Another way of saying this is that different goods are incommensurable in the pleasure they produce for each individual. In fact, they are incommensurable not only with regard to different people, but also with regard to the same people in varying circumstances. As a result, the whole enterprise of a scientific approach to happiness was left hanging in the balance.

Earlier on, Francis Ysidro Edgeworth (1994) had suggested that although we cannot strictly count "utils" making use of cardinal numbers, we could, nevertheless, observe that different things produce more or less "utils." In place of cardinality, then, ordinality, or the ranking of alternatives according to more or less, should be sufficient for our happiness or pleasure-calculus. Despite the fact that we could not arrive at common cardinal numbers to assign to specific goods, we could probably still reach a consensus that some goods bring more or less pleasure than others. In consequence, we could take this order of preference as an indicator of the path to follow in our choices. Yet, as any group of friends at an ice cream shop knows or soon discovers, one's preference is not necessarily the same as another's. Ordinal values assigned to goods cannot be generalized, once again blocking the road for a meaningful calculation of "utils" among individuals. This may also be called the problem of intersubjectivity: people's preferences vary.

Until Easterlin's time, the reaction of most economists had been to shift their attention from the calculation of "utils," plagued by the twin ills of cardinalism and ordinalism, to the calculation of output or income, in the measurement of happiness or welfare. The reasoning was that, although money was not equivalent to happiness, nevertheless, it could serve as a measure of one's resources or capacity to engage in activities which, in turn, would bring pleasure or happiness.

In the review of measurements of individual subjective wellbeing in the previous section, we saw that a common feature consisted in asking individuals to situate themselves in a happiness scale bearing several points. These self-reported "scores" or "ratings" were then subjected to technical manipulations and mathematical calculations in order to arrive at some purportedly generalizable conclusions. With varying degrees of audacity or temerity, psychologists, economists, and government experts could, in the end, provide recommendations on how people could improve their happiness levels.

But as McCloskey (2012) has straightforwardly denounced regarding modern happiness studies, despite the appearance of objectivity, precision, and rigor, "It's not science." She cites several reasons in support of her objection. Firstly, modern happiness researchers seem to have confounded the properties of "non-interval" scales with those of "interval" scales in gathering data. For instance, when an individual is asked to rate himself in terms of "very happy," "fairly happy," or "not very happy," he simply chooses, from a variety of options that are conveniently ranked, the one that best reflects or captures his subjective state or mood. This procedure uses a "non-interval" scale which merely arranges a conventional set of available choices. Regardless of how reasonable the choice may be, it does not cease to be arbitrary, in the same way that classifications or points in the scale are arbitrary. Contrast this with the use of "interval" scales, such as Fahrenheit, Celsius, or Kelvin, in measuring temperature in degrees. Comparing temperatures on any one of these scales does not yield arbitrary results. To try to draw scientific or quantitative inferences from "non-interval" scales in modern happiness studies is similar to attempting to measure temperature in experimental physics in terms of "hot," "nice," or "cold."

A related issue to the use of "non-interval" scales refers to the built-in upper limits of subjective wellbeing questionnaires. As we shall see later, a consistent finding in contemporary happiness research is the decreasing marginal utility of income: there is a level past which any additional income hardly raises one's level of wellbeing. This leads scholars to conclude that, from the happiness perspective at least, it makes no sense to try to increase one's income any more, once a certain point has already been reached. Exerting extra effort would be useless, a waste, for one's resulting happiness. Again, this is but a consequence, as McCloskey (2012) reminds us, of the pre-established limit in our "non-interval" scale. Because there is nothing beyond "very happy" in the scale, it would be impossible to know just how much individual subjective wellbeing could improve – or not – with additional income. This should not come as a surprise, as we have chosen to use a bounded scale in our investigation.

A third objection that McCloskey (2012) raises pertains to the confusion between "statistical significance" and "scientific significance." She regrets that even researchers as seasoned as van Praag and Ferrer i Carbonell (2008) are misled into taking the "sampling improbability of a result" for the "clinical or legal importance of the result." The first denotes the "sampling error," which is calculated from the size of the sample and the number of probable results, whereas the second indicates the "human error" or the "error in prediction." McCloskey (2012) cites that in the 2012 US presidential elections, for instance, the "sampling error" in surveys of whether people would vote for Obama or not was always between 2 and 3 percent. This figure derived from the sample size, normally 1,000 or 1,500 individuals, and the probability of an affirmative response, which was always around 50 percent. However, this "sampling error" or the "statistical significance" of the survey had nothing to do with its "predictive error" or "scientific significance," which depended on a host of other factors different from the sample size and the probable results. For instance, if the unemployment rate were to drop below 8 percent, foreseeably, Obama would win, in the same way that if Obama were caught committing adultery or any other major misdemeanor, he would lose, McCloskey (2012) surmises. Neither one of these factors is related to the "statistical significance" of the surveys, yet they have a considerable bearing on the "scientific importance" of the results, for reasons of an entirely different nature.

McCloskey (2012) riles against attempts to reduce happiness to a single dimension, such as "$H = 2.718$," instead of acknowledging that it is a multifaceted reality. For instance, how does one account for the enjoyment of a eating piece of a rich and moist chocolate cake, which relieves one's hunger and cravings, while at the same time feeling guilty, for not keeping one's diet, and anxious about the soon-to-be-released laboratory results of one's endocrinal condition? It does not seem as if the totality of the experience could be captured by a single number on a single magnitude or unit. McCloskey is joined here by Nussbaum, who unequivocally states, "it would not make sense to ask people to rank all their pleasures along a single quantitative dimension: this is just bullying people into disregarding features of their own experience that reflection would quickly reveal. People are easily bullied, particularly by prominent psychologists, and so they do answer such questions, rather than respond, 'This question is ill-formed'" (Nussbaum 2008: 86). This is a wise observation.

Indeed, accuracy and precision are desirable in measurement, but not to the extent of sacrificing the very nature of the thing to be measured, effectively transforming it into something else. It is very easy to fall into this trap when attempting to construct a science of happiness. In such a case, we should pay careful heed to Aristotle's advice in *Nicomachean Ethics* not to expect the same degree of accuracy or precision (*akribeia*) in everything (Aristotle 1985: 1094b). Certainly, accuracy or precision should not be expected from politics, the study of "*eudaimonia*" or human flourishing within the political community, which requires more flexible standards. A balance must be struck between mathematical rigor, on the one hand, and relevance or comprehension, on the other, in the effort to get a glimpse of the true nature of things. This principle surely applies to modern happiness studies, which, despite changes in methods or approaches, ultimately seeks to understand the same reality as Aristotle's version of politics had intended. But more on this later.

One may be surprised that even in such fundamental dimensions of the physical universe, such as mass or weight, we don't have an exact and constant standard (*The Economist* 2012). In the case of time, having established the earth's prime meridian in the London suburb of Greenwich, we can calculate the duration of a day, what it takes for the planet to cover a full rotation on its axis, and derived from that, the duration of an hour, a minute, and a second, successively. In the case of length, we can describe the meter as the distance between two scratches on a platinum–iridium bar kept at the *Bureau International des Poids et Mesures* in Sèvres, Paris. Nowadays, more precise methods for measuring time and length exist. We could use clocks with cesium atoms as pendulums for measuring seconds and, on the basis of that, calculate the distance covered at the speed of light for measuring length. But for mass or weight, we remain dependent on a lump of a platinum–iridium alloy also found in Paris, as the standard for the kilogram. And although we cannot verify whether the official standard for the kilogram has in fact gained or lost weight, due to the action of pollutants and subsequent efforts to clean it, what is certain is that it has not remained constant. If such is the case with the kilogram as a unit of measure of mass or weight, then perhaps it would not be too unreasonable to expect a lesser degree of accuracy or precision, in measuring happiness or subjective wellbeing.

The relative ease with which we now gather, accumulate, analyze, and correlate scientific data – whatever could be drawn from experience and subjected to mathematical calculations – has created several serious problems of its own. As Brooks (2013) warns us, there are significant limitations to what data can do. Data are useful to correct prejudices and intuitions often distorted by feelings and emotions in decision making. However, data also have inherent weaknesses. Firstly, data do not capture social phenomena well. By means of data, computers could readily measure the quantity of social interactions and relations, but not their quality. Social cognition – the process through which human beings are able to detect each other's emotional states, sensing the likelihood of cooperative behavior and evaluating things emotively – can hardly be represented by cold and hard data. Secondly, data tend to ignore the significance of contexts. They treat human events as isolated occurrences without regard for what happens before, during, and after them. They have great difficulty in taking into account multiple explanations and causations, such as those usually found at work within narratives. Thirdly, data gathering and analysis have a tendency to snowball, to create an avalanche of facts and figures that ends up burying what we were originally searching for in a barrage of "noise" or meaningless statistical correlations.

Moreover, with data alone, we find ourselves in deep frustration, unable to comprehend huge, complex human problems. It may not be challenging for super mainframes to crunch the numbers for main economic indicators such as GDP, income per capita, inflation or unemployment rates, given the right instructions or formulas for each. But these same machines would be in a terrible bind to determine levels of human happiness and misery, or to decide what state of affairs would be more in keeping with human dignity. No amount of data analysis would ever seem sufficient to arrive at such judgments. And that's primarily because data do not acknowledge or recognize values, which is, probably, their most important limitation in decision making. Insofar as data and the machines that deal with them are concerned, reality is just a series of ones and zeroes. There is no reason why I should prefer Shakespeare's collected works to the New York City phone book to keep me company on a deserted island. Neither is there a cogent explanation why one would first want to save his family before farm animals, from a barn set ablaze. When values are reduced to data, they are de-valued, they cease to be valuable, they simply stop being values. At the same time, we should also rid ourselves of the belief that data are objective, unquestionable "facts of nature," because in all certainty they are not. Like all other cultural artifacts, they are generated, processed, stored, interpreted, and transmitted by fallible human beings. Hence Gitelman's quip, "'raw data' is an oxymoron" (Gitelman 2013).

How do all of these considerations impact modern happiness studies and its quest for observable and measurable data on individual subjective wellbeing? Firstly, it would be cavalier to simply dismiss empirical and quantitative data as irrelevant to the study of welfare or wellbeing, reverting to the situation in which abstract, theoretical reasoning alone mattered. That would be tantamount to ignoring the evidence about some tangible signs or manifestations of happiness or wellbeing. However, it would be foolish to demand, from the empirical and quantitative data on individual subjective wellbeing, a degree of accuracy or precision in measurement with which not even purely physical attributes, such as weight or mass, are able to comply. Psychometrics surely deserves a place in the field, and its efforts in the construction and validation of measurement techniques and instruments concerning happiness ought not to be taken lightly. But then again, the theory behind these measurement techniques and instruments, as well as the data they produce, should not be regarded unreflectively. They are not to be treated as natural objects that stand alone by their own merits. Instead, they should always be set against a narrative background for their proper understanding and interpretation. We shall turn to this in the final section of the chapter.

THE NEED FOR A NARRATIVE

It could not be otherwise. The data or facts that one seeks, together with the tools or instruments of measurement one employs, cannot but determine the very object of study or measurement. Thus, when we focus on output or GNP, what we get is aggregate economic welfare, but not social welfare. (In fact, not even welfare, as some would object, since all that GNP measures, strictly speaking, is the value of monetary transactions, largely for tax purposes. Neither the work of housewives nor the value of illegal activities could be captured by these statistics, for instance. Yet no one can deny the impact of these endeavors, positive or negative, on welfare.) And when, together with income, we consider happiness self-reports, we then obtain a picture of individual subjective wellbeing without regard for the community or collective. This means that all individual experiences are but an amalgam of positive emotions, pleasant feelings, and good moods, collectively known as "affect." It also expresses conscious approval or satisfaction that such is effectively the case (the "cognitive element"). Several psychometric tests and techniques have been devised to ascertain subjective wellbeing from an overall, global or integrative perspective; but there are also others that view subjective wellbeing as domain-specific or episodic. The latter are dedicated to the precise measurement of utilities experienced by subjects in the exact time and place that they engage in particular activities. Apart from the discussion of whether individual subjective wellbeing is global or episodic, there is also the open question regarding its distribution throughout a person's lifetime. For instance, which is preferable: a relatively high but constant level of subjective wellbeing throughout one's life, or to start off in an objectively miserable state, but to progressively experience improvements in one's wellbeing, until a blissful moment at the end is reached?

Meanwhile, there have always been those who have firmly held on to the view that self-reports are not to be trusted as indicators of individual wellbeing. We should, rather, direct our attention to

choices and consumption behaviors, observable by neutral third parties, as unequivocal signs that reveal preferences. Thus, we regain an
objective handle or proxy on happiness, in line with current scientific convention: the amount of money spent on a particular basket of
goods, either in itself or compared to alternatives. Other non-verbal
signals of subjective wellbeing would be heightened electrical activity
in certain areas of the brain, as detected by fMRI machines, increased
heart rates while engaging in specific tasks or actions, and the concentration of certain neurotransmitters and hormones in the bloodstream. Accordingly, there is a tendency to reduce happiness to one's
consumption choices, to a matter of brain waves and increased heart
activity, and to the effects of biochemical substances. But as many
would agree, the subjective experience of wellbeing is never identical
to any one of these signs, or even to the combination of all of them.
These "scientific" descriptions of consumption behaviors, brain activity, and neurotransmitter and hormone concentrations explain wellbeing from the "outside," and are never equivalent to the actual, lived
experience.

All of these attempts that we have briefly described, meant
to provide undisputable data on happiness, are, in fact, riddled with
technical difficulties of various kinds. We have mentioned the problems of "cardinalism," the belief that the amount of utility, pleasure,
or satisfaction that can be obtained from a particular good could be
objectively determined, as well as those of "ordinalism," the idea
that negates the former and states that we could only infer subjective
preferences from comparisons and choices (Ng 1997). We have also
seen the arbitrariness involved in the pervasive use of non-interval
scales which, moreover, have built-in lower and upper limits. We
have become aware of the generalized confusion between statistical
error and scientific or clinical significance. Put together, they go to
show that despite the merits of acquiring happiness data, there are also
some disadvantages to the approach. This seems to reveal that happiness is a complex, human phenomenon with an inescapable social
dimension, where context and quality are of primary importance.

Happiness is tied up with meaning and significance. Its experience is value-laden in a way that does not lend itself to ordinary data measurement. Happiness largely depends on one's values, the results of free choices, against which events and experiences are compared and deemed favorable or not. Values provide height, depth, breadth, color, texture, and consistency to what would otherwise be plain, bland, or flat experience. Values establish an order of importance in life-events because we build our identities around them. Values acquire reality as they are lived in concrete situations, in human life that unfolds in time. In other words, in order to adequately capture and understand the nature of happiness, which is inextricably linked to values, data gathering needs the complement of narrative. Happiness is one of those "thick" concepts (Geertz 1983) that can be comprehended only insofar as it is embedded in a community's practices, which include assumptions and values.

As a research method, narrative is often contrasted with paradigmatic, discursive reasoning or the scientific method (Bruner 1986, 1990). Narrative means thinking through storytelling, trying to understand the particular case, some individual or personal experience that transpires in a specific context, event, or situation. As Mattingly says, "narrative thinking is our primary way of making sense of human experience" (Mattingly 1991: 999) because through it alone are we able to have a peek into the motives and reasons that truly explain human action. Abstract, discursive thinking, on the other hand, is concerned with transcending physical events by recognizing them as particular instances of general laws. Here the argument is logical and direct, based on empirical proof and relations of cause and effect. Physical forces enable us to perform human actions but do not explain them.

Mattingly explains further that "narrative makes sense of reality by linking the outward world of actions and events to the inner world of human intention and motivation" (Mattingly 1991: 999). Narrative "puts things together," "gives a meaningful structure to life through time" (Mattingly 1991: 1000–1002). Only in the form of a story may a person's actions be suitably accounted for, finding significance and coherence as part of a larger whole that continually unfolds, leading to an end, purpose, or *telos* (MacIntyre 2007). The narrative structure of human life and happiness requires a *telos*. Without narrative, human life and experience will just be a meaningless succession of events. Such events may, perhaps, be enumerated and analyzed physically, but not organized into something understandable or reasonable. And by means of narrative, each individual life intertwines with the lives of others, forming a complex unity also known as the history or tradition of a community. Not all communities value things in the same way, as each one establishes its own hierarchy. Following Ricoeur, we could affirm that it is through a process of "emplotment," the drawing out of a certain configuration from a mere chain of actions and events, that thought, sense, and meaning alight in one's life (Ricoeur 1984).

The quest in modern happiness studies to try to understand its object by means of empirical and quantitative data provided by economics and psychology, therefore, may be legitimate and helpful. However, there has to be a constant awareness in whoever decides to tread down this path of the limits of the chosen methodology. This should lead him to seek the complement of narrative, without which happiness would be reduced to a mere physical event, and thus lose its distinctive human significance or meaning. Closely linked to its purpose, happiness and life's meaning could only be comprehended in the interlocking of lives set against a background of community and tradition. But neither can data be translated into narrative nor narrative into data. Both are equally necessary for a full, evaluative account of happiness.

REFERENCES

Aristotle 1985. *Nicomachean ethics* (Irwin, T., trans.). Indianapolis, IN: Hackett Publishing.
Bentham, J. 2000. *An introduction to the principles of morals and legislation.* Palo Alto, CA: Batoche Books.

Brooks, D. 2013. "What data can't do," *The New York Times*, February 16.

Bruner, J. 1986. *Actual minds, possible worlds*. Cambridge, MA: Harvard University Press.

1990. *Acts of meaning*. Cambridge, MA: Harvard University Press.

Cantril, H. 1965. *The pattern of human concerns*. New Brunswick, NJ: Rutgers University Press.

Davis, J., Smith, T. and Marsden, P. 2001. *General social survey, 1972–2000: Cumulative codebook*. Storrs, CT: Roper Center for Public Opinion Research, University of Connecticut.

Diener, E., Emmons, R. A., Larsen, R. J. and Griffin, S. 1985. "The satisfaction with life scale," *Journal of Personality Assessment*, 49: 71–75.

Diener, E., Wirtz, D., Tov, W., Kim-Prieto, C., Choi, D., Oishi, S. and Biswas-Diener, R. 2010. "New measures of well-being: Flourishing and positive and negative feelings," *Social Indicators Research*, 39: 247–266.

Easterlin, R. A. 1974. "Does economic growth improve the human lot? Some empirical evidence," in David, P. A. and Reder, M. W. (eds.), *Nations and households in economic growth: Essays in honor of Moses Abramowitz*. New York and London: Academic Press, pp. 89–125.

2002. *Happiness in economics*. Cheltenham, UK/Northampton, MA: Edward Elgar.

Edgeworth, F. Y. 1994. *Mathematical psychics: An essay on the application of mathematics to the moral sciences*. Düsseldorf: Verlag Wirtschaft und Finanzen.

Fordyce, M. W. 1988. "A review of research on 'The happiness measures': A sixty second index of happiness and mental health," *Social Indicators Research*, 20: 63–89.

Frey, B. 2008. *Happiness: A revolution in economics*. Cambridge, MA/London: The MIT Press.

Geertz, C. 1983. *Local knowledge: Further essays in interpretive anthropology*. New York: Basic Books.

Gitelman, L. (ed.) 2013. *'Raw data' is an oxymoron*. Cambridge, MA/London: The MIT Press.

Graham, C. 2011. *The pursuit of happiness: An economy of well-being*, Washington, DC: The Brookings Institution Press.

Hektner, J. M., Schmidt, J. A. and Csikszentmihalyi, M. 2006. *Experience sampling method: Measuring the quality of everyday life*. Thousand Oaks, CA: Sage Publications.

Inglehardt, R., Basanez, M., Diez-Medrano, J., Halman, L. and Luijks, R. 2000. *World values surveys and European values surveys, 1981–1984, 1990–1993 and 1995–1997.* Ann Arbor, MI: Inter-university Consortium for Political and Social Research, study no. 2790 (http://faith-health.org/wordpress/wp-content/uploads/wvs.pdf, accessed February 19, 2013).

Johns, H. and Ormerod, P. 2007. *Happiness, economics and public policy.* London: Institute of Economic Affairs.

Kahnemann, D., Diener, E. and Schwarz, E. (eds.) 1999. *Well-being: The foundations of hedonic psychology.* New York: Russell Sage Foundation.

Kahneman, D., Krueger, A. B., Schkade, D. A., Schwarz, N. and Stone, A. 2004. "A survey method for characterizing daily life experience: The day reconstruction method," *Science,* 306: 1776–1780.

Kahneman, D., Wakker, P. and Sarin, R. 1997. "Back to Bentham? Explorations of experienced utility," *Quarterly Journal of Economics,* 112 (2): 375–405.

Larson, R. and Csikszentmihalyi, M. 1983. "The experience sampling method," *New Directions for Methodology of Social and Behavioral Science,* 15: 41–56.

Lucas, R., Diener, E. and Suh, E. 1996. "Discriminant validity of well-being measures," *Journal of Personality and Social Psychology,* 71 (3): 616–628.

Lyubomirsky, S. and Lepper, H. S. 1999. "A measure of subjective happiness: Preliminary reliability and construct validation," *Social Indicators Research,* 46: 137–155.

MacIntyre, A. 2007. *After virtue* (3rd ed.). London: Duckworth.

Mattingly, C. 1991. "The narrative nature of clinical reasoning," *American Journal of Occupational Therapy,* 45: 998–1005 (doi:10.5014/ajot.45.11.998).

McCloskey, D. N. 2012. "Happyism: The creepy new economics of pleasure," *The New Republic,* June 8 (www.tnr.com/article/politics/magazine/103952/happyism-deirdre-mccloskey-economics-happiness, accessed February 23, 2013).

Ng, Y.-K. 1997. "A case for happiness, cardinalism, and interpersonal comparability," *Economic Journal,* 107: 1848–1858.

Nussbaum, M. 2008. "Who is the happy warrior? Philosophy poses questions to psychology," *Journal of Legal Studies,* 37 (2): 81–113.

Nussbaum, M. and Sen, A. (eds.) 1993. *The quality of life.* Oxford: Clarendon Press.

Peterson, C. 2003. *Approaches to happiness questionnaire,* (www.authentichappiness.sas.upenn.edu/tests/SameAnswers_t.aspx?id=266, accessed February 5, 2013).

2005. *Authentic happiness inventory questionnaire,* (www.authentichappiness.sas.upenn.edu/tests/SameAnswers_t.aspx?id=266, accessed February 5, 2013).

Ricoeur, P. 1984. *Time and narrative,* vol. I. Chicago: University of Chicago Press.

Ryff, C. D., Singer, B. H. and Love, G. D. 2004. "Positive health: Connecting well-being with biology," *Philosophical Transactions of the Royal Society of London*, B, 359: 1383–1394.

Seligman, M. E. P. 2002. *Authentic happiness*. New York: Free Press.

2011. *Flourish*. New York: Free Press.

Stone, A. A., Shiffman, S. S. and DeVries, M. W. 1999. "Ecological momentary assessment," in Kahnemann, D., Diener, E. and Schwarz, E. (eds.), *Well-being: The foundations of hedonic psychology*. New York: Russell Sage Foundation, pp. 26–39.

The Economist 2013. "Measurement: Mass effect," January 12.

Urry, H. L., Nitschke, J. B., Dolski, I., Jackson, D. C., Dalton, K. M., Mueller, C. J., Rosenkranz, M. A., Ryff, C. D., Singer, B. H. and Davidson, R. J. 2004. "Making a life worth living: Neural correlates of well-being," *Psychological Science*, 15 (6): 367–72.

Van Praag, B. M. S. and Ferrer i Carbonell, A. 2008. *Happiness quantified: A satisfaction calculus approach*. Oxford: Oxford University Press.

Veenhoven, R. 1993. *Happiness in nations: Subjective appreciation of life in 56 nations 1946–1992*. Rotterdam: Erasmus University Press.

Watson, D., Clark, L. A., Tellegen, A. 1988. "Development and validation of brief measures of positive and negative affect: The PANAS scales," *Journal of Personality and Social Psychology*, 54: 1063–1070.

2   Happiness and income

How much happiness can money buy?

Why is it that, when told that "money can't buy happiness," humanities students respond with a big yawn, while their friends from the
business and economics departments come up with a deeply troubled
look? What seems to be evident to some, for one reason or another,
appears terribly puzzling to others. Why so?

At the root of the matter is what has popularly come to be
known as the "Easterlin paradox," according to which an increase in
income does not entail an increase in subjective wellbeing or happiness. (Easterlin's real position, as we shall soon see, is a lot more
nuanced.) But, indeed, it seems paradoxical only to those who subscribe to the neoclassical economic theory, about how an increase in
income necessarily expands an individual's "opportunity set": that is,
the basket of goods and services that are available for his consumption. Surely, the individual is under no obligation to consume any of
the goods and services offered; he could even dispose of all of them,
if he so wishes, in whatever way he deems fit. But if he chooses, at
least he would have the "opportunity" or financial resources needed
to purchase them, which is by far preferable to the contrary. To the
extent that subjective wellbeing or happiness is related to the enjoyment of certain goods and services, it therefore seems logical, and
even obvious, that an increase in income should bring with it greater
happiness for the individual. Thus, we could understand what counts
as the general reaction of business and economics students to the
proposition above.

On the other hand, humanities students appear to be thinking along the lines of certain psychological studies, which suggest
that higher income does not lead to increased happiness. Brickman,
Coates, and Janoff-Bulman (1978) compare the life satisfaction levels

of lottery winners who had made their windfall within the previous year and those of a control group. They found that the winners reported only a very marginal increase of 4.0 on a five-point life satisfaction scale versus the 3.8 registered by the control group. Moreover, the winners even admitted that they were significantly less pleased with positive, everyday events than the control group. They always seemed to expect more, and thus, were continually disappointed. In a similar study, Smith and Razzell (1975) also found that British football pools winners, after the initial euphoria, reported a significant drop in their happiness levels. This could be explained by several factors, such as the tendency for winners to leave their jobs, thereby falling out of supportive social networks, their missing opportunities to cultivate a sense of achievement, or simply, their letting go of comfortable work-related routines. It could also be due to the high levels of stress that come from the responsibility of now being expected to provide financial assistance to an endless stream of friends and relatives in need. Above all, winners seemed to get used to the consequences of their good fortune sooner than later; the spike experienced in their happiness levels immediately upon claiming the prize fizzled out in due course. In other words, humanities students appear to be convinced that money does not make for happiness – at least, not of the lasting sort.

In fact, there is no dearth of arguments for thinking that winning the lottery brings bad luck (Nocera 2012). An exceptional case is that of Jack Whittaker, then a 55-year-old president of a construction company from West Virginia, who won the biggest ever $315 million Powerball jackpot in 2002. At that time, he already had a net worth of more than $17 million. Whittaker pledged 10 percent of his prize money to several Christian charities and donated $14 million to the Jack Whittaker Foundation, a non-profit organization dedicated to providing basic needs to low-income families in his home state. As a sign of gratitude, he even gave the woman who worked at the convenience store where he bought the winning ticket a $123,000 house, a new Dodge Ram truck, and $50,000 cash. Less than a year later, thieves went away with $545,000 that was stashed in Whittaker's car while it was parked at a strip club. Not long afterwards, thieves once again broke into his car, this time running away with around $200,000. When asked why he carried around such huge amounts of money with him, Whittaker simply replied, "Because I can." Within a decade of his winning, his wife had divorced him, both a daughter and a granddaughter had died of drug overdoses, and he had become a respondent in several lawsuits, including one filed by the Caesars Atlantic Casino, for issuing $1.5 million worth of bouncing checks. He once confided to reporters about his stroke of fortune, "I wish I'd torn that ticket up."

How, then, could one altogether avoid, or at least neutralize, the curse of winning the lottery (McNay 2012)? Apparently, the answer lies in the struggle to remain "normal" and, to the extent possible, anonymous. Winners should try their best not to lose their sense of values and should resist the lure of extravagant living that comes with easy money. Keeping anonymity could present quite a challenge, as lottery promoters tend to draw public attention to the winners, taking pictures of them with oversized checks and transforming them into instant celebrities as a form of free marketing for their business. Getting the services of a professional financial adviser would be highly recommended, since winners tend not to be people accustomed to managing astronomical amounts of money. Apart from guiding winners to make sound investments, the financial adviser could also convince them to take the money out in annual increments, and spend it according to a plan and a purpose.

Returning to Easterlin (1974), we find that his pioneering empirical and quantitative research on the connection between income and happiness consists, in fact, of three different but very closely related questions. The first concerns "within-country comparisons," inquiring whether in a given country, the higher the income group, the greater the proportion of people who report themselves to be "very happy." The second deals with "international comparisons," trying to find out whether, in examining a group of countries, the wealthier the country, the happier are the people. And the third investigates "national time series": that is, whether the number of inhabitants of a given country who describe themselves as "very happy" increases as they grow richer in time. The first two questions, therefore, take snapshots or cross sections: in the first case, of different socioeconomic classes within the same country, and in the second, of countries as a whole. The third is more like a motion picture which tells the story of how a group of people fare in terms of happiness, as they grow richer in the course of time. Let us now study each of these queries separately.

IN A GIVEN COUNTRY, ARE THE RICH HAPPIER THAN THE POOR?

Easterlin's data for the United States, taken in December 1970, definitely affirm this, with the proportion of people belonging to the highest income group who consider themselves to be "very happy" being almost double the proportion of those belonging to the lowest income group (Easterlin 1974: 99–104). In fact, as income level rises, the proportion of people who claim to be "very happy" also rises steadily, lending support to the idea that income and happiness are, indeed, positively correlated. Similar results were obtained in previous studies carried out, aside from the United States, in nineteen other countries from all over the world, between 1946 and 1966.

The most remarkable finding, perhaps, from these studies is not the positive connection between income and happiness, which by and large fulfills general expectations. Rather, it is the discovery that, even among those belonging to the lowest income groups, there is always a sizable number of people who nonetheless still think of themselves as being "very happy." In similar fashion, a representative portion of those belonging to the highest income groups consistently report themselves to be "not very happy" at all. To add further to the dilemma, Frey and Stutzer (2002: 83–85) report that in Switzerland, between 1992 and 1994, the highest income-earners registered lower levels of life satisfaction than the income group immediately below them. How can we explain these phenomena in light of the above?

Although Easterlin expressed his inclination to believe that, on the whole, data suggested a causal relation running from income to happiness, he did not discount the influence of other factors; indeed, not even the possibility of causality running in the opposite direction. Apart from income, there seemed to be a pervasive association, in some pieces of research, between years of schooling and happiness, for instance. And it is fairly easy to imagine how greater income positively affects years of schooling, or even health, for that matter. In other words, it may not be income alone that is pushing happiness, life satisfaction, and wellbeing up to higher levels, but income in conjunction with or by means of its positive effects on other dependent factors, such as education and health.

Similar inferences may be drawn from the much later "Moving to Opportunity" experiment (Ludwig et al. 2008), where the mere fact of transferring to higher-income neighborhoods produced an improvement in life satisfaction levels together with better physical (lower obesity and diabetes rates) and mental health (fewer incidences of depression). Higher income seems to have a "halo effect," proving beneficial to those who live in the same environment, despite not having higher incomes themselves. This study, initiated in the early 1990s, involved moving 4,600 families from neighborhoods where half of the residents lived in poverty to others where only a third were poor, in several cities in the United States, such as Los Angeles, New York, Baltimore, Chicago, and Boston. Although the transferees, after 10 years, did not actually receive more education, get better jobs or earn higher incomes than the control group who refused to move, they had experienced a boost in their happiness levels equivalent to around a $13,000 increase in income. These improvements were attributed by those who transferred to greater safety and less stress, arising from having left dangerous and oftentimes violent as well as poorer neighborhoods. Moreover, regarding the direction of causality, Easterlin likewise remained open to the possibility that happy people, because they tended to be more successful in their work or profession, for example, turned out to earn higher incomes than those whose outlook wasn't as sunny. Certainly this could also be true, alongside the conclusion that higher income makes people happier, albeit through a weaker causal link.

On the other hand, despite later studies from the United States (1994) and Europe (1975–1991) confirming the positive correlation between income and happiness, Frey and Stutzer (2002) believe, nonetheless, that income by itself explains little of the differences in happiness among groups of people, and that other factors are more important (Frey and Stutzer 2002: 81). They do not deny income's positive effect on happiness, but simply try to nuance it. For example, they call attention to the fact that the strongest correlation between income and life satisfaction was observed in the depressed areas of Calcutta (Biswas-Diener and Diener 2001). Could it be, then, that income affects people's happiness differently? How, exactly?

Before proceeding further, let us summarize our findings so far. In general terms, we can say that the rich are happier than the poor (and that the richer one is, the happier he is likely to be) in any given country. We also know that income has a stronger effect on happiness than happiness on income. But the effect of income on happiness is not the same for all people. It seems to be stronger the poorer a person is, as attested by the study conducted in the Calcutta slums. Income has more weight and exerts a stronger influence in the happiness of the poor. This seems to be reasonable, given the usefulness of income to satisfy basic, material human needs, which become more of a challenge when one is poor.

However, this is not the whole story. Aside from absolute income, be it high or low, there is also the happiness arising from income relative to that of other people in the society where one lives. We tend to think of ourselves, in both our earning and spending behaviors, no less than in our pleasures or enjoyment, as isolated individuals who do best by ignoring the rest. The truth is, however, that we cannot help but compare ourselves to other people, as is proper to our nature as social animals. These interpersonal comparisons among people of varying income levels could help explain why the relation between income, on the one hand, and happiness, subjective wellbeing, or life satisfaction, on the other, isn't as straightforward as initially thought.

Several empirical studies bear this out. In a research involving 10,000 British workers, Clark and Oswald (1996) identified a reference group of people of the same sex, education, and job, and discovered that relative income mattered more than absolute income for their levels of life satisfaction. People are more satisfied with life as a whole, the lower the income level of the group with which they compare themselves. Comparisons, however, have to be made with regard not just to anyone, but to "relevant others." Hence, given two non-working married sisters, for example, the decision of one of them to seek employment is significantly affected by her husband's income relative to that of her brother-in-law (Neumark and Postlewaite 1998). The lower her husband's income compared to her brother-in-law's, the greater the incentive to work. Conversely, we may think that between the two sisters, the "happier" one is she whose husband earns more than her brother-in-law, no matter how small the absolute difference in incomes may be. She experiences less "need" to work. What is important is that her husband earns "more" in a relative sense: that is, compared to her brother-in-law. Having come from the same family of origin, it is understandable that two married sisters compare their respective husbands' incomes, and make decisions or gauge their happiness on the basis of that information, rather than by comparing their incomes or happiness to that of the queen of England, for instance.

The importance of relative income differences compared to "relevant others" could also provide us with a clue to why women report to be equally happy or, indeed, even happier than men in the workplace, despite suffering sex discrimination and receiving around 25 to 30 percent less pay for the same work, at least in countries like the United States, Great Britain, New Zealand, and Hungary (Sousa-Poza and Sousa-Poza 2000). This is what has come to be called the "gender/job-satisfaction paradox," especially prevalent in

Anglo-Saxon cultures. Some scholars try to explain this anomaly simply by saying that in general, regardless of the influence of all the different factors, such as income, on happiness, women are happier than men. Another version states that women "feel more obliged" than men to say that they are happy, even if this is false; that women are not as given to complaining as men are. However, a better explanation may be that women in fact compare themselves to other women, and therefore do not perceive or suffer so much as a result of income discrimination, instead of comparing themselves to their male colleagues (Frey and Stutzer 2002: 88). For women workers, the "relevant others" are other women, not their male work companions. Only when women compare themselves to men, performing the same work under identical conditions but receiving less pay, will they start to feel more dissatisfied and unhappy with their jobs. True enough, younger and better-educated professional women, especially those working in male-dominated environments, report comparable work satisfaction levels to their male counterparts (Clark 1997).

Actually, one of the biggest setbacks to happiness, not only in middle-income societies but also in rich ones, is inequality, not poverty or material deprivation (*The Economist* 2011b). The standard measure for inequality is the Gini coefficient, ranging from 0, when everyone has the same income, to 1, when all income is concentrated in the hands of just one person. The majority of countries register values between 0.25 (Nordic countries) and 0.6 (Latin America). Worldwide, inequality is falling, as poor countries on average grow faster than rich ones. But in many middle-income and rich countries, inequality has risen since the 1980s. In China, for instance, the Gini coefficient went up from under 0.3 to 0.4 between the 1980s and 2011, while in the United States it climbed from 0.34 to 0.38.

Let us take a closer look at the evolution of inequality in the United States. In principle, inequality could be traced to two causes: the wealthy getting wealthier or the poor getting poorer. In the case of the United States, the growth of inequality is overwhelmingly due to the first. During the 1970s, the income of the wealthiest 20 percent of Americans grew by 14 percent, while the income of the poorest 20 percent rose by only 9 percent. In the 1990s, the gap became even wider, with the income of the top fifth growing by 27 percent, while the bottom fifth saw theirs rise by just 10 percent. In a study of the income of the top 0.1 percent of the US population between 1913 and 1998 (with the latest update of tables and figures to 2011), Piketty and Saez (2013) discovered that these people were earning around 8 percent of the total income towards the end of the period, comparable to the Golden Years of the 1920s, and up by 2 percent from the 1960s. There seems to be a correlation between the income surge of the super-rich and the growth of financial services as a share of gross domestic product, which doubled to 8 percent between 1980 and 2000. For most of the last century, the rate of return on capital has been consistently above the rate of growth of the economy in general. This has resulted in capital receiving a disproportionately larger share of income than labor (Piketty 2014). Within this context, the rage and indignation of the "Occupy Wall Street" movement at Zuccotti Park in New York City at the height of the financial crisis in 2011 becomes a lot more understandable. Without questioning the dismal inequality figures, however, some social observers tend to interpret the problem essentially in terms of certain character defects and inappropriate lifestyle choices (Brooks 2014). Those who get left behind largely come from broken homes and have been raised by single mothers. Having failed to finish even high school, they have very poor job skills, making them unfit to participate in a postindustrial economy.

What adverse effects does income inequality have on happiness within societies? First and foremost, its acute forms seem to offend elementary notions of justice or fairness. Indeed, it is difficult to prove that the top 0.1 percent of the US population works eighty times as hard as the rest of the country, or that they contribute eighty times as much to the general welfare so as to justify their earnings premium. Secondly, income inequality has significant repercussions on health, leisure, and ultimately, life expectancy, as some data show (Fletcher 2013). For instance, St. John's and Putnam are neighboring counties in Florida, but incomes and housing values in the first are twice those of the second. Unsurprisingly, life expectancy at St. John's is 83 years for women and 78 for men, while at Putnam, it's 78 for women and 71 for men. There's a 5–10 percent difference in longevity, therefore, between the two counties, attributable, among other things, to income inequality. Some epidemiologists (Wilkinson and Pickett 2009) even claim that the winners in the income race levy some sort of "physiological tax" on the losers. Income inequality is said to cause chronic stress in the worse-off, making them secrete large amounts of a hormone called cortisol in the bloodstream, which during prolonged periods could produce damage to the brain and the immune system. At the same time, inequality may also hinder the secretion of another hormone, oxytocin, which is said to promote bonding and trust. Hence, unequal societies characteristically have lower trust levels. As a result, they spend a greater deal of resources on security, hiring different forms of guard labor, from police to security guards and door-men (Bowles and Jayadev 2014). Considering that the retirement age in both counties is the same, the working poor, then, collect even less retirement benefits than the rich, since they die earlier. In effect, the poor, with their contributions and taxes, end up subsidizing the Social Security retirement benefits of their richer, healthier, and longer-living neighbors. To summarize, huge income gaps within societies cause serious deterioration in health (drug abuse, infant mortality, life expectancy, mental illness, obesity), human capital (child wellbe-ing, high school dropouts, math and literacy scores, social mobility, teenage births), and social relations (child conflict, homicides, impris-onment, social capital, trust) (Wilkinson and Pickett 2009).

Easterlin (1974: 116–117) himself clarifies the much diminished relevance of absolute income to happiness and satisfaction by means of an analogy regarding comparisons of height among people. When asked, "In general terms, how tall would you say you are – not very tall, fairly tall or very tall?" most people would feel confused and unable to respond, unless given a standard with which to compare themselves. Does the question refer to how tall one is in respect to people of one's age, or of one's sex, or to the average height of people in one's country? If this point of comparison is not specified, it will be impossible to give a cogent answer. Something similar occurs with questions regarding happiness. When an individual evaluates his own happiness, he always needs to refer to a norm or standard, largely derived from his personal experience as a member of society: does the question refer to how happy he is compared to people of his age or sex, or to the average happiness of people in the country? Unfailingly, in these cases, it is the relative height, income, or happiness that matters. There is one major difference, however, between comparisons of happiness, on the one hand, and height and income, on the other. Objective standards for height (how many meters tall?) and income (how many euros a year?) exist, while there is none to be found for wellbeing, satisfaction, and happiness, as has been previously seen.

Let us now explore the roots of this concept of relative income, as it explains differences in happiness or life satisfaction among the income brackets. The origins of the notion of relative income in respect of utility or satisfaction may be found remotely in Marx and Veblen, in the late nineteenth century, and more proximately in Duesenberry, in the early twentieth century. While writing on the relation of wage labor to capital, Marx (2006) observes that the satisfaction or contentment that one derives from his dwelling depends not on its absolute size or dimensions, but on its size or dimensions relative to those of his neighbors:

> A house may be large or small; as long as the neighboring houses are likewise small, it satisfies all social requirement for a residence. But let there arise next to the little house a palace, and the little house shrinks to a hut. The little house now makes it clear that its inmate has no social position at all to maintain, or but a very insignificant one; [. . .].

Therefore, the satisfaction that one obtains directly from consumption and indirectly from the income that permits such consumption is more of a consequence of comparative social position: the size of one's house relative to those surrounding it, in Marx's example. The higher the place one occupies in the ranking, the greater the satisfaction or happiness.

Veblen, for his part, takes the argument one step further. In the book *The Theory of the Leisure Class*, he describes, in a critical tone, the habits and customs of the new social class that made its wealth in the then recent industrialization. He defines "conspicuous consumption of valuable goods" as "a means of reputability to the gentleman of leisure" (Veblen 2013). Marx had already called our attention to the link, given the social nature of human beings, between satisfaction and a favorable social position or status, largely dependent on economic power, wealth, and income. In order to acquire the benefits of a privileged status, however, it is not enough for economic power simply to be possessed. It needs to be publicly displayed. And what better way to achieve this aim than through ostentatious spending on luxury goods?

The object of conspicuous consumption, then, is no longer the intrinsic benefit that comes from the use of goods and services: that is, of food to satisfy hunger, drink to quench thirst, or clothing to protect from the external elements. Rather, the end is now none other than to send the unequivocal sign of a capacity for huge discretionary spending through extravagance, in the hope of gaining due recognition and admiration. To follow the previous examples, eating, drinking, and wearing clothes are now done not because one is hungry, thirsty, or cold, but for their own sakes, for show, as manifestations of extraordinary wealth, power, and prestige. Conspicuous consumption becomes the source of social status, the recognition, admiration, and honor accorded to a person. It answers a need which is more psychological than biological, yet very powerful just the same in boosting one's happiness or satisfaction. Although initially applied to characterize the behavior of the *nouveau riche*, conspicuous consumption could also be detected among the poor and is especially prevalent in societies of emerging economies.

In formulating the relative income hypothesis, Duesenberry (1949) presents an individual's consumption utility or satisfaction in a mathematical way. It is a function, not of one's absolute level of spending, but a ratio of his current spending to the average weighted spending in society. In simplest terms, the higher one's spending is compared to the national per capita average, the greater the utility, satisfaction, or happiness. Conversely, the lower one's spending relative to the average, the greater the disutility, dissatisfaction, or unhappiness. An interesting corollary of Duesenberry's investigations refers to the asymmetric structure of such comparisons. In principle, as long as one doesn't belong to the lowest rung of the consumption ladder, he could get a lift in satisfaction or happiness if only he were to look down. But unfortunately, however, hardly anyone does that, and the majority of people always look upward in comparing themselves to others, thereby diminishing their satisfaction or happiness levels instead. More often than not, people aspire to greater income and consumption despite its downward effect on their satisfaction, wellbeing, and happiness.

Discussions on the impact of relative income on satisfaction and happiness by means of (conspicuous) consumption and social status have evolved as of late into the consideration of the so-called positional goods (Hirsch 1976). Before introducing the concept of "positional goods," let us first recall the intrinsic connection between the economy and scarcity. If resources were not in any way scarce with regard to the needs and wants of agents, the economy would lose its reason for being. Hirsch (1976) begins with a characterization of two economies based on corresponding forms of scarcity. The material economy concerns goods that are physically or numerically scarce, but of which more could be produced by increasing inputs of time, effort, money, and raw materials. The positional economy, on the other hand, relates to goods that are scarce but only in a socially restrictive way. In some sense, no amount of time, effort, money, or raw materials would lead to an increased production of this class of goods. They could only be redistributed. Thus, Hirsch explains the positional economy as composed of "all aspects of goods, services, work positions and other social relationships that are either (1) scarce in some absolute or socially imposed sense or

(2) subject to congestion and crowding through more extensive use" (Hirsch 1976: 27).

The consumption or enjoyment of positional goods depends on their exclusivity and this happens in a twofold way. Firstly, it may be the case that satisfaction derives directly from the fact that others do not or indeed cannot possess the good – for instance, being the Secretary General of the United Nations, of which there could only be one at any given point in time. Secondly, it could also occur that the enjoyment of the good is subject to congestion or crowding out. Consider the value of having an MBA degree in the workplace, which is inversely proportional to the number of MBA graduates available. If there are too many MBAs around, the degree suffers from inflation as a work qualification and its value is substantially reduced. Neither case denies an intrinsic value to the good at hand, being Secretary General or having an MBA. Yet in both, we may say that it is the positional value that predominates. The benefit one achieves from positional goods, therefore, is always at the expense of others (granted that the majority, if not all people, find becoming Secretary General or having an MBA reasonably desirable).

It is clear from the above that a privileged social status, which manifests itself in conspicuous consumption made possible by relative income superiority, is a positional good. There is hardly any intrinsic value to it, yet it becomes most desirable for social and psychological reasons, as an object of pride for whoever possesses it, and an object of aspiration for the others. Simply earning more money or engaging in more opulent spending does not necessarily translate into a higher social status, as long as others are similarly able to keep up the pace. Privileged social status is a good which, by nature, could only belong to a selected few, and the fewer there are, the more valuable it becomes, and the better for its possessors. We could also see how high social status satisfies both conditions set for positional goods. In a relative sense, one could only maintain social status to the extent that his class does not become congested or overcrowded.

And in absolute sense, we could always imagine that even in the most exclusive club of high-net-worth individuals, there would always be one at the top of the class.

In addition, therefore, to what we have already seen, the rich are happier than the poor in a given country due to the positive effects of a superior income relative to their peers or relevant reference group. These benefits are boosted by the practice of conspicuous consumption, which signals wealth, power, and social status. Social status, in turn, may be characterized as a positional good insofar as its main value lies in its exclusivity: that is, in the fact that it cannot be possessed by others.

ARE RICHER COUNTRIES HAPPIER THAN POORER COUNTRIES?

With this second question, Easterlin (1974: 104–108) examined a cross-section of countries looking for differences in happiness linked to income or GNP per capita. Basing himself on studies from the late 1950s to the mid-1960s (Cantril 1965; Rosenstein-Rodan 1961), Easterlin concluded that even if there was, indeed, a positive correlation between income and happiness among countries, it was not very clear. It was certainly not as evident as one would expect from the results of within-country comparisons among socioeconomic classes. Countries tended to cluster within a narrow range of personal happiness ratings despite huge differences in income, with the ratings of outliers largely explicable due to some unusual political circumstances at the time of the survey. Also, the happiness levels of the lowest-income countries figured neither at the bottom nor at the top of the scale but somewhere along the middle. Cultural factors likewise seemed to exert a huge influence, with Canada, Australia, Great Britain, and the United States registering similar results. But even that had to be taken with the proverbial grain of salt, since to lump Thailand, Malaysia, the Philippines, and Japan together as having the same culture would appear to be quite a stretch. From the data then available, Easterlin inferred that although per capita income was important for the personal happiness ratings of countries, it was not the only factor to be considered.

In more recent times, Frey and Stutzer (2002: 74–76) report more robust findings in support of the positive correlation between income and happiness among countries (Diener, Diener, and Diener 1995; Veenhoven 1991; Inglehart 1990; Inkeles and Diamond 1986). That exchange rates and purchasing power parities have been used to control for differences in the cost of living among countries lends greater force to their argument.

Frey and Stutzer (2002) express their hope that such findings would help disabuse us of the romanticist belief that because people in poorer countries lead more "natural" lives, in the sense that they are less engaged with technology and the artificial world, they are happier. The biography of the French Postimpressionist Paul Gauguin (1985) immediately comes to mind. After having lost his fortune as a broker in the collapse of the Paris Bourse in 1882, he embraced his new passion, painting. His art brought him to several places, first, the Antilles, then Brittany, and lastly, Polynesia, where – while fleeing from whatever smacked of European civilization, the artificial and the conventional, including his wife and children whom he left in Denmark – he painted idyllic renderings of Tahitian women and landscapes. Undoubtedly, technological progress also entails costs, in terms of possible widespread environmental damage and depletion of natural resources or increased lifestyle stress, due to faster speed of change, relentless competition, and ever-growing expectations. Yet overall, the effects of technology on humankind have been beneficial. Not only has life expectancy grown tremendously and health conditions improved remarkably, for example, but also human beings have achieved greater freedom from the limitations of their physical environment, being able to channel their energies toward loftier pursuits. Both the development and the access to technology require high levels of disposable income. Returning to Gauguin, a little more money would have done him well in his final years, if only to enable him to receive proper medical care for the syphilis that he eventually contracted. Certainly, therefore, money is not the root of all evil – far from it. In fact, money is actually necessary for material wellbeing, an integral component of happiness, as the comparison among countries attests.

It is difficult for a country to be happy when it is poor; certainly, more difficult than when it is rich (although that, too, has its own share of challenges, as we will soon have a chance to examine). But what, precisely, does being poor mean? Nearly everyone has an inherent sense of what poverty entails: not having enough of certain things, those that the rich can afford to simply take for granted. Yet it is notoriously complicated to arrive at a shared definition of poverty among researchers, governments, and international agencies. That is why different countries and international organizations have come up with definitions of their own, and sometimes, countries may even have more than one, depending on the purpose (*The Economist* 2011a). Within the European Union, the poor are those whose income falls short of 60 percent of the median. For the World Bank, there are two standards, the $1.25 a day and the $2.00 a day (in 2005 US dollars), and a person is considered poor if his income is below either one, adjusted for differences in purchasing power. A country's poverty rate depends on the fraction of people who earn less than these income levels and who are, therefore, unable to buy a notional basket of basic goods and services. The United Nations, on the other hand, makes use of a far more complex tool, the "Human Development Index," which apart from income also assesses countries in terms of schooling and life expectancy. As for specific countries, in the United Kingdom, three measures are in use: one absolute, another relative, and a third that looks more into forms of material deprivation, such as a child's ability to celebrate his birthday. The United States has an official poverty threshold, developed in the 1960s, equivalent to the basic food costs of a household multiplied by three. A family is judged to be poor if its income fails to clear this barrier. However, in 2009, the "Supplemental Poverty Measure" was introduced, in order to determine a family's eligibility for government assistance programs. It is defined as "the value of cash income from all sources, plus the value of in-kind benefits that are available to buy the basic bundle of goods, minus necessary expenses for critical goods and services not included in the thresholds" (Renwick 2012). It corresponds, in effect, to the costs of food, clothing, shelter, and utilities, to which an additional 20 percent is added for other expenditures.

None of these measures is completely problem-free. Indeed, income is important, inasmuch as it represents the amount of resources available to satisfy needs and wants, but low income is only one aspect of poverty. For example, although a greater portion of India's population, compared to Tanzania, clears the World Bank's $1.25 a day hurdle, Tanzania seems to be more successful in getting its people fed, housed, and educated. Higher income, therefore, does not always imply better health or nutrition. So it makes sense to explore other, non-income-based indicators. Furthermore, a poverty threshold based mainly on food spending, such as that of the United States, egregiously ignores that groceries account for only about 8 percent of total family expenses in that country. That is why the "Supplemental Poverty Measure" was mooted, to better estimate a household's ability to pay for basic necessities. On the one hand, it includes, besides cash, other forms of income such as food stamps, tax credits, and other means of government support, from which tax payments, work expenses, and medical bills are subtracted. On the other hand, the measure is adjusted for differences in the cost of living across the country's regions, as well as for whether a family owns or rents its home.

Poverty, therefore, has several other facets apart from low income, and each of them may impact wellbeing in a different way. This is the philosophy behind the "Multidimensional Poverty Index" (Oxford Poverty and Human Development Initiative 2012), developed by the University of Oxford and adopted by the United Nations Development Program. Poor people experience deprivation, not only in terms of lack of income, but also as poor health, lack of education, inadequate living conditions, lack of sanitation and clean water, disempowerment, poor-quality work, social exclusion, constant threat from violence, shame, and so forth. Addressing each of these aspects specifically and in their interactions with one another could lead to a more holistic understanding of deprivation and more effective poverty alleviation strategies (Alkire and Foster 2009). An innovative feature of this measure lies in the participation of the poor themselves in defining what poverty means for them, rather than just depending on the judgment of experts (*The Economist* 2010). This matters a lot, because an apparent deprivation, such as a dirt floor instead of a concrete one, may turn into a condition for wellbeing, due to the fact that it expresses a person's choice or preference. For similar reasons, we understand that fasting during Lent or Ramadan out of religious convictions is all right, but persistent hunger or involuntary starvation is not, no matter how "normal" it may be. The "Multidimensional Poverty Index" also detects the particular contours of poverty across regions. For instance, it has been discovered that material deprivations weigh more heavily in the experience of poverty in sub-Saharan Africa than in South Asia, where malnutrition is a greater scourge. Nonetheless, this index seems to be less useful for middle-income countries, which may have solved problems such as malnutrition and lack of clean water, but still suffer from other forms of poverty.

The relation between average per capita income and happiness among countries has been described by Frey and Stutzer (2002: 75) as a curvilinear one. If income is represented on a horizontal axis and happiness or life satisfaction on a vertical axis, one finds that in the beginning, every increase in income translates into a proportional increase in happiness. However, past a certain level of income, the increase in happiness tapers off, until it becomes practically negligible. Income may continue to rise, therefore, but happiness remains flat, for all intents and purposes. Hence, we could speak of a "diminishing marginal utility" for income, since upon reaching a certain point on the graph, the satisfaction derived from every unit increase in income decreases. If we were to interpret the graph as "income pushing happiness," then we could say that upon reaching the point where happiness plateaus, income, apparently, ceases to produce its positive effect on happiness. Based on studies comparing income and life satisfaction levels in different countries in the 1990s, Frey and Stutzer locate the turning point at $10,000 per capita at purchasing power parity (PPP) in 1995 US dollars.

Granted the correlation between income and happiness, it is legitimate to ask whether it is income, indeed, or other factors associated with income that exert a favorable influence on happiness. For as Frey and Stutzer (2002: 75) suggest, higher-income countries are, in general, more likely to have stable democratic regimes, and thereby to be in a better position to guarantee the basic human rights of citizens. Perhaps, because of this, their people also tend to enjoy greater income equality. At the same time, as we have already seen, more income means greater access to technology, which is of paramount importance to health, for instance. In other words, we cannot discount the possibility, at this stage, that rather than income *per se*, it is a host of other social indicators normally associated with income, such as democracy, human rights, equality, and better health that contribute to the life satisfaction of a country's citizens (Easterly 1999).

The influence of these other factors could explain, to some extent, the proliferation of happiness and life satisfaction measures among countries. For instance, there is the "Happy Life Years" indicator (Veenhoven 1996), which merges the results of Gallup-type surveys on life satisfaction with longevity or life expectancy. If, in a country, people give themselves an average of 5 in a 10-point happiness scale, and life expectancy at birth is 60 years, then "happy life years" equals 30 years [(average happiness × 0.1) × life expectancy at birth in years]. Apart from purchasing power per capita, "happy life years" also seems to be positively correlated with freedom (economic, political, and personal), brotherhood (tolerance, trust, voluntary work), and justice (rule of law, civil rights). By contrast, it is negatively correlated with corruption. Another approach consists of the "Happy Planet Index" (New Economics Foundation 2013). Besides wellbeing and life expectancy, it also takes into account a country's ecological footprint, the per capita measure of a country's resource consumption in terms of global hectares (g ha) [wellbeing × life expectancy/ecological footprint]. Thus, the "Happy Planet Index" frames the development of each country in the context of real environmental limits, marrying sustainability with wellbeing. Whether these other goods, such as longevity or environmental sustainability, could be obtained at lower income levels, however, is a different, although related matter that would also be worth considering.

In particular, this seems to be the case with Costa Rica, which consistently ranks among the happiest countries by these standards, despite having a much lower per capita income than, for example, Denmark or the United States (Kristoff 2010). Such high marks in happiness rankings by country could be ascribed to both natural endowments and human decisions. Firstly, Costa Rica is blessed by lush tropical mountains and jungles, and bathed on both sides by sparkling oceans and beaches. Yet the decision to preserve them belongs to its citizens and government, just like the resolution to dissolve its army in 1949, investing the money instead in education. This has paid off handsomely for Costa Rica, which now boasts of a highly educated English-speaking workforce that competes in huge growth sectors of the global economy, such as information technology components, manufacturing, and services, as well as eco-tourism. Better education has likewise been identified as the driver for gender equality and healthcare improvements, allowing for longer and healthier lives. Undoubtedly, the country's Latino culture, with its tight-knit families, extensive social networks, and healthy attitude to the work–leisure balance is an enormous plus factor for overall happiness.

Among the thirty-four rich countries belonging to the Organisation for Economic Co-operation and Development (OECD) we once again discover that the United States, despite having the highest income and wealth, is not the country with the highest life satisfaction – an honor that belongs to Switzerland, according to the 2103 Better Life Index (OECD 2013). Besides income and life satisfaction, this index considers nine other topics – community, education, environment, civic engagement, health, housing, jobs, safety, and work–life balance – that together contribute to overall quality of life. The data therefore suggest that Switzerland is more successful than the United States in providing citizens with greater life satisfaction through a mix of these quality of life indicators.

Remember, however, that the graph comparing income and life satisfaction levels among countries only shows correlation; not causality or the direction of causality. Instead of "income pushing happiness," it could very well be the case that "happiness pushes income." Just like happier economic classes in the previous research question, countries with happier populations could be more inclined to work harder, exercising creativity and entrepreneurship, and leading to greater success, and ultimately, higher incomes (Kenny 1999). Equally possible is that causality is bi-directional. Not only does "income push happiness," but "happiness pushes income" also. At this moment, we will just have to remain open to all of these possibilities. And on the premise that, indeed, causality between income and happiness among countries works both ways, we will still have to investigate whether the force is equal in both directions or stronger in one than in the other.

Regarding the question, therefore, whether richer countries are happier than poorer ones, we seem to have overcome initial doubts in the research to the point that we could now respond with an unqualified "yes." A corollary consists of having unmasked the falsehood of believing that people in poorer countries are happier, because they purportedly lead lives closer to nature. We have seen that poverty and deprivation are complex human experiences that depend not only on income or material resources. We have also had a chance to appreciate the value of choice in determining what counts as poverty. The relation between income and happiness across countries could best be described in the form of a curve indicating a "decreasing marginal utility" for income. Besides income, there seems to be a host of other related factors which somehow affect happiness, such as longevity and environmental quality. These, in turn, have given rise to wider happiness measures among countries. Yet we have never really determined the direction of causality between income and happiness across countries.

DO COUNTRIES BECOME HAPPIER AS THEY GROW RICHER?

Perhaps Easterlin's (1974: 108–111) response to this question was the least conclusive among the three. He had data for only one national time series, specifically from the United States for intermittent periods between 1946 and 1970, and with significant variations in the wording of the questionnaires which vitiated comparability. This did not hinder him from affirming, nevertheless, that "for the United States, since 1946, higher income was not systematically accompanied by greater happiness" (Easterlin 1974: 118).

Frey and Stutzer (2002: 76) were more fortunate, gaining access to later studies (Blanchflower and Oswald 2000; Lane 1998; Myers 2000) which show that although per capita income in the United States soared during the last decades of the previous century, nonetheless, the fraction of people who reported themselves to be "very happy" decreased. In particular, from 1946 to 1991, per capita income in the United States rose by 150 percent, from $11,000 to $27,000 in 1996 dollars. But happiness ratings fell, from an average of 2.4 on a three-point scale in 1946 to 2.2 in 1991. This transpired at a time when nearly all households had experienced an amazing increase in purchasing power, allowing themselves to enjoy modern conveniences such as indoor toilets, washing machines, telephones, color televisions, and cars (Easterlin 2000; Lebergott 1993). Frey and Stutzer described the graph plotting per capita income and happiness through the years as like an open pair of scissors, with average happiness falling despite the rise in income.

In interpreting the data, as Frey and Stutzer (2002: 77) themselves point out, we cannot discount changes in the population (not the same interviewees) or changing standards in happiness even among the same people (experiences falling short of expectations) during the 45-year interlude. However, they agree with Easterlin (1974:

119) in citing adaptation as a possible explanation for these results. The observation that as economic conditions improve, because of greater income, so does the social norm (which is none other than the generalized economic experience), by itself does not seem to require further proof. People not only compare themselves with relevant others, as we have already seen, but also compare their present experiences with what they remember in the past and how they imagine the future to be. Both incomes and aspirations are evaluated against particular backgrounds of time and place. Thus, it is fairly understandable that, despite a rise in income and living conditions, experienced happiness or life satisfaction levels turn out to be disappointing, if aspirations or expectations are too high.

Beyond a certain threshold of income in which practically all basic needs are met, people do not become happier as they grow richer. In consequence, neither do countries. The reason for this comes by many names, such as "adaptation level theory" (Frederick and Loewenstein 1999), "aspiration level theory" (Michalos 1991; Inglehart 1990), and to a large measure, also "set-point theory" (Fujita and Diener 2005). As income rises, there comes an initial surge in satisfaction from its attainment. But since generally, aspirations also rise in proportion to the increase in income, one grows accustomed or adapts to the new, higher income level. As a result, therefore, after a given period, the individual returns to his original, "set-point" level of happiness, in case of complete adaptation, or even slightly below, if aspirations have exceeded attainments and adaptation has been incomplete. (That aspirations fall short of attainments is most unlikely.) In other words, the net effect of higher income on happiness has been zero, or even possibly negative. Some see this set-point of a person's ability to experience pleasure or satisfaction as one determined largely by genetic factors, as part of a homeostatic mechanism (Headey and Wearing 1992).

Hedonic adaptation has been studied mostly in reference to consumer goods. Easterlin (2003: 11180–11181) cites the case of individuals who have been tracked over 16 years, from early, middle, and late adult stages in the life cycle, and have been asked regarding their material aspirations and attainments in reference to the good life. They were asked, first, about the things in life that they "would like to have" (aspirations), then next, about whether they already had those things (attainments). The lists contained the usual big-ticket consumer goods such as a home, a car, a television set, a swimming pool, a trip abroad, a vacation home, and so forth. Predictably, as people grew older, they fulfilled more of their initial material desires as their income and purchasing power rose. But their aspirations for more goods also increased. In fact, the results suggest that as material aspirations were fulfilled, new ones arose in approximately the same proportion. Hence the constancy in happiness levels throughout the individuals' lifetimes.

Because material aspirations increase commensurately with attainments in income and other similar possessions, thereby upgrading an individual's frame of reference, happiness levels tend to remain constant. Frey and Stutzer (2002: 78–79) unpack this observation into four different components. Firstly, it implies the insatiability of human wants and desires, especially for money, wealth, and other material possessions. However, there is also a bright side to this trait, inasmuch as ambition could also serve as a motor or prod in the unending search for excellence. Secondly, it teaches us that although, in theory, future aspirations could go either way, in fact, they always adjust upwards. Thirdly, insofar as greater opportunities, by way of higher income, also generate superior aspirations, happiness levels may experience decline. This situation is described as being caught in a "hedonic treadmill" (Brickman and Campbell 1971), wherein increasing effort is demanded simply to remain exactly in the same place, in terms of satisfaction or wellbeing. Eventually, of course, one may reach the point of exhaustion and pleasures drop. The pleasures associated with higher income opportunities are neutralized or reduced by the repetition of stimuli, habit, or custom. Closely related is the "satisfaction treadmill" (Kahneman 2000) where changes wrought by higher aspirations produce a similar effect. And lastly, it likewise illustrates an asymmetrical perspective of the past, when people generally think themselves to be less happy, and the future, when they imagine themselves to be happier than the present. This ingrained optimism regarding the future may have to do with some evolutionary advantage, as belief in progress or advancement spurs us on. Most disturbing, however, is the equally plausible conclusion that all efforts to satisfy mankind become self-defeating, because every satisfied desire produces – hydra-like – several more. Where, then, does that leave most government policies, which focus almost exclusively on economic growth? Of what use will that promise be, if it fails to bring wellbeing and happiness?

Some of the theories we have already seen regarding interpersonal comparisons also serve to explain why raising everybody's income in a given country does not produce a parallel increase in happiness. Hirsch (1976) calls our attention to two issues concerning positional goods and offers a possible remedy. The first issue deals with the "paradox of affluence," also called the "tiptoe paradox." It describes the situation in which everyone's income has risen, but no one feels better off. That's because relative to everybody else who happens to be a "relevant other," one's income rank, position, or status has not improved, but instead, remains the same. Something similar occurs when everyone decides to stand tiptoe while watching a street parade, for instance. Despite all the extra effort, no one really sees any better in the end. It would even have been preferable for the people to stand squarely on their feet. The second refers to the "distributional struggle" for positional goods such as a higher income, which leads to the accumulation of wasteful secondary goods. Whereas in principle, an increase in income for everyone allows for the enjoyment of more goods, such enjoyment is reduced by the mere fact that everyone else is doing the same. Participants feel a compulsion to outdo, not only themselves, but also one another, engaging in dubious spending of limited resources, just to reach the very top. But since this is a target moving upwards without end, it becomes a constant source of disappointment, frustration, and anxiety for everyone.

The nugatory effect of increased income cannot be better illustrated than in the case of wealth-addiction. Sam Polk narrates how angry he was at the end of his Wall Street trading career because – at the age of 30, free from debt and family obligations – he was only given a $3.6 million bonus: "I wanted more money for exactly the same reason an alcoholic needs another drink: I was addicted" (Polk 2014). The possible remedy to both paradoxes lies in a form of "reluctant collectivism," since neither competition among isolated individuals in the free market nor outright collective provision of such goods seems to work. Institutional measures, therefore, have to be called upon, mediating among individual choices in order to reach desired outcomes.

These paradoxes surrounding positional goods may also apply to other things apart from income. Take, for instance, the informal competition for the title of having the "tallest building" in a country or in the world (Leslie 2013). The installation of a 408-foot spire on top of One World Trade Center in New York in May 2013 would, in principle, give it a claim to be the "tallest building in the US" at the symbolic height of 1,776 feet, although certification from the Council on Tall Buildings and Urban Habitat will have to wait until construction is completed. Until then, Chicago's Willis Tower (formerly called Sears Tower) keeps the title at 1,451 feet, as it has for the past 40 years. In fact, the Willis Tower used to be the world's tallest building, until the Petronas Towers in Kuala Lumpur, Malaysia were finished in 1998.

But how, exactly, is the height of a building measured? It so happens that the Council offers three different criteria: highest occupied floor, height to the tip, and "architectural top." This last one may include structures such as ornamental spires, but not antennas, signs, flagpoles, or other functional–technical equipment. Therefore, the spires of both the Petronas Towers and One World Trade Center count as "architectural tops," while the antennas of the Willis Tower do not. Otherwise, One World Trade Center would actually be 83 feet shorter than Willis Tower at 1,368 feet, if its spire with lighting were considered "functional–technical equipment," like the Willis Tower antennas. In the contest for the tallest building, then, it pays to invest in ornamentation, which may oftentimes be useless, rather than in function. In fact, in what seems to be a clear case of one-upmanship, the One World Trade Center spire was actually flown and bolted on to its structural top, not built from the ground up. This not only raised costs in terms of labor and materials, but also enlarged the whole project's carbon footprint, without providing any additional benefit. Given the prestige and symbolism associated with having the tallest building, we cannot depend on the players themselves to control their spending, however wasteful, in trying to obtain the title. Instead, we will have to rely on the efforts of an institutional agent, like the Council, to lay down the rules. Even then, however, there is no guarantee that players will not do their best to work around the system.

Frank (2007) provides a more pointed version of the dilemmas involving positional goods as well as their remedy. The consumption of positional goods produces a negative externality on others – what we want depends precisely on what other people have – leading to an "arms race" in spending that leaves everyone worse-off. It therefore gives rise to a "market failure" in which government should be called upon to intervene, concretely, by way of a progressive consumption tax. He illustrates his argument by means of a hypothetical choice between two worlds: A, where one lives in a 4,000 square foot house while everyone else lives in a 6,000 square foot house, or B, where one lives in a 3,000 square foot house while everyone else lives in a 2,000 square foot house. Despite objectively having a larger house in A, most people choose to live in B, because in relative terms, they are better off. Housing size, therefore, is an example of a positional good, and in B, it is not oneself but the others, who would be feeling a "relative deprivation."

In theory, there are two sides to the problem of "relative deprivation": one, represented by the homeowner who enjoys the positional good, and the other, constituted by everyone else in the community who suffers from it. The cause of "relative deprivation," then, could either be the envy that other people feel or the "context" that one creates. Although Frank (2007) acknowledges that "status hunger" is an innate condition in humankind, common to both the owner of the larger house and all the other neighbors, however, he prefers to deal with the "context" rather than with envy. That's because envy locates the source of harm on the less fortunate who already feel relatively deprived, while "context" situates it in the conspicuous consumers of positional goods. Thus, it makes sense to levy a progressive consumption tax on the creator of the unequal context, to discourage such behavior and better redistribute excess income. Consumers of positional goods, then, are no different from polluters of the environment who impose negative externalities of their reckless conduct on others, their innocent victims.

Having surveyed the different mechanisms which detract from happiness, satisfaction, and wellbeing despite an increase in income, we may now have a look at the variety of strategies available to combat them. First of all, if the "set-point" hypothesis were completely true, that in spite of occasional highs and lows, one always returns to a genetically pre-established level of happiness due to homeostasis, then actually, there would be very little, if anything at all, that one could do. At most, one should only be aware of this fact and try to act in consequence, not taking changes in mood or humor too seriously. It is almost an invitation to embrace the stoic ideal of apathy, according to which happiness consists precisely in keeping calm and staying away from disturbances caused by emotions and feelings. But if one does not find this entirely convincing, then there are two other general lines of action to be pursued. One refers to counteracting or diminishing adaptation to the degree possible, getting off the hedonic and satisfaction treadmills to some extent, and modifying the context or social norm of consumption behaviors, without necessarily having recourse to taxation. The other focuses more on dealing with one's own aspirations and expectations in the future, despite their known insatiability and upward trajectory, striving to keep envy in check. In truth, the best option would be to follow a combination of these three main strategies. To do so effectively, however, one would need courage to change the things that have to change, patience to accept the things that cannot change, and wisdom to know the difference, as the old adage says.

Let us begin with the first, concerning adaptation. We may learn from the experience of a young American couple, Tammy Strobel and Logan Smith, who after 3 years of conscientiously living more simply, both discovered that they had become a lot happier, against all odds (Rosenbloom 2010). In 2007, Tammy, like her husband, was 31 years old, and worked as a manager in an investment firm in Davis, California, earning $40,000 a year. They led a comfortable life, occupying a two-bedroom apartment, owning two cars, and having enough dinner china for two dozen guests. Yet the couple realized that they were caught up in a "work–spend treadmill" and that they weren't really happy. So they decided to take on the challenge of reducing personal belongings to just 100 items, effectively subjecting their lifestyle to a radical downgrade. That is, they modified their consumption behaviors by adapting to a strikingly more frugal social norm. Three years later, the couple had moved to a 400 square foot apartment in Portland, Oregon, from where Tammy worked as a free-lance web designer and writer, making around $24,000 a year, enough to cover their expenses as Logan finished graduate school. Instead of cars, they owned bikes, and kitchenware was limited to four plates and two pots. They had also gotten rid of a $30,000 debt. Surprisingly, they could even contribute money for the education of nieces and nephews. Aside from happiness, the only thing they had more of was time, which they spent outdoors, traveling and volunteering in outreach programs.

The first major lesson consists in the decision to step down the consumption treadmills. Above all, this means to stop buying more material things such as clothes, appliances, cars, and so forth, to which we immediately adapt or grow accustomed. Beyond the initial surge, which soon wears off, getting new stuff such as these does not really contribute to happiness in the long run. Going back to basics makes more sense. Secondly, as for the extra things that one already has, it would be best to donate them to charity. In several experiments involving students and even babies conducted in different countries such as the United States, South Africa, India, and Canada, the research team headed by Elizabeth Dunn and Michael Norton discovered that spending money on others ("pro-social spending") actually makes one happier than spending money on oneself (Dunn and Norton 2013). Generosity seems to be its own reward after all. In third place, it also pays more, happiness-wise, to spend money on experiences, such as excursions, vacations, entertainment, sports, and so forth, instead of on material things. Because we don't adapt to such experiences as quickly, satisfaction tends to be longer lasting. That's also the reason why clever marketers try to dress their products as experiences, transforming outdoor grills into elements of garden parties, for example, thus increasing the perceived value for consumers.

Fourth, it certainly is smart to use money on leisure, especially the kind that strengthens social bonds and interactions. In the wake of the economic crisis which began in 2008, many families hardly had a choice but to remain home for "staycations." They found out, however, that by merely being together, sharing meals, watching movies, playing games in the backyard, and simply having time to relax and talk to each other, they enjoyed themselves a lot more than by going off, perhaps, to some expensive trip at an exotic spot. Fifth, adaptation may likewise be held at bay by consuming many smaller doses of pleasure, rather than by taking it all in one big gulp. For instance, in place of a continuous 2-week vacation, one may take the option of several long weekend breaks. Or instead of spending disposable income on a big-ticket item, such as a luxury sports car, one may think of a country club membership, enjoying a whole range of services little by little, spread over a long period of time. Lastly, one could also harness the powers of anticipation to the benefit of happiness by delaying gratification. Rather than "buy now, pay later," happiness increases by postponing enjoyment. Before credit financing became generalized and came into vogue, people spent a lot of time planning, saving, and fantasizing about their purchases. They were already enjoying the merchandise or the experience, albeit only in their imagination, previous to actual consumption, thereby adding to their total net satisfaction.

The alternative action plan consists in properly managing one's aspirations and expectations, without leaving room for envy. From practically any imaginable angle, Pico Iyer's life may be judged to be an unqualified success (Iyer 2009). He was born in the late 1950s in Oxford, where his father was a philosopher and his mother, a religious scholar. By the time he was 8 years old, the family had moved to Santa Barbara, California. He won scholarships to Eton, Oxford, and Harvard, graduating with the highest marks and distinctions for his education. He briefly taught writing and literature at Harvard in the early 1980s, before embarking on a renowned career as a writer for *Time Magazine*. Since then, he has written several novels and essays with cross-cultural themes, regularly contributing articles to *Harper's*, *The New York Review of Books*, *The New York Times*, and many other distinguished publications. Upon marrying his Japanese wife, Hiroko Takeuchi, he decided to move to Kyoto, where he has been living for almost 25 years. He confesses to not missing his Park Avenue apartment or his Rockefeller Center office at all, not even his jet-set vacationing to sites as varied as Burma, Morocco, and El Salvador. Instead, he feels rather content, living in an almost monastic, two-room apartment, with no car, bicycle, television, cell phone, internet, or any form of understandable media.

About the time he was 30, Iyer was coming round to the realization that "happiness lies less in our circumstances than in what we make of them" (Iyer 2009). In other words, happiness depends more on our inner world, our aspirations, desires, and expectations, than on the objective material realities that surround us in themselves. The challenge, then, lay in getting hold of these interior yearnings and re-directing them toward other, perhaps scaled-down goals. Despite being very well placed in his chosen profession, it dawned on him that "always [...] there was some higher position I could attain, which meant that, like Zeno's arrow, I was guaranteed never to arrive and always to remain dissatisfied" (Iyer 2009). So, much like the young American couple in the previous story, Iyer resolved to adopt a lifestyle that was as simple as possible. To his amazement, he discovered how "happiness arose out of all I didn't want or need" (Iyer 2009). The lack of a car gave him the daily adventure of going around the neighborhood, and the absence of communication media gifted him with enough time to write long friendly letters, to read, and to play. All of these turned out to be immensely gratifying. It's not that he has lost interest in everything else in the wider world; at least, not in the results of the NBA finals. But he has reached the conviction that "Perhaps happiness, like peace or passion, comes most when it isn't pursued" (Iyer 2009). And although he wouldn't recommend a life based on renunciation indiscriminately, for him, it was certainly the right choice: "In New York, a part of me was always somewhere else, thinking of what a simple life in Japan might be like. Now I'm there, I find that I almost never think of Rockefeller Center or Park Avenue at all" (Iyer 2009). Iyer indeed comes close to the Buddhist ideal of happiness, maybe not eliminating desires, but reorienting them toward objectives closer in reach.

HOW MUCH HAPPINESS CAN MONEY BUY?

Surprisingly little. Very little. For whoever may be reading this work, most probably, hardly any more than what he already has. For one can reasonably suppose that such a person would have his basic material needs more than adequately covered. Money counts a lot for the happiness of individuals who are poor in absolute terms and for whom mere subsistence oftentimes requires a daily struggle. Beyond such a dire situation, however, the impact of money on happiness becomes less and less. This is reflected in the diminishing marginal utility of income for life satisfaction or happiness, when comparing a cross-section of countries on both fronts. Furthermore, we cannot discount the possibility that, whatever this contribution may be, it is attributable not to money directly, but to a host of other factors associated with money. In the case of individuals, we may refer to health-care or education, whereas for countries, we could think of access to technology, a functioning democracy, or environmental stewardship, aside from cultural features such as the strength of family ties, for instance. Money, which is, above all, a proxy for the opportunity set of material goods and services within one's reach, turns out to be a vital, necessary condition, but by no means a sufficient one, in achieving happiness. This holds equally true for individuals as well as entire countries. Exactly how much money is necessary, however, can only be determined by taking into account the particularities of time and place, the social norm, and most important, the scope and intensity of individual desires.

To a large extent, the amount of happiness money can buy depends not on the individual in isolation, but on such a person as a member of a community. That's why past a certain stage of absolute deprivation, happiness becomes more a function of income relative to that of other constituents of society, especially one's relatives, friends, and neighbors. Generally, the higher the position one occupies in the income ranking, the more satisfied he is, and the lower, the more miserable. For this reason, it makes sense to speak not only of income poverty, but also of poverty in other dimensions, and above all, of inequality as a great source of unhappiness. However, not all forms of inequality possess the same relevance. Perhaps the unhappiness one suffers for not having as many cars, yachts, or vacation homes as one's neighbors is not as justified as that of another who cannot afford basic health services or does not have enough funds to send his children to school. It's when inequality arises from injustice or is accompanied by it that it becomes a scourge. This just goes to show that human beings, in accordance with their social nature, could only attain happiness by entering into a relation of codependence or solidarity with their like. In a similar fashion, by refusing to acknowledge the consequences of one's choices, decisions, and actions on others, human beings are able to inflict a great deal of misery on the rest of their kind and ultimately, also on themselves.

As we have seen, money is not related to wellbeing and satisfaction in a univocal way. Instead, it could even occur, as it does quite frequently, that net happiness diminishes in society despite high levels of income. Take, for instance, when these resources are used for conspicuous consumption or for the enjoyment of purely positional goods. Although, for a short period of time, whoever happens to be ahead in the conspicuous consumption contest or on the positional goods curve may experience a burst of happiness, that is not long lasting. It fades away as soon as someone else outdoes him, by however little an amount. And by then, a much greater and ever-increasing effort will be required to regain an ephemeral and marginal lead. That's why, in spite of the increase in income evidenced by growing expenditures, less happiness results, for resources are spent on items which are largely useless by themselves. Their only utility lies in their capacity to signal wealth, status, and power.

One may, of course, remark that the competition for positional goods would only take place if there were at least two willing players. If the rest of society ignored, shunned, or even looked down upon one's signaling, that individual's balloon would pop and no escalation of useless expenditures would take place. Consider, for example, how members of the old moneyed class tend to frown on the ostentation and opulence of the parvenus and Johnny-come-latelies, never accepting them into their fold. Instead, they prefer to go around in inexpensive and even shabby clothes, to mark out the difference in what amounts to be a form of reverse snobbery. Unfortunately, however, such a reaction does not take place as often as we would like, and in the majority of cases, it is the positional goods "arms race" that carries the day. In other words, people love to show off, to flaunt their wealth, to strut their stuff. And the rest have a very difficult time to control their envy, time and again battling to keep up with the Joneses, regardless of the odds of winning.

Greater income also fails to result in greater happiness, because it may be the case that we have a genetic set-point for happiness, to which we always revert after occasional blips. An increase in income then becomes useless. Similarly, due to a process of adaptation or because aspirations are in an upward spiral, more wealth and consumption does not translate into increased satisfaction with life. A few recommendations have been offered to keep adaptation at bay, such as investing more in experiences than on objects and indulging in such experiences in smaller doses, spread out through longer periods, thus effectively delaying gratification. As for aspirations, they may be kept in control by putting a stop to the compulsive buying of superfluities, by giving away whatever one holds in excess, or by spending on others instead of oneself. That means rational spending, keeping budget discipline, not being covetous or selfish, and having the ability to say "no" to the temptation of easy pleasure. But then again, no matter how clear and convincing the theory may be, all this is much easier said than put into practice.

REFERENCES

Alkire, S. and Foster, J. 2009. "Counting and multidimensional poverty measurement," *Oxford Poverty and Human Development Initiative (OPHI) Working Paper*, no. 32 (www.ophi.org.uk/wp-content/uploads/OPHI_WP32.pdf? 9700ef, accessed May 29, 2013).

Biswas-Diener, R. and Diener, E. 2001. "Making the best of a bad situation: Life in the slums of Calcutta," *Social Indicators Research*, 55(3): 329–352.

Blanchflower, D. G. and Oswald, A. J. 2000. "Wellbeing over time in Britain and the USA," *NBER Working Paper*, no. 7487.

Bowles, S. and Jayadev, A. 2014. "One nation under guard," *New York Times*, February 15.

Brickman, P. and Campbell, D. T. 1971. "Hedonic relativism and planning the good society," in Appley, M. H. (ed.), *Adaptation level theory: A symposium.* New York: Academic Press, pp. 287–302.

Brickman, P., Coates, D. and Janoff-Bulman, R. 1978. "Lottery winners and accident victims: Is happiness relative?" *Journal of Personality and Social Psychology*, 36(8): 917–927.

Brooks, D. 2014. "The inequality problem," *New York Times*, January 16.

Cantril, H. 1965. *The pattern of human concerns*. New Brunswick, NJ: Rutgers University Press.

Clark, A. E. 1997. "Job satisfaction and gender: Why are women so happy at work?" *Labour Economics*, 4(4): 341–372.

Clark, A. E. and Oswald, A. J. 1996. "Satisfaction and comparison income," *Journal of Public Economics*, 61(3): 359–381.

Diener, E., Diener, M. and Diener, C. 1995. "Factors predicting the subjective well-being of nations," *Journal of Personality and Social Psychology*, 69(5): 851–864.

Duesenberry, J. S. 1949. *Income, saving and the theory of consumer behavior*. Cambridge, MA: Harvard University Press.

Dunn, E. and Norton, M. 2013. *Happy money: The science of smarter spending*. New York: Simon and Schuster.

Easterlin, R. A. 1974. "Does economic growth improve the human lot? Some empirical evidence," in David, P. A. and Reder, M. W. (eds.), *Nations and households in economic growth: Essays in honor of Moses Abramowitz*. New York and London: Academic Press, pp. 89–125.

2000. "The worldwide standard of living since 1800," *Journal of Economic Perspectives*, 14(1): 7–26.

2003. "Explaining happiness," *Proceedings of the National Academy of Sciences of the United States of America (PNAS)*, 100(19): 11176–11183.

Easterly, W. 1999. "Life during growth," *Journal of Economic Growth*, 4(3): 239–276.

Fletcher, M. A. 2013. "Research ties economic inequality to gap in life expectancy," *Washington Post*, March 11.

Frank, R. H. 2007. *Falling behind: How rising inequality harms the middle class*. Berkeley: University of California Press.

Frederick, S. and Loewenstein, G. 1999. "Hedonic adaptation," in Kahneman, D., Diener, E. and Schwartz, N. (eds.), *Well-being: The foundations of hedonic psychology*. New York: Russell Sage Foundation, pp. 302–329.

Frey, B. S. and Stutzer, A. 2002. *Happiness and economics: How the economy and institutions affect human well-being*. Princeton, NJ/Oxford: Princeton University Press.

Fujita, F. and Diener, E. 2005. "Life satisfaction set-point: Stability and change," *Journal of Personality and Social Psychology*, 88: 158–164.

Gauguin, P. 1985. *Noa Noa: The Tahitian journal*. New York: Dover Publications.

Headey, B. and Wearing, A. 1992. *Understanding happiness*. Melbourne: Longman Cheshire.

Hirsch, F. 1976. *The social limits to growth*. Cambridge, MA: Harvard University Press.

Inglehart, R. F. 1990. *Culture shift in advanced industrial society*. Princeton, NJ: Princeton University Press.

Inkeles, A. and Diamond, L. 1986. "Personal development and national development: A cross-cultural perspective," in Szalai, A. and Andrews, F. M. (eds.), *The quality of life: Comparative studies*. Ann Arbor: Institute for Social Research, University of Michigan, pp. 73–109.

Iyer, P. 2009. "The joy of less," *New York Times*, June 7.

Kahneman, D. 2000. "Experienced utility and objective happiness: A moment-based approach," in Kahneman, D. and Tversky, A. (eds.), *Choices, values, and frames*. New York: Cambridge University Press and Russell Sage Foundation, pp. 187–208.

Kenny, C. 1999. "Does growth cause happiness, or does happiness cause growth?" *Kyklos*, 52(1): 3–26.

Kristoff, N. 2010. "The happiest people," *New York Times*, January 7.

Lane, R. E. 1998. "The joyless market economy," in Ben-Ner, A. and Putterman, L. (eds.), *Economics, values, and organization*. Cambridge: Cambridge University Press, pp. 461–488.

Lebergott, S. 1993. *Pursuing happiness: American consumers in the twentieth century*. Princeton, NJ: Princeton University Press.

Leslie, T. 2013. "Heights of fancy," *New York Times*, May 30.

Ludwig, J., Liebman, J. B., Kling, J. R., Duncan, G. J., Katz, L. F., Kessler, R. C. and Sanbonmatsu, L. 2008. "What can we learn about neighborhood effects from the moving to opportunity experiment?" *American Journal of Sociology*, 114 (1): 144–188.

Marx, K. 2006. *Wage labour and capital* (www.marxists.org/archive/marx/works/1847/wage-labour/ch06.htm, accessed May 21, 2013).

McNay, D. 2012. *Life lessons from the lottery: Protecting your money in a scary world*. Key Biscayne, FL: RRP International.

Michalos, A. C. 1991. *Global report on student well-being. Volume 1: Life satisfaction and happiness*. New York: Springer.

Myers, D. G. 2000. "The funds, friends, and faith of happy people," *American Psychologist*, 55(1): 56–67.

Neumark, D. and Postlewaite, A. 1998. "Relative income concerns and the rise in married women's employment," *Journal of Public Economics*, 70: 157–183.

New Economics Foundation 2013. *Happy planet index* (www.happyplanetindex.org/about/, accessed May 28, 2013).

Nocera, J. 2012. "The bad luck of winning," *New York Times*, November 30.

OECD 2013. *Better life index* (www.oecdbetterlifeindex.org/#/21111111511, accessed June 3, 2013).

Oxford Poverty and Human Development Initiative 2012. *Multidimensional poverty index* (www.ophi.org.uk/policy/multidimensional-poverty-index/, accessed May 29, 2013).

Piketty, T. 2014. *Capital in the twenty-first century.* Cambridge, MA: Harvard University Press.

Piketty, T. and Saez, E. 2013. "Income inequality in the United States, 1913–1998" (with the latest update of tables and figures to 2011), *Quarterly Journal of Economics*, 118(1): 1–39.

Polk, S. 2014. "For the love of money," *New York Times*, January 18.

Renwick, T. 2012. *What is supplemental poverty measure and how does it differ from the official measure?* (http://blogs.census.gov/2012/11/08/what-is-the-supplemental-poverty-measure-and-how-does-it-differ-from-the-official-measure/, accessed May 29, 2013).

Rosenbloom, S. 2010. "But will it make you happy?" *New York Times*, August 7.

Rosenstein-Rodan, P. N. 1961. "International aid for underdeveloped countries," *Review of Economics and Statistics*, 43: 107–138.

Smith, S. and Razzel, P. 1975. *The pools winners.* London: Caliban.

Sousa-Poza, A. and Sousa-Poza, A. 2000. "Taking another look at the gender/job-satisfaction paradox," *Kyklos*, 53(2): 135–152.

The Economist 2010. *A wealth of data*, July 29.

2011a. *Measure by measure*, January 20.

2011b. *Unbottled Gini*, January 20.

Veblen, T. 2013. *The theory of the leisure class* (www.gutenberg.org/files/833/833-h/833-h.htm, accessed May 21, 2013).

Veenhoven, R. 1991. "Is happiness relative?" *Social Indicators Research*, 24(1): 1–34.

Veenhoven, R. 1996. "Happy life-expectancy: A comprehensive measure of quality of life in nations," *Social Indicators Research*, 39(1): 1–58.

Wilkinson, R. and Pickett, K. 2009. *The spirit level.* London: Allen Lane.

3 Choice, desire, and pleasure

Is happiness getting what you want or
wanting what you get?

Unless one happens to have the misfortune of living at subsistence
level, money by itself accounts for fairly little, much less than what
we usually imagine, in happiness. There are a host of other factors
to bear in mind, such as one's income relative to that of other members of the community or in comparison to one's aspirations. Adaptation or growing accustomed to the pleasures and satisfactions derived
from income likewise merits consideration. But beyond these issues
already discussed in the previous chapter, we would also have to look
into consumption decisions, into how income is spent and its surprisingly predictable impact on happiness. By so doing, we move beyond
the realm of what has heretofore been understood to be strictly material and economic, into the more nebulous region of psychology. In
particular, we shall be analyzing the psychological mechanisms that
enter into play, whenever we evaluate options and make decisions
with regard to pleasure, satisfaction, and ultimately, happiness. None
of this would occur, however, were it not for the underlying principle
of desire, which is the moving life force in all human beings.

Robert Frank (1997) has long defended the idea that happiness
is not a matter of how much money is available, but of how the available money is spent, such that it benefits not only the individual,
but also all the other members of the community at the same time.
He believes that happiness is some form of "public good," meant to
be enjoyed by all individual members of society in a non-excludable
and non-rivalrous way. And for this reason, he finds it fully justified
for government to adopt a more interventionist stance, by way of
implementing a progressive consumption tax, for example, instead

of leaving purchasing decisions to market coordination through the pricing system exclusively. Thus, affluent consumers will be discouraged from spending discretionary income on things that serve only to boost their satisfaction at the expense of others, in what amounts to a "zero-sum game" or a "nuclear arms race." He provides a series of thought experiments which, when melded with inputs from neuroscience, physiology, and psychology, show how certain consumption choices could indeed, on the contrary, give way to higher levels of subjective wellbeing for everyone (Frank 1997: 1836–1839).

Frank offers for our consideration two societies, A and B, which are identical in all respects except that in A, people live in a 5,000 square foot house, while in B, they live in a 3,000 square foot house. Those in society A, because they have bigger homes, live farther from their place of work and have to go through a 1-hour commute daily, driving through heavy traffic. Those in society B, because they have smaller homes, live at a shorter distance and only have a 15-minute journey on a commuter train. Which society would have higher life satisfaction levels? The question here is whether it would be better to spend on housing (more room) or on transportation (shorter commute), holding everything else constant. While it may appear to some that a larger home is preferable, psychological and neurophysiological studies suggest that people, in due course, almost always completely adapt to more spacious homes, such that they no longer provide them with any significant, long-lasting pleasure. We quickly tend to fill up whatever empty space is left in our homes with all sorts of knick-knacks, and even end up having to rent extra storage space, just to keep things we neither really need nor use. No such adaptation takes place, however, with the stress that comes from the longer commute, or with the noise, tiredness, annoyance, and other irritants that accompany it. They result in a prolonged elevated blood pressure and higher concentrations of stress hormones such as cortisol and norepinephrine, which weaken the immune system and make people more vulnerable to illnesses, effectively shortening life-spans. From the happiness perspective, therefore, it pays to invest more in efficient public transportation than in enormous housing units or "McMansions."

Let us return once again to societies A and B, and this time consider that residents of A, because they spend so much time traveling, do not have time for daily exercise, whereas residents of B, because they live closer, could afford 45 minutes of exercise daily. Which society would be happier? The trade-off now concerns the size and distance of homes and the time available for physical exercise. Frank then tells us that regular aerobic exercise produces enduring physiological and psychological benefits, including better health (less heart disease, strokes, diabetes, hypertension, and so forth), longer lives, and more frequent and intense positive feelings. And although initially, one may regard exercise as unpleasant, oftentimes one adjusts to it, and eventually finds it enjoyable. Money, therefore, would be put to better use in regular aerobic exercise that develops endurance and lessens stress than in buying larger homes, especially if this means longer commutes.

In recent years, experiments with rats have shown that exercise stimulates the growth of new brain neurons that are biochemically better equipped to cope with stress (Reynolds 2009). Rats that have been running for several weeks registered lower activity levels of serotonin, a neurotransmitter, when subjected to laboratory stressors than slothful rats. As a result, exercising rats manifested less anxiety and helplessness. Similar findings have been obtained from experiments with another neurotransmitter, dopamine. Furthermore, it has been demonstrated that moderate exercise attenuates the deleterious effects of oxidative stress on neurons as well as on other types of cells. These health benefits in rats, however, were not produced instantly. They required sustained exercise efforts during at least 6 weeks. Although no immediate exercise recommendations for human beings could yet be inferred from the experiment with rodents, it seems reasonable to think that regular, moderate aerobic exercise, such as running, swimming, or cycling, by triggering physiological and biochemical changes, effectively helps combat stress in people.

Going back to Frank (1997: 1838–1839), in a third scenario he again proposes societies A and B, where residents of A, because they own bigger houses, have to work longer hours to pay for them, and thus have little time to socialize with friends, effectively doing so only once a month. Residents of B, on the other hand, because of their smaller and more economical houses, don't have to work as hard, and instead, can afford to get together with friends four times a month. Who are happier? Is it worthwhile to work longer hours, in order to support a bigger household, at the expense of cutting down on social life? Apparently not. The loss of pleasures deriving from frequent, varied, and deep social contacts cannot be offset by those that come from a higher income or a more spacious home. In order to be happy, therefore, it may be better to spend time socializing with friends than slaving it out in work and other income-generating activities.

Despite the evidence that investing resources on more efficient transportation, regular aerobic exercise, and social relationships produces higher levels of subjective wellbeing than using them for larger homes and longer work hours, why do so many people behave as if it were otherwise? Frank (1997) suggests two possible explanations which have already been alluded to. The first concerns the difficulty of deciding with incomplete information, particularly on the degree of future adaptation to a chosen good. This may be reflected in the common dilemma between going to work on Saturdays, for instance, just in order to earn extra income to buy a more expensive car, or staying home and relaxing with family and friends. One does not easily imagine, at the time of making the decision, how quickly he will grow accustomed to the new sports car, and consequently, how much he will miss out on the more desirable social relations.

The second, more complicated issue relates to the interaction between individual decisions that oftentimes results in a "positional goods arms race." In the United States, for example, spending money to buy a house in a neighborhood with purportedly better schools for one's children may only result in driving up real estate prices, without producing any of the imagined educational benefits, especially if everyone else decides to behave in the same way. (Remember that, in the United States, public schools are usually funded through real estate taxes, so that the more expensive the homes, the greater the budget for public schools.) It may be a wiser choice to allocate money to a different end, therefore, such as to investments for one's retirement. Moreover, while there will always be loans available for education, there are none for retirement. So by short-changing retirement investments, one can, in fact, simply be increasing the likelihood of having to depend on one's children for support later in life (Carrns 2014).

Sometimes, individual interests as reflected in a private consumption decision may prove detrimental to those of society as a whole, thus creating the need for government to step in. Instead of taxing savings, for example, it would be better to levy a progressive tax on consumption. That would discourage individuals from spending on luxury goods for the sole reason of improving their social status. Such behaviors give rise to certain forms of competition in which everyone loses and are, therefore, highly unproductive from the overall perspective.

There are other behaviors that reflect this same principle of how looking out exclusively for one's own advantage leads first to harming others and, eventually, to harming oneself as well, due to the waste of resources. Think of standing out on the curb to watch a street parade. It may occur to one individual that by standing tiptoe, he may a get a better view of the pageantry. But inevitably, this means blocking the view of those behind him. These people, then, will come around to the trick and start tiptoeing as well. In the end, when everyone is tiptoeing, they will see exactly the same thing as if they were more comfortably standing flat on their feet, but with greater effort. In other words, no one wins and everybody loses. Similarly, we could imagine an office situation wherein workers excessively value "face-time," so they linger around even beyond work hours to create a favorable impression on their bosses, as is often said to happen in Japan and Korea. It could even be the case that they are not really engaged in any productive activity, but are simply seated, doing extra time in front of their computer screens. If only one or just a few workers were to do this, it might function. But if most people or everyone did it, then the overtime would be to no avail. It would only result in a waste of resources, of time, effort, and money, without benefits for anyone, not to mention the missed opportunities of being with family and friends, engaged in other, more pleasant activities instead.

We could also set aside the possible harms, both to others and to oneself, and consider, instead, the possible benefits. Spending money on others rather than on oneself has been shown to be highly effective in boosting personal happiness (Dunn and Norton 2013). Such pro-social behavior, also known as "philanthropic giving," has produced the same positive effect on happiness, regardless of the amount of money spent, the items bought, and the culture or country of residence. There is a qualified sense, therefore, in which money can be said to "buy happiness": paradoxically, to the extent it is spent on benefitting other people.

In a sense, Frank's proposals are a special case of "internalizing negative externalities": that is, taking into account those harmful side-effects of one's purportedly private decisions and actions. This is a similar response, then, to policy recommendations coming from James Buchanan's school of "public choice," which justifies collective political action in order to eliminate, or at least diminish, the external costs or negative externalities arising from individual behaviors, while ensuring certain external benefits or positive externalities for all (Buchanan and Tullock 1962; Buchanan 1975). In contrast to Buchanan's libertarian leanings, however, Frank may find in Amartya Sen's "social choice" option, which tries to compatibilize inalienable individual rights and freedoms with the consequences of concrete economic behavior, a more kindred progressive spirit (Sen 1999).

SPOILED FOR CHOICE

Among modern happiness scholars, Tibor Scitovsky (1992) stands out by proposing a solution which does not side with either the unreconstructed individual or the all-knowing and imperial state, but with education. The problem that he deals with can be phrased in several ways. Can a market economy or, better still, a consumerist brand of capitalism, characterized by an almost infinite variety of choices catering to individual whims, by itself make us happy? If not, can it at least guarantee us greater happiness than that promised by the alternative of a state-controlled, centrally planned economy? Implicit in the question is the belief that freedom is a necessary condition for happiness, and therefore, the greater the freedom, in terms of the variety of choices available in the market, the easier it is to satisfy personal needs and desires, and ultimately, the better it is for happiness. To make his case, Scitovsky goes through three steps. First, he questions the widespread assumption in the dominant neoclassical economic theory regarding the sovereignty of individual choice. Next, he develops a careful analysis of the challenges and pitfalls of opulent societies, of societies of abundance. And thirdly, he delineates recommendations on the role of education, especially in early childhood, to better equip people in combating the dangers of abundance and opulence, in such a way that positively influences their chances of achieving happiness.

The neoclassical economic belief that Scitovsky challenges could be stated as follows: the individual consumer knows what is best for himself and always seeks to achieve it rationally – that is, making the best use of the means available at his disposal Scitovsky (1992: 7–8). Economists take for granted that, when it comes to preference-formation, in tastes, desires, and inclinations, each consumer is his own master, uninfluenced by others. For this reason, economists are loath even to analyze the motivations of consumer behavior, lest they inadvertently impose their own standards on other people, which would be highly inappropriate. Consumer preferences are simply beyond the scope of an economist's competence, and therefore must be treated as givens or inalterable facts. It is not for economists to judge whether such preferences conform or not to proper standards by their own reckoning, for this would violate an elementary freedom, the freedom of choice. The only thing expected of economists, and of the market as a whole, is to efficiently deliver the goods and services that consumers want, for the purpose of their own satisfaction and happiness. Similarly, economists assume that, as market players, consumers know exactly what they are doing, and that they are doing it the best they can, as befits resourceful, individual-preference maximizers (Jensen and Meckling 1994). Consumers need not be told what is the best way to proceed in order to protect or further their own self-interests. They are more than capable of looking out for themselves. That is already deeply ingrained in their nature, as its proper logic or rationality.

The contrary position that Scitovsky adopts consists of two elements (Scitovsky 2002: 59). Firstly, it acknowledges that, in making, stating, and acting on preferences, individual consumers can and do commit mistakes. Tastes and inclinations are often affected by experiences (either vicarious or one's own), recommendations, and customs, as well as prices and availability of goods in the market. In fact, many people ignore or may even be completely unaware of things and activities that could bring them enjoyment and happiness. In brief, they don't necessarily know what's best for them. Their situation could be likened to that of the prisoners in the allegory of the cave in Plato's *Republic* (514a–520a). Accustomed to merely seeing the shadows of those who pass by the mouth of the cave, they could not even suspect the variety and richness in color and form of the outside world. And when, eventually, one of them breaks free, goes out of the dungeon, and experiences the real world in its fullness, his other companions refuse to believe what he relays to them. They prefer the comforts of their familiar, black and white environment to the thrill and excitement of the kaleidoscopic world outside. That is too much of a risk. The returned escapee, more than a deliverer, has become a nuisance, an instigator, a rabble-rouser. For the good of all, it is best that he be silenced and the matter put to rest. Sadly, this happens more often than we care to admit. As this allegory teaches, tastes and inclinations in themselves are not infallible, therefore, and we frequently seek satisfaction from the wrong things. Certain objects of desire may even positively do us harm and thereby detract from our long-term happiness.

Moreover, for Scitovsky, we must not confuse freedom of choice, the ability to decide what to buy, where, and in what quantities with one's own money, with consumer sovereignty (Scitovsky 1992: 8). He expresses a fairly negative view of consumer sovereignty, especially when it is taken to mean that, as with the freedom of choice, all consumers are equally sovereign. Not all individual consumers have the same capacity to influence the market with respect to kind, quantity, price, and so forth of the goods to be produced. He likens the market to a voting machine, where the money consumers spend is counted as votes. The more a consumer spends, the greater his voting power, and consequently, the more of the good or service that he desires will be produced. Rather than as a democracy, the market or free enterprise system, then, functions more like a plutocratic regime. A consumer's influence is determined by his purchasing power, and not all consumers possess the same amount by a long shot.

The second element of the critique casts doubt over the unfailing rationality of the individual consumer's decision making. Not only do we sometimes desire the wrong things, but we also desire – even the right things – the wrong way. For Scitovsky, consumers are nearly always subject to a myriad of desires, and inevitably, these desires enter into frequent conflict with one another. We experience these conflicts under different names – most commonly, as a "lack of self-control" or a "weakness of will." We find this, for instance, whenever we have to go on a diet for health reasons. We are torn between the desire to assuage hunger or to indulge in a craving, on the one hand, and the equally strong desire to maintain or improve bodily strength, on the other. Some other examples can be found in the struggle to rid oneself of unwholesome addictions in whatever form. The sensation of being pulled apart in opposite directions could indeed be excruciating. Apart from the lack of self-control, other causes of failure could be the lack of information, attention, or cognitive ability. Consider the difficulty in deciding the best cellphone model or service-contract for our particular needs, for example. As a result, instead of a single, self-interest maximizing model, in reality what we have is a wide variety of decision-making rationalities: egoists, altruists, misers, spendthrifts, ambitious, unambitious, scientifically minded, artistic, and their respective gradations (Scitovsky 2002: 59). The *homo economicus*, an individual who thinks and chooses unfailingly well, is a mere figment of our imagination; real human beings have weaknesses and often make mistakes (Thaler and Sunstein 2008: 6). Moreover, warm-blooded human beings happen to have two decision systems: an automatic system located in the most primitive part of the brain, on which we rely for rapid, instinctive responses ("fight or flight"), and a reflective system found in the more evolved part of the brain, responsible for the slower, more self-aware, and deliberative reactions. Oftentimes, one gets in the way of the other, leading to hasty conclusions which we end up regretting. Instead of being error-proof, we should then at least accept that our decision-making process, given these rival rationalities, often becomes error-prone. Furthermore, as Ariely (2010) alerts us, in the same way that, willy-nilly, we are subject to optical illusions regarding length or color, for instance, we also fall prey irremediably to cognitive illusions and biases in many of our decisions. What's more, being aware of them does little to change outcomes or results. We have a knack for always stumbling on the same obstacles. Hence, in pursuing choices under these constraints, we are not in control and instead behave in a manner that becomes, ironically, "predictably irrational."

Most of Scitovsky's intuitions have been borne out by recent empirical research on the impact of choices on consumer behavior. We normally think that, as rational agents, we have a fairly good idea of what we want, and that as long as we get it, there's no reason why we shouldn't be happy. Sheena Iyengar persuasively argues how little aware we are of our own preferences and how sometimes, the best choices we make from the viewpoint of happiness are quite disengaged from those preferences (Iyengar 2010). In the first experiment, students from New York and several Scandinavian countries were shown pictures of two women, one blonde, the other, brunette, and were asked whom they thought was prettier. Next, they were shown the pictures again and were asked for the reason behind their choice. Unbeknownst to the subjects, however, experimenters switched pictures, showing the picture of the blonde when they had chosen the brunette or the other way around. Eighty seven percent did not even notice that pictures had been switched, and simply replied, "Because I prefer blondes" or "Because I prefer brunettes," when asked. Of course, one may say that preference for blondes or brunettes when asked casually is not really a life-altering choice requiring one's full attention. But it still drives home the point of how distracted we are, forgetting about our preferences when we choose or adapting our previously stated preferences to our actual choice.

The second experiment concerns members of the graduating class from eleven universities in the United States who went through three waves of interviews, in September, December, and May of the academic year, about the characteristics they looked for in a job (Iyengar 2010). Responses were then ranked: first, interesting work, second, autonomy, and third, security, for instance. By December, both the responses and the rankings had changed compared to September, with security and income becoming more important than autonomy, for example. And finally, in May, preferences changed once again, reflecting adjustments to the job offers still available or to the jobs which they had already accepted, as was the case of some. Because of this, the correlation between what these seniors said they wanted in September and what they said in May was utterly insignificant, about 0.06. But more interestingly, those who remembered their preferences in September were less satisfied with the choices they made in May, and were even already thinking of changing jobs the following year. It also turned out that these same people received fewer job offers, despite or perhaps because they were so sure of their preferences. By contrast, those who did not remember their preferences in September received more job offers and were happier with their choices later in

May. There may be some truth to the saying, then, that happiness lies more in wanting what you get: that is, adapting your preferences to actual results, than in getting what you want or sticking to your preferences.

Besides Iyengar (2010), other authors have denounced the excessive importance Western society nowadays attaches to freedom of choice for happiness, to the point that it has become self-defeating. As sociologist Nikolas Rose writes, "modern individuals are not merely 'free to choose', but *obliged to be free* to understand and enact their lives in terms of choice. They must interpret their past and dream their futures as outcomes of choices made and choices still to make. Their choices are [...] seen as realizations of the attributes of the choosing person" (Rose 1999: 87). Barry Schwartz (2004) enumerates several reasons for the deleterious effect of too much choice on our own happiness: it facilitates regret, especially when one calculates the "opportunity costs" of actual choice against those of other options (dwelling on what one is missing out); it produces an escalation of expectations, which then become more difficult to fulfill; and it creates opportunities for self-blame, for the burden of the results or outcomes fall squarely on one's shoulders. Renata Salecl, in turn, speaks of the "tyranny of choice," which overwhelms us and produces in us a boundless anxiety to the point of paralysis; in effect, it has become the ideology of the West (Salecl 2010). She reminds us also of a few overlooked points regarding choice: that it is never a solitary act, inasmuch as we are always subject to the influence of other people; that there is no such thing as a "perfect choice," and that every choice entails a loss, or as the seventeenth-century Dutch philosopher Baruch Spinoza would have it, "*omnis determinatio est negatio*" (every determination is a negation).

Of course, we value choice insofar as it is an expression of individual freedom, and our distinctive personality and uniqueness. But we should not be blind to the fact that its exercise could often get in the way even of our own satisfaction and happiness. Iyengar (2010) illustrates this through a couple of familiar anecdotes. One refers to her husband, who expressed a birthday wish for the latest iPhone, but in black, "because it doesn't get as dirty and it looked sleeker than the white option available." But just as she was about to make a purchase, he rushed to her and switched the order to white. "Everybody is picking black," he reasoned. "I can't have what everybody else is having." In other words, despite his previous preference and the reasons for it, he changed his choice at the last minute, only to assert his individuality. Similar things happen when placing orders at restaurants with friends and colleagues. We may be sure of our preferences when reading the menu privately, only to change orders once we hear what others are having, in order not to seem like a copycat. In a particular study involving orders at a microbrewery, researchers compared what happened when customers made their choices privately with the results when they did so sequentially: that is, knowing what the others had picked before them (Iyengar 2010). When ordering privately, customers choose their actual preferences. They later turn out to be more satisfied or happier with their beers, even though they were more likely to ask for the same thing as everyone else. When ordering sequentially, however, clients tend to choose something different from their initial preferences for the sake of uniqueness. They also end up being less satisfied or less happy with their choices. The desire for individuality and uniqueness in our choices oftentimes trumps our preferences, thereby diminishing satisfaction and happiness.

Furthermore, there is an interesting twist even in our desire for uniqueness (Iyengar 2010). We would all like to be "sufficiently unique" in our choices, avoiding looking too bizarre or seeming like an outcast. That's why everyone tends to huddle in a "comfortable middle" when choosing names for our children, clothes, accessories, and so forth. We are always faced with the same dilemma: wanting to stand out, without being left alone, however. It is certainly difficult to balance rational preferences with actual choices, the desire to express one's individuality and, at the same time, the need to belong to the group, with satisfaction or happiness in view.

There also seems to be a limit to the number of options that would be beneficial to our own welfare, satisfaction, or happiness. More is not necessarily better. That's because choosing could itself become quite a chore, requiring its fair share of time, effort, and other valuable resources, set against expected or projected benefits. Way back in the mid-1950s, George Miller (1956) had set this magical number at "seven, plus or minus two," beyond which our mind encounters serious difficulties in processing additional information. Iyengar (2010) relates the results of an experiment she conducted at an upscale grocery store in California, which offered 348 different varieties of jam. She set up tasting booths, alternately displaying six and twenty-four different flavors. When were people more likely to stop and sample the jam? And once they did, who was more likely to buy a jar? Her findings show that, with twenty-four kinds of jam on display, 60 percent of the customers stopped to try the samples, whereas with six kinds on display, only 40 percent stopped. However, as for their actual purchasing behavior, only 3 percent bought jam when there were twenty-four kinds on display, compared to the 30 percent who did, with just six kinds on display. Analogous results turn out for experiments involving ice cream. Baskin-Robbins, the world's top ice cream retailer, attracts customers on the basis of its offer of thirty-one different flavors, although 50 percent of its sales are accounted for by the three most popular ones: plain vanilla, chocolate, and strawberry. So having a wide variety of options is good for generating a lot of foot traffic and making people stop, although a more limited number is, in fact, more effective in having people actually buy the merchandise. That's because too many options translate into such an unwieldy complexity in trying to distinguish alternatives and weigh them against one another, that people just freeze and decide to give up, for fear of regretting a bad decision later. No doubt some choice is good, it is certainly better than none, but there's also a point past which "choice no longer liberates, but debilitates" (Schwartz 2004:2). The French proverb is even more stark: "*Trop de choix, tue le choix*" (too much choice kills the choice).

So how are we supposed to navigate the numerous perils of choice, such that it works to our advantage? The answers would be different, depending on whether we put ourselves into the shoes of the buyer or the seller. From the perspective of the buyer, at least three different strategies can be employed (Iyengar 2010). One consists in "choice training": that is, going through a series of choices from the easier to the more difficult ones to combat "decision-fatigue." This technique is backed up by the experience of a German manufacturer of customized cars, where clients go through around sixty different decisions, with a variety of options for each, such as four different kinds of engines or fifty-six different colors for the exteriors, for instance. The company discovered that when clients go through the easier or "more shallow" options to the more difficult or "deeper" ones, say, from the exterior colors to the kind of engines, there was less likelihood for them to succumb to "decision-fatigue" and just choose the default option. These clients also reported to be more satisfied or happier with their choices than those who proceeded the other way around. That's because they have learned to make choices, excluding the irrelevant options and becoming more engaged and motivated as they see the final product take shape on their computer screens.

Another strategy lies in going for more limited, but expertly made options. Take, for example, choosing a bottle of wine to take to a dinner invitation at a friend's house. Instead of going to a wholesaler, "Wines-R-Us," with thousands of different labels, it would be better to head for a boutique cellar, which may stack, perhaps, even less than a hundred specialties. These specialties, however, would probably be better categorized, albeit with fewer options under each category. That way, it would be easier for one to disregard the fruity and the reds, which he dislikes, and concentrate on the whites and drys, which he prefers, for example. He would be more satisfied for the simple reason that he understands his choice better.

And lastly, one also needs to discern when choices are trivial and simply a waste of time and energy, saving resources instead for the more meaningful and transcendent decisions. Compare the choice between two shades of gray, "pearl gray" and "anthracite," for the tie at one's wedding, and the choice of a "best man." Surely it would pay to go for the default option in the first and give the second more careful thought and deliberation.

Similarly, in the case of sellers, there are several techniques to keep in mind in the choice structure, lest they want to appear unresponsive to consumers or, even worse, dictatorial, by hardly offering any options (Iyengar 2010). As we have already seen in the case of jams and ice cream, a wide variety of options serves to attract customers, although the cash cows are a limited few, and usually, the same old familiar ones. In fact, some businesses deliberately limit consumers' choices, yet still manage to be highly profitable. That's the case with the budget supermarket chain Aldi, which normally carries only around 1,400 products in its outlets, compared to the bewildering 48,750 items that, according to the Food Marketing Institute, the average American supermarket stocks on its shelves (The Economist 2010). Obviously, Aldi would only have one offer for certain categories of products, such as baking powder or plastic spoons, yet consumers seem to perceive good value for money and keep loyal to the chain.

Another instance in which sellers get away with more limited options is by offering a personal shopper service or establishing boutique luxury stalls at upscale department stores, since this is usually perceived as a sign of exclusivity by clients. The same goes for shorter set menus or fewer options for appetizers, entrées, main courses, and desserts, at fine dining restaurants. In this case, guests seem to value the previous selection of dishes made by the chef on their behalf and give it a vote of confidence.

Another possibility would be to improve product categorization. Surprisingly, the more sellers categorize products, the fewer options they actually offer per category, yet customers perceive this differently. For customers, it seems as if they are being given a wider choice and a greater variety, all because of the effort in product categorization. Apparently, human beings are able to handle categories better than choices per category. Thus, a magazine aisle with 334 well-categorized titles could be perceived to offer more options to the reader than one with 661 poorly categorized titles.

A fourth trick concerns branding. The more options proliferate, the more important brands become, because they simplify choices, making shopping easier. Brands offer an anchor of identity and consistency in what is, often, a fast-moving and confusing market. Consumers trust quality brands, and they become their default choice or option.

In summary, sellers ought to frame choices more appropriately so as to gently nudge consumers toward options in their best interests, in an exercise of what has come to be known as "liberal paternalism" (Thaler and Sunstein 2008). No legitimate option should be expressly forbidden in respect of customer freedom, although a certain prodding should also be exercised toward expert recommendations. For this, some familiarity with psychological principles concerning decision making is in order. One concerns "anchoring and adjustment," according to which one should begin with what is easier, then move in the desired direction. When fund-raising, for example, better results may be expected when options are set for $250, $1,000, and $5,000 than when they are established for $50, $75, and $100. Another principle refers to "availability," or the assessment of risks by what more readily comes to mind, rather than real probabilities. That's why it would be easier to sell travel insurance by reminding passengers about the chances of missing a flight, losing luggage, or falling sick on a trip, although these events, in fact, are less likely to occur. And a third plays with the notion of "representativeness," or the mistaken belief that past performance determines future action, when results are, in truth, random. For this reason, casinos are happy to extend credit lines to hot-handed gamblers on a winning streak, all the better to fleece them.

For both buyers and sellers, it is interesting to note that choices are heavily influenced by culture (Iyengar 2010). Collectivist cultures, such as the traditional ones found in Asian countries, don't seem to be too fixated on individual choices and would very much rather give up on them and blend in with the crowd. Asian-American schoolchildren, for instance, were discovered to perform better in tasks believed to have been assigned to them by their mothers, while their Anglo-American counterparts did best in tasks they themselves had chosen. It's not that people of Asian heritage do not want to choose, but the better choice for them is what harmonizes, rather than distances, the self from the others. It could also happen that, given the limited exposure to the market of formerly communist countries in eastern Europe, consumers there are not as sensitive to differences within categories of products as the individualistic consumers are in the West. For instance, they do not discriminate too much among different brands of soft drinks. For them, soft drinks or fruit juice or milk would be the meaningful and relevant options under the general category of "beverages"; differences among soft drinks, on the other hand, would be trivial and not worth their attention.

Granted the costs attached to discerning preferences and making decisions, on the individual as well as at the group level, the number of options we consider and the choices we undertake have to be set against the benefits. There may be certain techniques to help us maneuver in our decision making, either as consumers or as sellers, but the crucial difference lies in a value judgment regarding which options are truly worthwhile, from the perspective of human flourishing. For this no foolproof procedure has yet been devised. But before exploring other proposals for taming unwieldy choices, let us turn our attention to the sources from which preferences arise. That is, let us study desires and their satisfactions, in the form of comforts and pleasures.

We shall do so once more by the hand of Scitovsky. Against the tenets of neoclassical economics regarding the sovereignty and infallibility of individual choice and decision making, Scitovsky affirms that individuals often make mistakes about what is good for them and choose or decide wrongly. Having vested themselves with what were formerly considered divine attributes, human beings now discover that their freely chosen ends may, indeed, be the very source of their own unhappiness. This paradox lies in the background of his analysis of affluent societies or "societies of abundance."

COMFORTS, PLEASURES, AND THE EDUCATION OF DESIRE

In the first edition of *The Joyless Economy* in 1976, Scitovsky centered his critique on the opulent societies of Western nations in advanced stages of development, with high incomes and historically unimaginable levels of wellbeing. Nowadays, we would call them "postindustrial societies" or "service economies" (Bell 1973), where problems of survival and basic material necessities concerning food, clothing, and shelter have given way to those of boredom and ennui: that is, a deep-seated malaise arising from people simply not knowing what to do with so much extra time on their hands. These are societies where physical pain has been practically eliminated or, at least, doesn't last for long. They boast of stratospheric standards of material wellbeing. But at the same time, their citizens confess to suffering an interior void, a lack of joy and pleasure, which seem to come only through receiving proper stimulation and exposure to change, novelty, and variety (Scitovsky 1992: 182). It is as if people had grown numb and led anaesthetized lives. Why is this so? How did it come about?

For Scitovsky, this sorry state is the product of two closely related social trends that have increasingly gained prevalence (Friedman and McCabe 2002: 48). The first is that, in seeking excessive comfort, people have unwittingly become insensitive to what we could call the "normal" pleasures in life. And the second, led again by the misguided search for comfort, is that people have tended to choose only what is simple and easy, thereby losing out on the challenge and stimulation that bring joy. Let us explain each of these phenomena in turn.

Much as we are used to hearing them together in a line of a famous Christmas carol, comfort and joy do not mean the same thing. In Scitovsky's understanding, comfort is the opposite of pain, while joy is the opposite of boredom. Comfort is associated with the absence or satisfaction of a want or a need (Scitovsky 1992: 64, 71–78). Joy or pleasure, on the other hand, has to do with the right stimulation, level of excitement, or arousal (Scitovsky 1992: 18–25, 31). Citizens of affluent societies are too preoccupied with avoiding pain, which comes from the experience of a want or need, that they make comfort their ultimate refuge. Their pursuit of comfort in the satisfaction of material wants has become almost like an addiction. The everyday or normal dose is no longer enough to get by; each time they feel the need to consume more, only to profit less.

Consider the following examples. It is often said that hunger is the best seasoning, since it makes any kind of food taste good and satisfying. It is indeed a pleasure to eat when one feels hungry. But how about eating when one does not feel hungry at all, when one is simply forced to eat, say, by an overly doting mother or mother-in-law? Remember having to face the buffet table on your nth Christmas party? Doesn't it actually feel more like a torture? Or how about going to bed when you're neither tired nor sleepy? How does it feel to be tossing and turning round the sheets, just listening to the alarm clock mark the seconds? Don't we understand, then, why tiredness and exhaustion are the best sleeping pills? Yet in societies of abundance, people have grown accustomed to precisely these things, eating without being hungry and going to bed without being tired from physical exertion. They have become too successful in banishing pain or suffering from material want. What they fail to realize is that by doing so, by attaining so much comfort, they have banished a great deal of pleasure and joy in their lives by the same stroke.

Even worse, however, is that people of these societies have almost completely forgotten that a certain level of stimulation is necessary to achieve joy or pleasure. In principle, that should be fairly easy. What they need to do is to leave their comfort zones and open themselves up, once again, to change and variety. For instance, they could start to engage in other activities besides work, which are not immediately directed to satisfying material wants or needs. But in the case of still a large swathe of the population of the United States, their Protestant Calvinist and Puritan heritage impedes them from doing just this (Scitovsky 1992: 90). Any activity that is unproductive or unprofitable is seriously frowned upon or censured. It is deemed superfluous, wasteful, and even dangerous to the salvation of souls. Such an attitude is what closes doors to the experience of joy and happiness. Although set in nineteenth-century Denmark, the movie *Babette's Feast*, based on the eponymous novel by Isak Dinesen (Karen Blixen's pseudonym), masterfully portrays this outlook in life and its dire consequences, as well as the possibility of redemption, through something as accessible as a dinner banquet prepared by a French Catholic cook.

When it comes to clothes, to cite another everyday need, this mind-set is reflected in what amounts to the United States' national costume of "practical dressing": something of a cross between a tracksuit and pajamas, with sports shoes or flip-flops as footwear and a baseball cap. It's unisex and comes in all sizes; it's so comfortable and versatile that it could be worn the whole day, regardless of place, occasion, or activity. It may not score very high in terms of beauty and elegance, but it certainly serves the purpose of covering the body. After all, what else is the point in wearing clothes?

Another consequence of this overly pragmatic mentality is the short and staggered vacations that American workers normally take, compared to the six continuous weeks that their French colleagues enjoy, for instance. Almost literally, time is taken to be gold, and it should not be wasted, therefore, in idle holidays.

The second trend that characterizes affluent societies is the avoidance of whatever smacks of a challenge or complexity, since that is a source of discomfort. Instead, people should be choosing what is plain, simple, and easy. So when one needs to relax, he watches television, period, although in fact, that usually means hopping from one channel to another, until he eventually dozes off. Reading long Russian novels with their endless list of characters and complicated plots is completely out of the question, because that only adds to the stress and the strain, and besides, they're terribly boring, anyway.

Indeed, rest and relaxation for many, if not for the majority, consists in the same fail-proof popular distractions. People have become obsessed with watching and practicing sports, because they have become obsessed with the way their bodies look and the way their bodies feel. At least during the time they spend at the gym, all their troubles and worries are kept at bay. Sex continues to be another all-time favorite. And just in case the environment is still not erotically charged enough for one's taste, he could always turn to the internet for mind-boggling variety and customization, all available at the click of a mouse.

Then there's the compulsion to be always up to date with the latest fad, whatever that may be, in the realm of fashion, the private lives of the rich and the famous (for no other reason than being rich and famous), and the social media. That, too, is a popular pastime, and it may very well be the cause of the epidemic in attention deficit and hyperactivity disorder (ADHD), not only among kids, as suggested by Dr. Michael Rich, director of the Harvard Center on Media and Child Health Studies (Richtel 2010), but also perhaps among the general population. After all, just how many adults are unable to put down their cellphones even during dinner, for example? Little by little, we begin to gather evidence that digital technologies aren't unambiguously a godsend in the education of the young. Their improper use frequently contributes to uncontrollable distraction, shortened attention spans, and poor social adaptation, as juvenile brains grow addicted to instantaneous results and gratification (Richtel 2010).

Last but not least is the fascination with gratuitous and unprovoked violence, true to life or virtual (video games), which a ready access to guns in countries such as the United States has only helped to aggravate, often leading to fatal consequences. These are the means with which the majority of people in societies of abundance combat tedium and boredom: sex, drugs, and rock and roll.

It comes as no surprise that the worst-off in affluent societies, not only materially, but even in the access to joy and pleasure, continue to be the urban poor (Scitovsky 2002: 61–62). We know that most of the juvenile crime is committed between the time students are dismissed from school and the time adults arrive home from work; in other words, during the period when kids are left alone at home. We also know that there's a very strong correlation between single-parent homes and poverty (Garfinkel and McLanahan 1986). Single mothers, especially, have to work extra hours just to be able to put enough food on the table. Because of this, they hardly have enough time to supervise their kids' schoolwork. As a result, the odds are stacked against their children doing well in school. Poverty, a lack of parental attention, and a dearth of educational role-models are a recipe for a disastrous school performance. These disadvantages, carried over from home, usually give rise to unmotivated and disengaged students who are uneasy in formal learning environments and often cause teachers a lot of trouble. These kids feel left out in class and eventually drop out of school. In the past, grave penury and the threat of starvation may have led young people such as these to resort to theft. But in this age of food stamps and welfare, that is no longer the case. What may happen, instead, is that they steal, and even kill, simply for the thrill, because they are bored and don't know what else there is to do. That's why the urban poor so frequently suffer a double penalty. Besides the drawbacks of material poverty, they also have to endure the effects of a cultural, intellectual, and moral impoverishment because of their dysfunctional family background.

When analyzed coldly, the solution to the problem seems clear. To remedy their restlessness and boredom, people ought to consider resorting to the endless trove of high culture and the fine arts, where they are bound to find something personally satisfying. But then, the taste and appreciation for such cultural products seldom come naturally, often requiring a certain level of guided exposure, gradual training, and cultivation instead. For example, before falling in love with Shakespeare's plays, one first has to learn to read, and then perhaps move on from fairy tales and children's books to adventure stories for adolescents, until he finds himself in a position to understand the complex structure and dynamics of human relationships as portrayed in Elizabethan theater. These are exactly the skill sets and dispositions of which poor children coming from dysfunctional homes are so often deprived. It is nearly impossible for them to develop a fondness for reading, if the only book available in their homes is the phone directory. The treasures of high culture and the fine arts, in effect, become inaccessible for them, due not so much to the monetary price as to the "moral" price, in terms of the previous effort in the training of taste.

With the above, we do not wish to condone the obsessive, "tiger mother" brand of parenting, often associated with traditional Asians, and especially the Chinese, which consists in relentlessly pushing children to overachieve, in school and elsewhere (Chua 2011). But between that and the ultra-permissive Western kind of parenting, where for fear of hurting children's self-esteem, whatever they do is said to be "okay," there has to be some middle ground. Healthy, happy kids are neither overworked nervous wrecks nor self-indulgent and spineless good-for-nothings. Rather, they tend to display a certain level of conscientiousness – in terms of order and self-control – in accordance with their years. Where both approaches agree, however, is in the crucial role of early childhood education in cultivating the right inclinations, tastes, and desires; in taking delight in what is noble and fitting; and in rejecting what is base. And in this regard, Scitovsky once more has plenty of valuable things to say.

Surprisingly for an economist, Scitovsky's treatment of education focuses less on its productive aspects than on its civilizing effects. At the minimum, this refers to the ability of education "to instruct in the harmless activities of life so as to divert people from harmful, violent ones" (Scitovsky 2002: 61). His desire is that access to leisure through high culture and the fine arts, which used to be the preserve of nobles and the privileged class, now be made available to as many ordinary people as possible. Only thus will they be able to find constructive outlets to relieve their boredom and, more importantly, get a fair and equal shake at life's better joys and higher pleasures. Lest he be accused of populism, however, Scitovsky unequivocally defends the need for earnest effort and perseverance in education and training, in order to reach this worthy objective.

In a nutshell, despite more than acceptable levels of material welfare and comfort, many people in affluent societies are not as happy as they could be, because they have not been trained to experience, since their early childhood, the "joy of learning," which happens to be the prerequisite for superior achievements and satisfactions in life. Although an infant brain is only around a quarter of the volume of an adult's, it quickly grows to 70 percent by age 1 and 85 percent by age 3, even developing more "synapses" or connections between neurons than an adult's (Reddy 2013). Unless the child uses those synapses soon, he may lose them, probably forever. For instance, if the connections in the visual cortex aren't used, these may be reduced and cause the child to later develop vision problems. Something similar occurs with the child's other learning processes. Scitovsky then goes on to describe the three main phases of child rearing, setting down the objectives for each and discussing their impact on successful adaptation (Scitovsky 2002: 62–63).

The first is the spectator phase, when infants already begin to learn simply by observing the behavior of people around them. At this stage, children may seem to be very passive and hardly aware of what is going on, judging by their reactions or lack thereof. But nothing could be further from the truth. They are more like sponges that eagerly soak up everything, almost indiscriminately. We are told, for instance, that even while in the womb, babies are already primed for language, and as soon as they are born, they are eager to continue with the task (Karcz 2013). The mother's womb, therefore, is no soundproof booth, since babies at birth already know enough phonology to distinguish their mother's native tongue from other languages. That's why it's very important to interact with them and to provide them

with the proper sensorial and mental stimulation while neural connections are maturing, although it may appear that they don't understand or even mind what's happening around them. If not, besides cognitive impairments, infants risk suffering from "attachment disorder"
affecting mood, behavior, and social relationships, due to a failure to
form normal attachments to primary caregivers (Chaffin et al. 2006).
This failure is associated with early experiences of neglect, abuse,
and abrupt separation from caregivers, between 6 months and 3 years
of age. This syndrome has been commonly detected, for instance,
among wards coming from orphanages in the former Soviet Union
and satellite countries. Because of the lack of resources, babies were
often left alone in their cribs for hours on end, untended by nurses.
As a result, they suffered some form of severe and incurable retar-
dation. Apparently, there is no substitute for real, physical contact
with adult caregivers. It has even been shown that simply letting kids
watch television actually prolongs this initial phase and delays their
development.

The next stage is the participator stage, when children begin to
imitate adult speech and behavior that they have observed. The role of
parents at this point lies in encouraging, helping, correcting, praising,
and guiding children as they learn to speak, stand, move around, and
perform all sorts of activities. Nothing pleases a child more than a parent imitating its behavior, as brain-imaging technologies can confirm
(Reddy 2013). A sterling moment usually comes when the child is able
to stand or walk by himself for the first time. Although most of the
people around him do, in fact, stand and walk on their two legs, the
child experiences a grand sense of achievement when this happens.
What is important is that he is doing it for the first time. Parents and
other primary caregivers need to be present for the child literally to
take his first steps. A similar thing occurs when the child pronounces
his first words. Even before the age of 1, most babies can already understand the meanings of about a dozen words, and by age 2, thanks to
adult interactions, they can pronounce around 200 (Karcz 2013). True
enough, toddlers characteristically omit words and endings, yet they

know enough syntax to say words in the right order, such as "baby drink milk" rather than "milk drink baby." Surprisingly, findings suggest a connection between a child's motor skills and memory, and his verbal ability. A greater concentration of gray and white matter, or nerve cells and fiber tracts in the hippocampus and the cerebellum – parts of the brain usually associated with motor abilities and memory – at 7 months happens to predict better verbal skills in 1-year-olds (Can, Richards, and Kuhl 2013). None of this would be possible without the example and encouragement of committed adults.

In third place comes the initiator phase, when preschoolers take the initiative in performing actions and carrying out activities they have just recently learned. It is during this stage that children start to discover their own identity, finding out how they look, what they like, how it feels to be in various situations, and what their limitations and possibilities are, in such a way that they begin to develop their own personality. Once more, the assistance of parents or primary caregivers is irreplaceable at this crucial moment, when children discover and mold their own tastes, inclinations, and desires. At a very basic level, for instance, children ought to be exposed by their caregivers to a variety of foods, tastes, and textures for them to develop healthy eating habits in the future. In fact, scientists at the Monell Chemical Senses Center in Philadelphia even claim that eating habits begin in the womb; since mothers, who keep a varied diet during pregnancy and breast-feeding, tend to have babies who are more open to a wide range of flavors (Wartman 2013). What's more, these babies carry these taste preferences over through infancy and into adulthood; while changing food preferences beyond toddlerhood has proved to be extremely difficult. Giving children always or only the food they like would in fact do them harm in the long term, making them prone to obesity and other diet-related diseases, although for the moment, they may certainly find it more pleasant. That's one way of spoiling them. Also, research shows that parent–child discourse about emotions during picture-book reading helps develop empathy, the ability to help and share with others, among infants between 18 and 30 months old (Brownell et al. 2013). More importantly, it has been discovered that infants are endowed with empathy, compassion, guilt, shame, righteous anger, and a sense of fairness which they develop from very early in their lives (Bloom 2013). They understand that helping is morally good, and that harming, hindering, or thwarting another's goals is morally bad. And although at first, they think of justice simply in terms of an equal distribution of resources, proper upbringing through reasoning and example allows them to realize, little by little, why someone who has worked harder or is in greater need actually deserves more. None of this would be possible without close interaction between small children and committed, caring adults.

There are a couple of takeaways that we can glean from Scitovsky's description of the three stages of parenting, of paramount interest to the way in which we handle preferences and choices that spring ultimately from pleasures and desires. The first refers to the role of education in shaping our tastes and wants. Although the basic impulses in our nature are innate, still they are subject to modification, in both direction and intensity, through the education we receive. Education consists not only in learning to carry out activities that satisfy our needs and to perform tasks that are useful to others and, therefore, economically productive. On a deeper level, there is also a "domestication" or "civilizing" of our primal urges, so as not to cause harm to others or to ourselves, and instead contribute to our own joyful fulfillment in society as human beings. Tastes, desires, and the will itself, as well as the ability to experience joy and pleasure, are all equally subject to the ennobling power of education. Education allows us to discern, therefore, what is best among competing options. It also enables us to differentiate meaningful and relevant choices from the trivial and insignificant ones.

Secondly, this education has to take place as early as possible, even before children start attending school. It is most effective when it begins at home, under the careful guidance of parents and other committed caregivers who interact with the child, provide him with worthwhile role models, and encourage and correct him through his first steps and initiatives. Not instilling this "joy of learning" in a child before reaching formal school age means leaving him severely handicapped for the rest of his life. It radically limits his available options, both at work and in leisure. It spells the difference between acquiring self-control and successful adaptation, on the one hand, and being a slave of one's whims to no tangible profit, on the other. On it depends whether a child's attempt at happiness and flourishing will eventually reach fruition.

Implicit in the above is the recognition that the individual does not necessarily know what is best for himself. Other people who are acknowledged experts in a field, such as chess grandmasters and ordinary parents, may have a better idea of what is truly good and useful, as in the case of novices and children, respectively. At times, the rational thing to do, therefore, when making a choice, is not to insist on following one's preferences, but to defer to others. It may be best that we allow ourselves to be gently prodded to make the right choices (Thaler and Sunstein 2008). Take for granted designing a building such that the stairs are in full view as the immediate option, rather than hiding them somewhere and making the elevator the default choice. The extra exercise could do wonders for people's health and the building would still comply with code requirements for those with mobility difficulties. Another example would be to display first or at eye-level healthy food options, such as fruits and whole-grain cereal snacks, in school cafeterias, rather than fizzy drinks and candy. It would be hard to think of a more effective measure to combat childhood obesity, while at the same time providing variety to cater to individual tastes. That's how education, the observance and transmission of best-known science and standards, takes place. In economic terms, this entails admitting, at the very least, the possibility of a difference between "objective" wellbeing or utility, which may be determined by conspicuous others such as experts, and "subjective" preference satisfaction, which can only be settled by oneself (Friedman and McCabe 2002: 51).

Scitovsky invites us to reconsider the blind faith normally deposited in free market capitalism, in the realm of economics, and in democracy, in the realm of politics, where the sum total of individual subjective preferences is believed to automatically result in the optimum state of objective wellbeing or utility for everyone. Neither a free market nor a democracy has room for experts, because the sovereignty of individual choice means that we are all our own self-appointed experts. Insofar as a democratic regime (especially of the populist sort), like the free market, is more likely to pave the way for the aggregate of untutored, popular desires to prevail, in fact, it results in something closer to a plutocracy, the government of the wealthy. Scitovsky expresses serious doubts, therefore, on the intrinsic worth of both capitalism and democracy, plumping up, instead, for their instrumental value with regard to wellbeing and happiness. In effect, he joins the position previously espoused by Hirschman (1970) concerning the strategies of "exit" or "voice" in the face of discontent with an organization or society as a whole.

In later years, Sen (1999) adds his own twist to the debate by studying "procedural utilities," referring to the mode of choice associated with democratic regimes, for instance, as distinct from "outcome utilities," referring to the menu of reasonable options actually available in "social choice theory." In other words, for Sen, democratic politics is choiceworthy because it entails respect for individual freedom (intrinsic or procedural value) while at the same time preventing famines (instrumental or outcome value) within states, which is, of course, a reasonable and desirable option. Democracy works best, not when it merely enables us to choose, but when it enables us to choose what we should reasonably value. For we do not recognize this value spontaneously; it requires critical reflection and examination of what we really desire in life: as we know from Socrates, an unexamined life is not worth living (Sen 2002: 230–231). Primarily, for this reason, we need culture, exposure to the proper forms of stimulation, and the chance to develop the appropriate consumption skills; in a word, education.

* * *

We began the chapter by considering the ways in which happiness depends, not so much on the amount of money spent, but on how it is spent. Consumption decisions are best taken when the public good perspective is adopted, since they invariably affect both the individual and the community to which he belongs. Every effort must be taken, then, to internalize the negative externalities of individual consumer behavior and to foment its positive externalities. To this end, it helps to bear in mind the degree of adaptation experienced to particular market goods. This should not be taken to mean, however, that spending money wisely is enough to guarantee happiness, as if it were simply a commodity to be bought. Happiness is never just the result of astute portfolio management or a canny investment strategy.

We have also seen how greater freedom, in terms of a wider variety of choices, does not necessarily lead to more satisfaction or, ultimately, to greater happiness. Against the dictum of the sovereignty of consumer choice, we have learned that individuals do not always know what is best for them; nor do they unfailingly proceed in a rational manner in its pursuit. In many fields there are some people who are more expert than others, and it pays to heed their advice. Part of this expertise includes discerning the relevant number of choices, distinguishing the trivial from the significant ones, and structuring choices in such a manner that takes the particularities of human psychology and culture into account. Conversely, proper choosing can be learned. There exists an education of desire which, when instilled in early childhood, enables the individual to achieve greater joys and pleasures – rather than mere comforts – in his choices and behaviors throughout his lifetime. A political consequence of such a principle is the need for certain universal, rational values to accompany and guide democratic procedures.

REFERENCES

Ariely, D. 2010. *Predictably irrational*. New York: Harper Perennial.

Bell, D. 1973. *The coming of the post-industrial society*. New York: Basic Books.

Bloom, P. 2013. *Just babies: The origins of good and evil*. New York: Crown Publishers, Inc.

Brownell, C. A., Svetlova, M., Anderson, R., Nichols, S. R. and Drummond, J. 2013. "Socialization of early prosocial behavior: Parents' talk about emotions is associated with sharing and helping in toddlers," *Infancy*, 18(1): 91–119.

Buchanan, J. M. 1975. *The limits of liberty*. Chicago: University of Chicago Press.

Buchanan, J. M. and Tullock, G. 1962. *The calculus of consent*. Ann Arbor: University of Michigan Press.

Can, D. D., Richards, T. and Kuhl, P. 2013. "Early gray-matter and white-matter concentration in infancy predict later language skills: A whole brain voxel-based morphometry study," *Brain and Language*, 124: 34–44.

Carrns, A. 2014. "Save for retirement first, the children's education second," *New York Times*, February 28.

Chaffin, M., Hanson, R., Saunders, B. E., Nichols, T., Barnett, D., Zeanah, C., Berliner, L., Egeland, B., Newman, E., Lyon, T., Letourneau, E. and Miller-Perrin, C. 2006. "Report of the APSAC task force on attachment therapy, reactive attachment disorder, and attachment problems," *Child Maltreatment*, 11: 76–89.

Chua, A. 2011. *Battle hymn of the tiger mother*. New York: Penguin.

Dunn, E. and Norton, M. 2013. *Happy money: The science of smarter spending*. New York: Simon and Schuster.

Frank, R. H. 1997. "The frame of reference as a public good," *Economic Journal*, 107(445): 1832–1847.

Friedman, J. and McCabe, A. 2002. "Preferences or happiness? Tibor Scitovsky's psychology of human needs", in Easterlin, R. (ed.), *Happiness in economics*. Cheltenham, UK/Northampton, MA: Edward Elgar, pp. 45–54.

Garfinkel, I. and McLanahan, S. S. 1986. *Single mothers and their children: A new American dilemma*. Washington, DC: Urban Institute Press.

Hirschman, A. O. 1970. *Exit, voice, and loyalty: Responses to decline in firms, organizations, and states*. Cambridge, MA: Harvard University Press.

Iyengar, S. 2010. *The art of choosing*. New York: Hachette.

Jensen, M. and Meckling, W. 1994. "The nature of man," *Journal of Applied Corporate Finance*, Summer, 7(2): 4–19.

Karcz, S. 2013. "A way with words," *Handed Down*, 86, 3 (Autumn), (http://hms
.harvard.edu/news/harvard-medicine/harvard-medicine/handed-down/
way-words, accessed January 8, 2014).

Miller, G. A. 1956. "The magical number seven, plus or minus two: Some limits on
our capacity for processing information," *Psychological Review*, 63: 81–97.

Plato 1941. *Plato's The republic* (Jowett, B., ed.). New York: The Modern Library.

Reddy, S. 2013. "Wise beyond their years: What babies really know," *Wall Street
Journal*, February 11.

Reynolds, G. 2009. "Why exercise makes you less anxious," *New York Times*,
November 18.

Richtel, M. 2010. "Growing up digital, wired for distraction," *New York Times*,
November 21.

Rose, N. 1999. *Powers of freedom: Reframing political thought*. Cambridge:
Cambridge University Press.

Salecl, R. 2010. *The tyranny of choice*. London: Profile.

Schwartz, B. 2004. *The paradox of choice: Why more is less*. New York: Harper
Perennial.

Scitovsky, T. 1992. *The joyless economy: The psychology of human satisfaction*.
New York/Oxford: Oxford University Press.

2002. "My own criticism of *The joyless economy*," in Easterlin, R. (ed.), *Happiness in economics*. Cheltenham, UK/Northampton, MA: Edward Elgar,
pp. 55–65.

Sen, A. 1999. "The possibility of social choice," *American Economic Review*, 89
(3): 349–378.

2002. 'Rationality, joy and freedom', in Easterlin, R. (ed.), *Happiness in economics*. Cheltenham, UK/Northampton, MA: Edward Elgar, pp. 226–239.

Thaler, R. H. and Sunstein, C. S. 2008. *Nudge*. New Haven, CT: Yale University
Press.

The Economist 2010. "The tyranny of choice," December 16.

Wartman, K. 2013. "Bad eating habits start in the womb," *New York Times*,
December 1.

4 The biotechnology of happiness

Not just a "quick fix"

Michael Oxley, a mechanical engineer, is founder and president of Foc.us, a London-based manufacturer of transcranial direct current stimulation (tCDS) devices (Murphy 2013). The company has been doing brisk business. In May 2013, it sold out of its initial production of more than 3,000 units online, each costing $249, in less than a month. Not bad, considering that tCDS has no approval at all from public health authorities. These gadgets, looking much like headbands with button-sized electrodes, are said to improve reaction time, mood, computational ability, and memory, according to some internet forums.

It is common knowledge that all sorts of skills, be it in sports or music, or of the cognitive kind, such as fluency in a language, require long hours – the proverbial 10,000 – of training and practice. The repetition of actions is said to create neural pathways in the brain, giving rise to more automatic forms of behavior. It has been found that low-level electrical current (equivalent to 0.1 percent of the charge used in electroconvulsive therapy) primes neurons somehow to learn and retain information better. By directing these electrical impulses to specific regions of the brain, tCDS may then help establish those desired neural connections more quickly, acting much like jump-starter kits. Dr. H. Branch Coslett, cognitive neurologist at the University of Pennsylvania School of Medicine, claims that tCDS helps people remember proper names, enhances creativity, and boosts reading efficiency. Other research shows that tCDS may also be useful in treating stroke victims and patients with Parkinson's disease, depression, and obsessive–compulsive disorders.

The problem, however, lies in do-it-yourself tCDS sessions without the adequate supervision of clinicians. Healthy people may resort to tCDS as a short cut or competitive advantage in gaining requisite skills, without going through the time and effort of traditional methods. As Dr. Sarah Lisanby, psychiatrist and director of brain stimulation and neurophysiology at the Duke University School of Medicine warns, tCDS is still very much at the infancy stage, and we still don't know about its long-term effects. Besides itching, redness, and burns under the electrodes, experts worry about more permanent damage, in the form of cognitive and motor function impairments, which people who self-administer tCDS may cause to themselves. Perhaps the greatest promise of tCDS lies in its combination with cognitive training, as Dr. Roi Cohen Kadosh, neuropsychologist at Oxford University, confesses.

Anecdotal as it may seem, the fascination with tCDS is highly indicative of the interest generated by biotechnological methods in relation, not only to cognitive abilities, but also to moods, wellbeing, and ultimately, happiness as a whole.

IT'S ALL IN THE MIND

For the past few decades, happiness has been a hot topic for what has been known collectively as "brain science," a host of experimental and quantitative approaches in a range of disciplines from psychology (positive psychology, cognitive psychology, neuropsychology, evolutionary psychology, clinical psychology) to economics (behavioral economics) to medicine (psychiatry, pharmacology), among others. In the next few pages, we shall try to make sense of the multiple and varied inputs from these different branches of knowledge, especially insofar as they all converge on that distinctive organ which is the brain, regarding the nature of happiness. To some degree, we shall also try to spell out the science behind therapies and interventions purportedly designed to improve one's level of happiness and discuss their possible ethical impact.

But before all this, we will have to explain some basic notions regarding brain anatomy and physiology (Aamondt and Wang 2008). The typical adult brain, about the size of a small cantaloupe, weighs around 3 pounds or 3 percent of the total body weight. Yet it consumes 17 percent of the body's total energy requirements, most of it in mere "stand-by" or maintenance mode: that is, without performing any particularly difficult task. The brain is mainly composed of two kinds of cells: glial cells, which provide support or "housekeeping" functions within the organ, and neurons, of which there are around 100 billion. Neurons communicate with one another and the rest of the body through electrical signals or impulses, produced by the uneven distribution of positive and negative ions in their makeup. Neurons have receptors, called "dendrites," and transmitters, called "axons." The spaces between axons and dendrites, called "synapses," are filled with chemicals known as "neurotransmitters." In the most general of terms, it can be said that all basic functions and abilities of human beings – sense knowledge, moods and emotional responses, individual personality traits, thought patterns, and so forth – come about thanks to these synapses or chemical connections between neurons. Synapses vary in number, strength, and location in the brain. Each neuron or group of neurons is responsible for controlling specific tasks and activities, such as detecting visual motion and planning eye movements, for instance. These particular functions have been discovered by tracking brain activity under different conditions, by stimulating concrete regions in the brain, or by tracing connections from certain regions of the brain to other areas of the body *in vivo*.

Both anatomically and functionally, we can distinguish several discrete regions in the human brain. The brain stem is located at the bottom of the brain, attached to the spinal cord. It controls critical life functions, including reflexive movements of the head and eyes, breathing, the heart rate, digestion, sleep, and arousal, most of which take place even without one's noticing. The hypothalamus likewise acts as a thermostat or control center for satisfying basic needs such as hunger, thirst, body temperature, and daily sleep, besides regulating sexual behavior by releasing sex and stress hormones. The almond-shaped amygdala, located just above the ear, is the seat of emotions – in particular, those of fear and anxiety, causing reactions of "fight

or flight" in the face of imminent danger. The hippocampus is responsible for long-term memory, storing information regarding facts and
places. The cerebellum is a large region at the back of the brain, and it
integrates sensory information necessary to guide movement. At the
center of the brain lies the thalamus. It receives and filters sensory
information, relaying data to the cortex. The cortex, in turn, is the
largest part of the human brain, occupying three-fourths of its total
surface at the top and sides. The cortex is subdivided into four lobes.
The occipital, at the back, takes care of visual perception. The temporal lobe, above the ears, regulates hearing and understanding of speech.
Together with the amygdala and the hippocampus, it plays a crucial
role in learning, memory, and emotional responses. The parietal lobe
receives information from the skin and other senses, directing one's
attention to a particular event. And finally, there's the frontal lobe,
which generates commands, produces speech, and selects the appropriate conduct in regard to one's objectives and circumstances.

In addition, research shows significant differences between the
right and the left hemispheres of the cortex. The left side is associated
with speech, math, problem solving, logic, and order; it also makes
artistic and emotional interpretations of events. The right side, for its
part, is linked with spatial perception, the tactile analysis of objects,
sight–motor coordination, and the recognition of factual knowledge.

Judging from the brain's perspective, what, then, is happiness?
Granted that it has neither color nor sound nor smell nor taste nor
tactile quality, it doesn't seem to be any particular kind of sense
information. Almost everyone, however, associates happiness with
something pleasant. Could it be, then, pleasure? A positive mood
or an exhilarating emotion, perhaps? How about beliefs and ideas?
What part do they play, if any, in happiness? Can judgment, reasoning,
and other conscious decisions affect happiness? If so, how? Is there
any specific behavior or conduct that one can deliberately undertake
which leads to happiness? Is happiness a goal, or is it, instead, something that one serendipitously runs into? Let us now explore each of
these possibilities in turn.

BEYOND PLEASURE AND SATISFACTION

There are three main contenders in the attempt to provide an apt description of happiness: pleasure, satisfaction, and the normative ideal of a good life (Nettle 2005). We shall now focus on the first of these. Given its link with pleasant sensations or states of mind, it comes as no surprise that among the pioneers in the study of happiness were "hedonic psychologists," those specializing in pleasure (Kahneman, Diener, and Schwartz 1999). For them, the key to happiness lies in the attainment of pleasure and the avoidance of pain, to which is often added the experience of joy. Pleasure comes when a desired object or state is reached. Aristotle believes that pleasure results from an unimpeded action itself, as the fulfillment of desire, while Bentham thinks that subjects stand passively with regard to pleasure as a sensation (Kenny and Kenny 2006). However that may be, the emphasis lies in the present "liking" of the object or state achieved rather than in its "desiring"; for it could very well happen that we do not actually like what we previously desired, because we had a false notion of it, for example. Pleasure refers to the experience, not to the activity that leads to it.

The difference between pleasure or "liking," on the one hand, and "desiring" or "wanting," on the other, is reflected in the two distinct pathways through which each of them takes place in the brain (Berridge and Kringelbach 2008). For instance, serotonin, the neurotransmitter responsible for feelings of pleasure or satisfaction, is actually found to suppress the effects of dopamine, which increases desire. Depending on their sources, we could speak of both "physical pleasures" (food, drink, sex, and so forth) as well as "mental pleasures" (success in different domains of human life and activity, friendship, and so on).

We cannot underestimate the role of beliefs about what things really are and their origin in our experience of pleasure (Bloom 2010). Pouring the same wine from a more expensive bottle improves its taste, compared to serving it from its original container, for instance.

In the same way, the value of an artwork, measured in the amount of money one is willing to pay for it, depends mostly on whether it is an original or a copy (or even worse, a forgery): that is, on beliefs regarding its origin or the process surrounding its creation. And although monetary value is not the same as the pleasurable experience associated with either wine or a painting, it may indeed serve as a relative measure.

Besides pleasure, the other major component in this account of happiness is joy. Joy is a positive affect, emotion, or feeling; it is a subjective, psychological state to which there is no object or referent in the physical world, although it is generated by an encounter with something in the physical world (Gilbert 2006). People attest to experiencing a number of different negative emotions, such as fear, anger, sadness, and disgust, but there is only one positive emotion, commonly called "joy," in the opposite side of the balance. Joy is a sign that something good has occurred that one is loath to change, lest joy be lost.

Certain states of the brain, facial expressions, and behaviors correspond to joy (Argyle 2009). There is increased activity in the left frontal cortex and a greater concentration of the neurotransmitter serotonin. Individuals break into a "Duchenne smile" (distinguishable from a forced smile), noticeable not only in the lower part of the face, but also in the upper part and in the eyes. Joyful people are also more prone to engage in social activities such as play and are more willing to explore. Joy makes one ignore other things or events vying for his attention, such as pain (the "analgesic" effect), dedicating himself instead to the activity he is currently pursuing.

The sequence of events may be narrated as follows. First, an external occurrence arouses the emotion, triggering some inner state in the brain and, perhaps, also some memories. This activates nerves which control muscles that produce emotional expressions, such as a smile in the face, a quickening of the heart rate or a reddening of the skin. Other nerves controlled by cognitive processes may also react, modifying these emotional expressions. And lastly, feedback mechanisms intervene, between the face and the brain, for instance, likewise affecting the actual emotional experience.

Joy has also been found to display a strong correlation with a personality trait called "extraversion," which is partially innate and very stable, and has a documented physiological basis. What isn't clear at this point, however, is the direction of causation, whether it goes from extraversion to joy or the other way around. Do we smile because we are happy or are we happy because we smile?

Indeed, positive affect or joy is partly conditioned by several personality traits or temperamental dispositions (Ryff 1989). Extraversion, optimism, high self-esteem, a sense of purpose, and an internal locus of control all contribute to positive feelings, whereas their opposite traits, such as neuroticism, pessimism, a lack of purpose, and an external locus of control, respectively, detract from them (Myers 2002; Argyle 2009). Extraverts, by reacting more strongly to positive stimuli, reinforce the joy or positive affect that these produce. These people are also more outgoing and sociable, investing time and effort in situations in line with their dispositions and avoiding those which are not. Neurotics, on the other hand, seem to be more sensitive to punishments than to rewards, thus accentuating the downward spiral of their emotions. Similarly, they tend to seek situations that feed their negative dispositions. Because they expect favorable outcomes, optimists work harder to achieve their goals, in what amounts, almost, to an instance of a self-fulfilling prophecy. They even enjoy better health. By contrast, pessimists, in anticipation of failure, are often quite disengaged from the tasks they perform. Generally, they are more cynical and less trusting.

According to some studies, self-esteem or self-acceptance is the best predictor of overall life satisfaction. In fact, people spend on average 60 percent of conversations talking about themselves, even rising to 80 percent in social media platforms such as Facebook and Twitter (Ward 2013). That's because self-disclosure is intrinsically rewarding, with the nucleus accumbens and the ventral tegmental area of the brain, associated with pleasure, motivation, and reward, experiencing greater activation, together with the medial prefrontal cortex. Not only is self-related thought more pleasurable than thinking about others. Telling others about oneself also gives one an additional high, compared to merely private ruminations. There are several reasons for this, based on the adaptive functions of communicating about oneself to others. It may increase interpersonal liking and social bond formation, crucial to physical survival and team-related activities. It can also contribute to personal growth and development by eliciting external feedback. That's why "selfies" have become so popular, because people find them immensely gratifying. Contrary, therefore, to what Descartes may have held, joy or contentment is not a purely private mental state where individual judgment is infallible. Rather, it is communicable through language and behavior. In fact, in order to understand human emotion, we require a certain coherence among language ("I am afraid"), context (one stands alone before a roaring lion), and behavior (one starts to run) (Kenny and Kenny 2006).

With luck, in the West, self-esteem doesn't pose much of a problem, since most people consider themselves better than average, anyway. In more collectivist Eastern cultures, however, there seems to be a greater premium on group harmony than on self-esteem, with regard to positive feelings. Purposeful or goal-driven individuals experience more joy and do so more intensely than drifters. And being in control, or at least believing oneself to be able to choose one's destiny (self-mastery), leads to greater positive affect than thinking oneself to be pulled apart by circumstances. Some research says that this may even be the basis of a widespread desire for freedom, self-rule, and democracy among human beings. Of course, these personality traits are modulated by characteristics such as sex and age. Nonetheless, they are fairly robust predictors of the state of affect or emotion.

A common feature between pleasure and joy is their transience or fleetingness. (This, in essence, is the Buddhist critique; as pleasure and joy, all happiness is ephemeral.) Their experience makes one want to freeze the instant forever in order to live it to the full. Change, which is inevitable, is also their worst enemy. Thus, in accordance with the hedonic perspective, happiness consists in maximizing these hedonic moments or episodes, effectively giving rise to a calculus or physics of pleasure. Kahneman (2000a) distinguishes two meanings of utility or pleasure: experienced utility, which refers to the actual pleasure (or pain, which is "disutility"), and decision utility, which refers to the pleasure (or pain) inferred from one's choices and decisions. Such is the difference between the two that each gives rise to a distinct subject, the "experiencing self," who lives in the present, and the "remembering self," who takes into account the past as a storyteller and is responsible for making decisions regarding the future. The main problem lies in that we constantly confuse one with the other, and thus end up in a bind when speaking of happiness. Do we refer to the happiness, in terms of enjoyment or liking, of the "experiencing self" or, on the contrary, to the happiness, in terms of wanting or desiring, of the "remembering self"? For not only does each subject have its own version of happiness, but also, what contributes to the happiness of one may, in fact, detract from the happiness of the other. In other words, the happiness of the "experiencing self" may be in conflict with that of the "remembering self."

Consider, for instance, the pain or disutility associated with colonoscopy, a fairly routine medical procedure (Kahneman 2000a). The total experienced (dis-)utility can be objectively measured by asking the patient about his experience and other diagnostic techniques at regular intervals throughout the length of the procedure and aggregating all these values. The longer the procedure and the more intense the spikes of pain, the worse the actual, total experience. This is the perspective of the "experiencing self." But if we were to ask the "remembering self," we would get an entirely different, more subjective evaluation of the procedure. First of all, the duration of the colonoscopy (at least within a range of 4–69 minutes) would hardly count ("duration neglect"). Secondly, the determining factor would be the average pain between its most intense level and over the last 3 minutes at the end, such that a patient with a higher peak-end average would retain a more aversive memory than one with a lower ("peak-end rule"). Consequently, the patient with a more painful or "traumatic" recollection would be less inclined to undergo the procedure again in the future. The predicted (dis-)utility is none other than a belief about future experienced (dis-)utility, but, in fact, it is based on the decision (dis-)utility of the "remembering self." It is something like an "anticipated memory." Thirdly, adding a period of pain, but of lower intensity to the colonoscopy, so as to decrease the peak-end average, actually makes the remembered experience less painful ("violation of dominance"), despite obviously prolonging it. This explains why medical technicians do not abruptly stop the procedure when pain is foreseeably at its height, extending it, instead, for a couple of minutes longer, but with pain at a lower, more tolerable level.

These same rules regarding the "remembering self" and decision utility apply to other more pleasant experiences and events, such as holidays or vacations. From the viewpoint of memory, there isn't much of a difference between a 1-week and a 2-week break, despite the double duration. Most of our experiences (experienced utilities), especially the less pleasant ones, are air-brushed away, and we are largely left with reminiscences of its climactic moments and how it ended (decision utilities). That's why it is best to end holidays with a bang, rather than a whimper, to raise the peak-end average of the decision utility and subjectively derive more pleasure and enjoyment from what were, objectively, the same events. Many tour operators are aware of this, for on it depend a large number of their repeat customers (predicted utilities). The mash-up between the "experiencing self" and the "remembering self," along with their respective utilities, is one of the cognitive traps into which we invariably fall, together with the so-called focusing illusion, according to which whatever it is we think necessarily affects our own happiness or wellbeing.

Other such cognitive illusions affecting the "remembering self" and its decision utilities are endowment and contrast effects, on the one hand, and forecasting errors, on the other (Tversky and Griffin 2000). While endowment and contrast effects refer to how the present is evaluated in comparison to the past, the optimism–pessimism pair refers to expectations regarding the future. According to the endowment effect, individuals tend to attach a higher value – a proxy for "liking" or the pleasure of ownership – to things they presently own, and a lower value – indicative of "wanting" or desire – to things they do not, as yet, possess (Thaler 1980). For this reason, people tend to command a significantly higher price to sell an object which they already own, such as a mug, for instance, compared to the price at which they would be willing to buy it (Kahneman, Knetsch, and Thaler 2009). This same phenomenon has been documented for sports championship tickets (Carmon and Ariely 2000) and performance bonuses, where workers have been found to exert greater effort when these are framed as probable losses, because they have already been provisionally awarded, compared to when they are presented as merely possible gains (Hossain and List 2012). This is another way of saying that human beings are generally more "loss-averse" or "conservative" of what they already have, than "acquisitive" or "desirous" of things they still have to attain.

Contrast effects, for their part, explain why after a positive experience, a similar subsequent event may seem less gratifying (a "negative contrast"), while after a negative experience, a similar subsequent event would seem less mortifying (a "positive contrast") (Tversky and Griffin 2000). In the first case, consider having dinner at a Michelin-starred restaurant one night, then at an unpretentious neighborhood eatery on the next. One cannot help but compare the eatery meal with that of the previous night and thus actually experience less pleasure. And for the second case, one can imagine suffering from a severe migraine headache one day, then getting a brain-freeze while eating ice cream later on. The pain from the brain-freeze would be negligible compared to that from the migraine headache. In both cases, the hedonic evaluation of the present hinges either negatively or positively on a recent, similar experience in the past, and memory unfailingly enters into play. Assessment is never independent or absolute.

Finally, regarding the forecasting errors of optimism and pessimism, both are due to the fact that one does not take adaptation into account, and therefore exaggerates long-term benefits and costs of future behaviors (Kahneman 2000b). For this reason one is often surprised when told that, after some time, lottery winners think that their prize has been a curse, or people who have become paraplegics usually revert to their happiness levels before the mishap (Brickman, Coates, and Janoff-Bulman 1978).

Therefore, despite the insistence on transient pleasures and joy as the main constituents of happiness, further research on decision utilities and the "remembering self" has made it necessary to broaden the scope of happiness to include life satisfaction. To some extent, we have already referred to this second level of happiness when speaking of individual subjective wellbeing in Chapter 1. Initially, we distinguished individual subjective wellbeing (positive emotion, pleasant feelings, good moods) from objective measures (GNP, per capita income, and so forth). Then we introduced two different perspectives in measuring individual subjective wellbeing: the global, life satisfaction approach and the domain-specific or episodic approach. From the aforementioned, we now realize that even individual subjective wellbeing has an objective component, through the moment-based assessment of the actual utilities of the "experiencing self" (the domain-specific or episodic approach). This sheds a new light on the understanding of the mathematics or physics of individual subjective wellbeing, as mainly the balance between positive affect and negative affect. And despite the cognitive errors attributed to memory and the "remembering self" in the evaluation of decision utilities, we also acknowledge that such inputs cannot simply be ignored. In other words, actual pleasures and joy cannot be a stand-alone account of happiness and should, instead, be incorporated into a broader perspective of life satisfaction. After all, although we take great pains to distinguish the "experiencing self" from the "remembering self," it cannot be denied that both form part of the same self or individual. And this individual, as the subject of happiness, happens to live not only from one moment to another, but also in a continuity. Thus, logic demands that the moment-based and transient account of happiness revolving around pleasures and joy be complemented by a more comprehensive and lasting version called "life satisfaction," despite its own challenges.

In the same way that pleasure and joy have been the focus of hedonic psychologists, life satisfaction has been the rallying point of "positive psychologists." As one of the founders of this school, Martin Seligman (2002), explains, "positive psychology" has nothing to do with "positive thinking," which is some form of self-delusion. Rather, it is an approach in modern psychology that centers on strengths (instead of pathologies or weaknesses), with the aim of building better lives for human beings (instead of repairing damage); it addresses the needs of normal people and seeks to nurture those of exceptional talent (genius) through appropriate interventions.

We are already familiar with the constitutive elements of happiness within Seligman's PERMA model: positive emotion, engagement, relationships, meaning, and accomplishment or achievement (Seligman 2011). Within this context, "life satisfaction" could be defined as a combination of a pleasant life (pleasures and positive affect), engagement (absorption in work or some other activity in which one excels, without feeling anything), and, above all, meaning (using signature strengths to serve the transcendent, something larger than oneself). A pleasant life is the least important in overall satisfaction for at least two reasons. A good mood is, largely, a heritable trait, and thus, not very modifiable. As for pleasure, we already know that it is subject to habituation, thanks to which its positive effect diminishes over time, unless an increasingly stronger stimulus is available. Engagement, then, may prove to be more significant, inasmuch as it enables us to identify our signature strengths and to reconfigure our lives to use them as much as possible. But insofar as it attaches us to a greater whole, meaning is what turns out to be most satisfying in one's life. Examples of interventions in this regard would be realizing "gratitude visits" or engaging in philanthropy, among others, both of which have been demonstrated to produce long-lasting positive effects on individual life satisfaction.

Still within positive psychology, we have scholars such as Mihaly Csikszentmihalyi (1990) and his notion of "flow." Akin to Seligman's "engagement," "flow" describes a state of complete concentration in an activity, such that nothing else – not even time, food, or the self – seems to matter to the individual. It differs from a pleasant life because, in the state of flow, the subject does not really feel anything. It is as if the nervous system had suffered an overload and, as a result, could no longer process any additional input or information. Csikszentmihalyi himself defines "flow" as "being completely involved in an activity for its own sake. The ego falls away. Time flies. Every action, movement, and thought follows inevitably from the previous one, like playing jazz. Your whole being is involved, and you're using your skills to the utmost" (Geirland 1996).

For Csikszentmihalyi, people are happiest when they find themselves in this state of "flow" (being "in the zone" or "in the groove" would be equivalent expressions). He has enumerated several characteristics of what this state entails (Csikszentmihalyi 1990). One is completely involved, focused, or immersed in what he is doing. There is a sense of ecstasy: that is, being outside of oneself and everyday reality; as if the body disappeared from one's own consciousness and existence were suspended. One possesses great inner clarity, a knowledge of what exactly needs to be done and how; awareness merges with action, and an immediate and uninterrupted feedback loop is established between the two. There is also an adequacy of skill to the challenge at hand, which is neither too difficult nor too easy; with effort, one rises to the task. Next comes a feeling of serenity or peace, the absence of care or worry about oneself, a transcending of the ego. There is also a transformation of time to the point of timelessness: one is thoroughly fixed in the present and does not notice the passage of the minutes or the hours. And last but not the least, "flow" is achieved when the individual performs an activity, not in order to attain any external goal, but because it is intrinsically

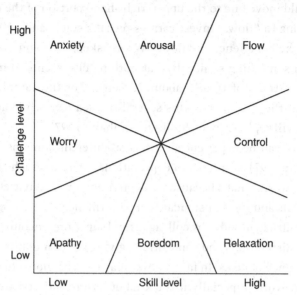

FIGURE 4.1 "Flow" in relation to other mental states
Source: copyright 1998, Csikszentmihalyi, Mihaly, *Finding flow: The psychology of engagement with everyday life.* Reprinted with permission of Basic Books.

rewarding or fulfilling (an "autotelic experience"). Indeed, the activity becomes its own reward and one experiences intrinsic motivation at its finest. Individuals who have a propensity to flow are said to possess an autotelic personality, which includes traits such as curiosity, persistence, and humility. This allows them to experience flow even in situations which other people would find daunting or miserable.

In a chart comparing a subject's skill level on the x-axis and the challenge level represented by a task on the y-axis, the state of "flow," in relation to other states, could be located as follows (Csikszentmihalyi 1997; figure 4.1).

At the center of the graph is the "mean level" or one's "set point." Thus, surfing channels on television would normally situate one in the lower, left-hand region of "apathy," where both skill and challenge levels are low, while doing what one really wants and doing it well would move one to the upper, right-hand portion of the chart, corresponding to "flow." Investigations reveal a stable and universal pattern in the experience of "flow." When asked, "Do you ever get involved in something so deeply that nothing else seems to matter and you lose track of time?" about 20 percent of the sample will respond that they experience this several times a day, while around 15 percent will reply "never" (Csikszentmihalyi 1997).

"Flow" can be experienced in several different domains (Csikszentmihalyi 1997). Contrary to expectations, there is much "flow" to be had at work. That's because work often involves activities with clear, set goals and rules or standards of performance. These, together with the feedback provided by colleagues and superiors, encourage one to set aside distractions and concentrate, giving the best of himself to the performance of tasks. In fact, "flow" may even be more elusive at play than at work, especially if the kind of leisure activity involved does not require any particular level of skill or challenge, nor does it propose any definite goal, as is the case in many forms of media consumption, such as aimless netsurfing. Engaging in active leisure, such as pursuing hobbies, playing musical instruments, or participating in sports, predisposes one better to episodes of "flow," particularly when one devotes to it a comparable amount of attention and ingenuity as he would to work. Active leisure often demands specific preparation and training before it becomes enjoyable, much along the lines that Scitovsky (2002) suggested in the education of desire. Social "flow," too, is possible; in fact, even chronically depressed people revive when they are in the company of others and are immersed in activities that require their full attention. Interaction with others and the performance of engaging tasks draws their focus from themselves and gives them a chance to foster their skills. Indeed, there are few experiences as gratifying as a good conversation, where interlocutors have compatible goals and help each other develop their thoughts freely and creatively.

The trick in achieving "flow," then, seems to lie, primarily, in the ability to harness and direct one's attention or mental energy to the activities in which one excels. (Stress, precisely, is associated with a "lack of control" over one's life.) Writing a journal, having a change of surroundings, or altering one's daily rhythms may help identify what those exact activities are. Next, one has to learn to organize his day around such activities, trying to maximize the time spent in these optimal experiences. This requires prioritizing objectives, eliminating distractions, and delegating, perhaps, other worthy but not very important aims. There are many ways to learn to control one's attention, such as meditation, prayer, aerobic exercise, martial arts, and so forth. It is essential, though, to enjoy the particular activity for its own sake, knowing that it's not the result that counts, but the mental control or discipline that one develops.

Recently there has been a lot of interest in "mindfulness," in the effort to "disconnect to connect," in the corporate world and beyond (Hochman 2013, *The Economist* 2013). It basically consists in taking time out from the tumult of daily activities for relaxation and meditation. Among the triggers is 24/7 connectivity through ubiquitous electronic devices which overwhelm our senses and attention, leaving us feeling drained. The deeper reason is, of course, not wanting to lose a beat in the ever-escalating competition for material success. Mindfulness responds to this heretofore repressed craving for ease and reflection, the desire not to be hyperstimulated or entertained in every possible way, the wish to abandon the chase. Such techniques bring about significant physiological and psychological benefits, from lowering blood pressure to relieving psoriasis; they could even help one get a promotion at work, perhaps. Inasmuch as it can decrease employee healthcare costs, mindfulness has begun to attract the attention of managers. All this, of course, favors the cause of happiness. Ironically, however, mindfulness could have turned into a management fad (and cottage industry) in its own right, promising the latest competitive advantage in the professional rat-race.

Thus, the ideal of happiness consisting mainly of "flow" differs from that of pleasures and joys proposed by hedonic psychologists. Pleasures and joys depend largely on external factors in the environment, while "flow" comes from within (Csikszentmihalyi 1997). More significantly, "flow" leads to growth in skill and ability, greater control over one's attention, and an increase in the depth and richness of one's consciousness and personality. None of these is assured by pleasures and joys in themselves. However, not everything related to "flow" is positive either, as it can be perfectly channeled to destructive ends. For instance, some soldiers claim to experience very intense "flow" while manning machine guns at battle front lines, just like some teenagers in the midst of some gratuitous acts of violence or destruction of property. Besides, merely concentrating on "flow" may lead one to neglect other less gratifying, but perhaps, equally necessary activities for the sustenance of life or the service of others. Exclusively aiming at "flow" may cause certain isolation. That's why, despite Csikszentmihalyi's insistence on the importance of "flow," it is best understood as a mere constituent, not as the totality of life satisfaction.

An account of happiness hinging on a normative ideal of the good life is the virtual third rail in all modern psychological approaches. Almost everyone acknowledges its presence, but few come near, and even fewer are those who fully engage with it. This may be due to the reluctance to veer away from the standard, social science perspective that seeks to build knowledge, little by little, from the bottom up, through tiny bits of empirically verifiable information (Ryan and Deci 2000a). A normative ideal for happiness implies a grand theory, perhaps too grand to be considered truly scientific. But at the same time, the question of what a good life is, or what makes one kind of life better than another, will simply not go away. In other words, it is still worth investigating what the normative or moral basis of satisfaction is, even in judgments regarding "life satisfaction."

Those who struggle with the normative dimension of happiness or the "good life" are said to subscribe to a "eudaimonic" view, borrowing a term from Aristotle (whose use of *eudaimonia* is often translated as "flourishing"). Taking off from the work of those who studied human potential, Waterman (1993) affirms that happiness is achieved when one fulfills or realizes his true nature or potential. This contrasts with the hedonic view, for it is possible to experience pleasure without developing human potential. It also differs from the life satisfaction perspective, insofar as the activities which realize human potential, apart from engaging, likewise have to be congruent with some firmly held values. Thus, the "flow" experiences of the trigger-happy soldier or the drug-crazed youth in a fit of vandalism would not be constitutive of the good life. Waterman calls this state of human fulfillment "personal expressiveness," a condition in which one feels intensely alive and in accordance with his authentic self. Unlike hedonic states, which relate to being relaxed and free from difficulties, "personal expressiveness" is reached when one feels challenged and exerts effort in tasks which afford growth and development.

Other scholars have advanced their own versions of how this ideal life ought to be. Ryff and Keyes (1995) speak of "psychological wellbeing" as a construct that touches on six different dimensions of human fulfillment: autonomy, personal growth, self-acceptance, life purpose, mastery, and positive relatedness. They show how psychological wellbeing affects the body's immunological system in a manner that promotes health. Ryan and Deci (2000b), in their "self-determination theory," identify three basic psychological needs – autonomy, competence, and relatedness – whose fulfillment leads to psychological growth, integrity, wellbeing, and vitality. Although certain activities, such as those in which one is pressured to succeed, give rise to a sense of satisfaction or "subjective wellbeing," however, they do not result in vitality, which is an element of eudaimonic wellbeing. While Ryff and Keyes (1995), through their notion of "psychological wellbeing," provide an expert definition of what the good life consists in, Ryan and Deci (2000b), by means of their "self-determination theory," limit themselves to describing the principal factors that promote or foster wellbeing. Although both teams of researchers agree that happiness lies more in functioning fully than in the fulfillment of desires, Ryff and Keyes seem to adopt a more normative slant.

In some measure, happiness researchers belonging to the school of evolutionary psychology may likewise be included, albeit unwittingly, in the normative option. Happiness would be an aim that human beings seek, even unconsciously, for in any case, it always ends up imposing itself as the overarching objective of all our activities. Nettle (2005) explains happiness as an evolutionary goal, something imaginary that gives direction and purpose to our lives. Similar to the notion of "fitness," happiness keeps us striving and competing in order to survive and pass our genes on to the next generation. It does so without being real or tangible.

Apparently, the brain is in control of happiness, yet as an organ, it is known to be very flexible and adaptive to the environment. For instance, our brain makes us believe that happiness is, indeed, what we want and that we can increase our own personal happiness by doing certain things. Several psychological changes could then ensue, with the brain reducing the impact of negative emotions, heightening the effect of positive ones, or changing the focus of attention. These techniques come under several names, such as cognitive behavior therapy, mindfulness training, and connecting with the transcendent through nature, art, and religion. Our mind, then, constantly plays tricks on us, disguising evolutionary advantages as "happiness," even when there is actually no such thing. The brain's only interest lies in achieving evolutionary fitness, to which happiness simply serves as a ruse. The positive emotions that we so desire are nothing else but the brain's responses to different evolutionary challenges. We seek them in the belief that they will eventually lead to happiness, although this latter part may never be fulfilled.

As an evolutionary psychologist, Nettle (2005) criticizes the hedonic account of happiness as being too trivial, and the equivalent of the life satisfaction account as being too broad. He also declares himself to be unconvinced by those who propose happiness as consisting in the fulfillment of human potential. For, among other things, what is "full potential"? Who is to judge when it is "fully realized"? How can we explain why someone who has not realized his full potential is, nonetheless, happy, or why another, who has in fact actualized it, is not? Yet, Nettle must have in mind some better version of what happiness is in reality, for otherwise, he could not even formulate his critique. And what he does, from then on, is to explain what happiness, as an evolutionary objective, may seem like. Certainly, he may not be imposing or dictating his version of happiness, but, indeed, he proposes what he believes to be a better account or explanation of the good life. And that, precisely, is what defines a normative ideal, although in this case, it may not be conscious or even teleological, strictly speaking.

Joining Nettle is fellow evolutionary psychologist Gilbert (2006), who may also be described as putting forward, albeit inadvertently, a normative account called "synthetic happiness." Again, just like Nettle, Gilbert (2006) informs us that, in truth, happiness is not a goal or an objective we can deliberately pursue. Rather, it is more like something that we stumble upon by chance, thanks to certain strange workings of our brain. Put briefly, we reach happiness not by getting what we want, but by "learning" to want what we get. It is less about the careful, calculated use of freedom and rationality in our choices, as allowing the brain to have its way, which is inevitable, after all (although we may not know or agree with it).

Gilbert (2006) then describes the several, different ways in which our brains fool us in our search for happiness. He attributes most of these charades to the prefrontal cortex, responsible for simulating future experiences and therefore involved with planning and the sensation of anxiety. Patients who have undergone a prefrontal lobotomy perform well in standard intelligence tests, but are unable to think about the future or the consequences of their actions, thus running into serious problems in their personal relationships. It is as if they lived in an eternal present, immune to worries.

The first systematic error lies in "prospection," in imagining the future too much like the present, but at a later date. That's why when children are asked what they want to be when they grow up, their response actually corresponds to what they want to be now. Since their prefrontal cortex has not yet fully developed, they are unable to think about the future. To some extent, we cannot help but think about the future in order to be prepared and to try to control it. For this reason people prefer to choose the number of their lottery ticket, as if by so doing, they would be able to influence the results. But the problem is that we are often wrong in gauging future pleasures and pains, as we have seen in the calculation of decision utilities (Tversky and Griffin 2000). Nonetheless, the mere illusion of control seems to provide the same psychological benefits as genuine control. We reap these benefits when we postpone a positive future experience, such as a dinner date or a leisure trip, because just thinking or daydreaming about it already affords us pleasure. We therefore double the pleasure in summing up the prospective and actual, for the price of one single experience.

A second systematic malfunction in the quest for happiness refers to the subjectivity of experience. We seem closed to the fact that experience is opaque to everyone else but the person who has it (Gilbert 2006). Gilbert (2006) narrates the story of conjoined twins, Lori and Reba Schappel, who express what apparently is a universal desire among those in their condition: they are happy as they are and would like to remain together always. Such a feeling is, of course, difficult, if not impossible to understand, for anyone who is not a conjoined twin. Gilbert (2006) clarifies that, in comparing our feelings or subjective experiences with those of others, we tend to confuse three related but different realities. There is an emotional happiness ("feeling happy") which is non-transferrable and irreducible to any other phenomenon, although it generates a similar pattern of neural activity in all individuals. Similarly, although yellow is light with a wavelength of 580 nanometers, the experience of seeing the color yellow cannot be reduced or substituted by merely projecting light with these characteristics. Next comes moral happiness ("feeling happy because...") which indicates actions which, according to a set of beliefs, produce those feelings. For instance, within the Aristotelian ethical framework, we could refer to virtuous action as that which brings about *eudaimonia*, or flourishing. Then there's judg-mental happiness ("feeling happy about...."), which reveals a cog-nitive stance or position regarding something we acknowledge as a potential source of pleasure, but without actually experiencing such pleasure. In varying degrees, these three senses reflect the impregnable subjectivity of happiness. This makes it overwhelmingly difficult to describe and evaluate other people's claims about the experience.

To further complicate matters on subjectivity, we discover that people can be mistaken even about their own feelings (Gilbert 2006). There are non-pathological cases, as when individuals very quickly decide on the basis of their intuitions or hunches, coming from a more primitive part of the brain designed for "flight or fight" responses to certain stimuli. Such hasty judgments can be wrong, of course, although they would have caused the brain just the same to pro-duce a ready state of arousal in the organism, when both blood pres-sure and heart rate rise, pupils dilate, and muscles grow tense. Sim-ilarly, arousal caused by fear or excitement may be confused with that produced by sexual attraction, such as when one thinks he has fallen in love with a female companion on an adventure trip. Then we have the pathological cases. A "blindsighted" person is one who sees, in the sense of experiencing light and knowing its location, without being aware of seeing. And an "alexythymic" person (from the Greek *alexythymia*, or "absence of words to describe emotional states") is one who displays the appropriate physiological responses of an emotion without being aware of experiencing it. When asked, "How do you feel?" he responds, "Nothing" or "I don't know." Fal-libility regarding sensations and feelings is such that one may even experience them without knowing it.

"Realism," the belief that reality is as it appears to the mind, is another error that persistently plagues the quest for happiness (Gilbert 2006). People tend to believe that their memories are accu-rate accounts of past events, when they are, in fact, heavily altered. Past experiences are compressed, reduced to a few critical features, and then unconsciously re-fabricated when we try to retrieve them.

We fill in the blanks of our remembrances with details from our pre-existing worldview and prejudices. Our memory acts as some sort of automatic form-filling application, such that we remember the past as we want to remember it, willy-nilly. For this reason, as every judge and lawyer knows, even the testimonies of eyewitnesses need to be cross-examined and verified. Something akin occurs with how we imagine the future, through what counts as an "anticipated memory." There are lots of missing details, yet we tend to emphasize positive features and neglect negative ones, giving in to an excess of optimism in our evaluations and judgments. Such misperceptions are aggravated, the greater the distance of the memory or image from the present.

By "presentism" Gilbert (2006) understands the tendency for actual experience to condition and disfigure one's perception of both the past and the future. When widows are asked about their grief at their husband's demise 5 years ago, their memories are influenced inevitably by how they feel at present. In the same way, teenagers tend to miscalculate how they would feel, several years down the road, about the tattoos and body-piercings which they now have made. There is a difference between actual vision (coming from the sense of sight) and mental imagery (coming from memory), although both are produced in the visual cortex of the brain. Yet we often confuse the emotional experience originating from one with the emotional experience originating from the other. This explains why we imagine those living in sunny places to be happier than those living in cloudy ones, despite similar responses in actual life satisfaction surveys. It's also the reason why we often mistake a future event to be the cause of present distress or unhappiness.

Given that the human brain is more sensitive to relative differences than to absolute magnitudes of a stimulant – such that one can be asleep with the television at full blast yet be awakened by a knock on the door – "presentism" can also be harnessed for some beneficial uses (Gilbert 2006). Think of haggling or asking for donations, for instance. In haggling, a well-known strategy consists in opening with very high stakes, then reducing the bid considerably. The buyer first bids at half the price, and then moves to a 25 percent discount, which instantly becomes much more palatable to the seller. In like manner, when soliciting a donation, by starting with double the target amount, then slashing it significantly, the donor becomes better predisposed to fulfill one's petition. Human beings are more sensitive to losses than to gains, as we already know. Besides, by framing the purchasing or soliciting strategy as the above, the other party tends to compare the present with the fictitious past (50 percent discount or double the target donation) rather than with the possible future (full price or target donation).

"Rationalization" is another such systematic error that makes the path to happiness largely a serendipitous one. It may be defined as unconsciously making something seem more reasonable than it really is (Gilbert 2006). This happens because most stimuli (facts and experiences) are by themselves ambiguous, and we clarify their meaning based on context, frequency, or recentness. For example, upon hearing the word "shoulder," a bus driver would most probably think of the side of the road, while an orthopedist, the place where the arm connects with the torso. Given this margin, we inadvertently choose to interpret stimuli in the best possible way, even if we have to cook our data. Such are the workings of our psychological immune system, that it fosters resilience. As a result, for instance, very few of those who have suffered the loss of loved ones actually fall into chronic depression, difficult as it may be to imagine beforehand. Our minds are programmed to make us practically immune to the dark side of reality.

Another consequence of "rationalization" is the search for a scapegoat, for someone else to blame, when a tragic accident occurs. It could have very well been brought about by bad luck, but that wouldn't be as emotionally satisfying as when we are able to attribute the fault to someone else. There is greater relief in finding an explanation for our misfortune, no matter how incongruous, than in blaming destiny. And the worst possible outcome is not to have anybody to shoulder the responsibility for the tragedy but ourselves. Self-blame and regret are highly negative and destructive emotions which our psyches try their best to avoid, regardless of the cost. That makes denial highly tempting and widespread, and also, utterly difficult to overcome.

Even for indifferent or neutral results, our minds endeavor to adjust levels of satisfaction so as not to leave a margin for remorse. Gilbert (2006) recounts an experiment involving college students, some of whom were stuck with photographs they had developed, while others had a chance to change the prints they wanted to keep. It turns out that those who made irreversible decisions were significantly happier with their photographs, precisely because it was not possible for them to experience remorse, while the others suffered notably with their doubts regarding alternatives. Remarkably, this goes against our firmly held belief that the more choices, the better. In fact, we are even willing to pay more to keep our options open, as in department stores with a "no questions asked" return or exchange policy, as compared to those which don't offer this possibility, although the shopping experience is actually more satisfying in the latter than in the former.

It appears, then, by virtue of the "rationalization" principle, that our minds almost force us to see the world through rose-tinted glasses. We tend to pay more attention to positive or favorable pieces of information, taking them in almost to the point of gullibility, and we love to surround ourselves with people who satisfy this craving (Gilbert 2006).

In the midst of all these systematic psychological errors, it is nothing short of a miracle, indeed, that anyone ever finds happiness. Gilbert (2006) acknowledges some degree of corrigibility in our experiences, through awareness and the mechanisms of practice and coaching, but offers no guarantees. Why, then, are so many false beliefs transmitted from one generation to the next? Here is where his evolutionary perspective comes in. These false beliefs promote stable societies which, in turn, help propagate these same beliefs further. In particular, were it not for the belief that the plethora of choices, characteristic of market economies, offered a way to greater happiness for individuals, endowed with seemingly insatiable appetites for material goods, then not only the economy, science, and technology, but the whole of social life would grind to a halt. If people, all of a sudden, were to become content with what they already had, this world would come to a full stop, for indeed, desire is the motor and essence of life.

Thus, as Gilbert (2006) concludes, happiness is not something to be found in nature; rather, it is something that we "synthesize" or "stumble into." We do this when, in Buddhist-like fashion, we finally see the light and are able to overcome or transcend desire. For as Prince Hamlet comments to his companions Rosencrantz and Guildenstern, "there is nothing either good or bad, but thinking makes it so" (*Hamlet* Act 2, scene 2, 239–251). For all we know, therefore, we may already be staring at happiness in the face, although we don't realize it. But which is actually better, to strive for something that may not exist or to be enlightened and cease all striving?

WHEN ALL ELSE FAILS

After exploring the three main psychological accounts of happiness – a pleasurable feeling, a judgment concerning life satisfaction, and a conformity to a normative ideal of the good life – and becoming aware of their strengths as well as pitfalls, we could now ask what, exactly, could be done to achieve the best outcomes or results in this peculiar quest. The responses could be grouped into two major types of interventions: the use of pharmacological agents and the modeling of behavior through the development of habits. Although these instruments could be employed jointly, it would be best to analyze them separately, for each presents its own set of challenges. Let us now turn to the first of these.

The ability of alcohol, opium, marijuana, coca, and other naturally occurring psychotropic drugs to drown sorrow and uplift spirits has been known to human beings far and wide, almost since the dawn of civilization. In recent times, however, we have been able to synthesize substances which offer not only temporary pleasure and relief, but also precise and long-lasting alterations in the human psyche. These are the "betablockers" (beta-adregenic receptor antagonists), which act on the memory, and the "SSRIs" (selective serotonin reuptake inhibitors), which influence our mood. It has become possible, therefore, to attain a pharmacologically induced happiness, in which unpleasant memories have been erased and emotional dispositions or moods have been brightened. But does this amount to authentic human happiness? Is this the kind of happiness that we could rightly desire for ourselves?

In the foregoing, we have understood how happiness entails close interaction between the mind and the heart, among sensation, desire, passion, feeling, memory, imagination, understanding, and reason, among others. Happiness is bound to personal identity, and thus, intimately linked to memory (President's Council on Bioethics 2003). The role of memory consists in assimilating present experiences into the remembered narrative of the past. As we have seen, a good memory does not require a perfect recall of events, but a selective reconstruction that distinguishes the important from the trivial in order to serve as a guide for action. Accuracy and completeness, therefore, are sacrificed to salience and meaning. Memories also change as life unfolds. Childhood memories acquire a different color and texture when remembered in one's senior years; they may become less vivid, but they gain depth of significance. Insofar as human beings pursue happiness as creatures immersed in time, memory plays a major role. However, for the very same reason of being time-bound, the happiness they achieve is never complete. Nonetheless, what is certain is that one's identity can never be detached from memory, which serves as a living archive of past experiences and an orientation for future conduct.

The pathologies affecting memory are varied. Weak memories, both inborn and acquired through alcohol abuse, for instance, give rise to cognitive disabilities. Memory loss, a failure of one's capacity to remember recent events, either through trauma (amnesia) or age

(Alzheimer's disease, senile dementia) is particularly dreadful because it results in the dissolution of personal identity. But a healthy memory could also become an obstacle to happiness, insofar as it retains exceptionally tragic events that may even prove life crippling. In these cases, pharmaceuticals such as "betablockers" may be prescribed in order to edit the terrible or destructive memories and to restore a certain tranquility and peace of mind.

Immediately after a new experience comes a period of memory consolidation (President's Council on Bioethics 2003). An event accompanied by strong emotional arousal triggers the release of stress hormones such as adrenaline in the brain. These substances, in turn, activate the amygdala, embedded in the temporal lobe, and together they determine how vivid and permanent the memory will be. It has been discovered that the introduction of "betablockers" in the amygdala counteracts the stress hormones and produces the opposite, memory-numbing effect. In the case of people suffering from "post-traumatic stress disorder" (PTSD), each time they remember their trauma, a fresh flood of stress hormones is released, thus producing recurrent and increasingly intrusive and debilitating memories. The use of "betablockers," therefore, could help these patients soften their painful memories and detach themselves from the strong, negative emotions they experience.

However, "betablockers" so far have been proven effective only when administered during, or shortly after, the occurrence of a traumatic event. This raises a number of difficult questions. Who is to judge that an event is "traumatic enough" to merit the prescription of "betablockers?" And, granted that not everyone eventually suffers from PTSD, for whom? For example, shall we inject all soldiers before entering into combat, or relief workers as they rush to a disaster zone, as some form of "preventive medicine"? These issues are further complicated by the possibility that the use of "betablockers" may interfere with the normal psychological recovery process, amounting to a short-term gain for a long-term loss (Schacter 2001). In the end, memories, no matter how painful, have to be faced, acknowledged, and lived through, before they are overcome and put to rest. By artificially interfering with memory formation through "betablockers," we may indeed ease probable pain. But only at the expense of falsifying one's perception of the world and, to some extent, altering one's life and identity. Furthermore, what would stop violent criminals and executioners from using these same drugs to render themselves immune to empathy, compassion, and remorse in perpetrating dreadful and brutal deeds? It seems that a happy life cannot consist exclusively of sweet and beautiful memories, with everything else deleted.

Some other pharmacological quick-fixes, this time acting on moods, are "SSRIs" (best known under the commercial name, "Prozac"), which are purportedly safe, non-addictive, and most important, legal, and their more sinister relatives, "MDMAs" (methylenedioxy-n-methylamphetamines, or "Ecstasy") (President's Council on Bioethics 2003). SSRIs prevents the "re-uptake" of the neurotransmitter serotonin, making more of it available for neurons to communicate with one another in the brain. Without being opiates or euphoriants, SSRIs nonetheless induce calmness, a background sense of wellbeing, and a generally brighter mood. Thus, they are prescribed in mood disorders such as depression, for which there are no biochemical, genetic, or biophysical diagnostic procedures. MDMAs also make more serotonin available in the brain, but instead of inner tranquility, what they produce is extreme sensory and social openness, intense affection, and bliss. There have been cases in which people high on Ecstasy have professed love and proposed marriage to a perfect stranger, on the basis of what is, in fact, a groundless emotion.

Indeed, there is a danger in reducing happiness to a mere mood, and in thinking that whatever elevates the mood necessarily increases happiness as well. Moods, which are transient states of feeling, and temperaments, which are more persistent dispositions to action, not only inform a person of his inner self, but also of the outside world. The knowledge they provide is of the self in connection with the external environment. Through the use of substances such as Prozac and Ecstasy we are now able to sever this link, producing a joyful mood which does not correspond to the unmedicated self's perception or judgment of its surroundings. One can create a false, but sunny disposition, introducing doubts, for instance, about a person's real character. Moreover, emotions tend to be redefined exclusively in biochemical terms: vehement desire indicates a high concentration of peptides in the hypothalamus; just indignation, elevated levels of serotonin in the temporal lobe; and happiness, simply a question of neuron activity (President's Council on Bioethics 2003). All of this promotes a detachment from other people and an estrangement from the real world. Interpersonal emotional bonds are weakened, for their roots become shallow.

Just like traumatic memories, sorrowful emotions may also hold some value. For example, grief and mourning at the death of a loved one reveal the genuineness of affection, and it would be profoundly inhuman to completely avoid this difficult stage through the help of drugs. Similarly, experiencing emotional hardship and discontent in worthy enterprises could often act as a spur to self-improvement, while Prozac-induced calm could breed complacency and apathy. Dependence on pharmacological means to assuage emotional pain and misery leads, at once, to a solipsistic and slavish existence (President's Council on Bioethics 2003). One lives in a manner preoccupied exclusively with his own comfort and elation, unmindful of others and the world at large.

There seem to be certain conditions that positive emotions – in the form of memories or moods – need to fulfill in order to contribute to authentic human happiness (Gruber 2013; Rodriguez 2013). The first refers to moderation, measure, and proportion. Too much of a positive emotion produces a manic state which makes one prone to reckless and unhealthy behavior. A balance with negative emotions and a diversity of genuine experiences, varying in flavor and intensity, have to be achieved for the best results or outcomes. Unpleasant feelings and enjoyable ones are equally crucial in evaluating experiences and making sense of life's ups and downs. Moreover, taking positive emotions together with negative ones helps detoxify the latter and promote psychological health.

A second requirement concerns context. Whether positive or negative, all emotions are tied to a specific set of circumstances in which they are deemed "appropriate." That means they are supposed to help one perform a concrete, adaptive function. Being worked-up or even angry may be the right attitude when one is engaged in a competitive activity, instead of being cheerful and relaxed. Also, negative emotions could provide vital signals regarding health or relational issues that require attention, thus aiding survival.

And thirdly, setting up positive emotion as an end-goal proves to be counterproductive. Those who do so unconsciously raise the threshold for their own joy and pleasure, eventually experiencing greater disappointment and a stronger tendency toward depression. It seems to be advisable to focus not on the positive emotion itself, but on the activity it naturally accompanies. For pleasure and satisfaction are more like signs that "life is good and going on as it should" than goals in themselves. At best, one's attitude toward pleasure and satisfaction should be one of "mindful acceptance" rather than a directed search or, even worse, an obsessive fixation. Suppressing thoughts and emotions can be harmful, so it's best that we acknowledge and accept them, positive and negative alike.

A more low-tech alternative to the use of pharmacological agents lies in the modeling of behavior through habits. By developing positive habits and overriding negative or destructive ones, individuals should be able to achieve their desired outcomes of fuller, more accomplished, and happier lives. Based mostly on William James's "pragmatism," it starts off from the idea that a substantial part of the actions we perform daily – close to 40 percent, according to recent studies (Verplanken and Wood 2006; Neal, Wood, and Quinn 2006) – are not the result of actual, carefully deliberated choices or decisions, but rather, the fruit of habit (James 1975, 1981). When we do things for the first time, normally, we encounter difficulties and need to dedicate a fair amount of attention. But through repetition and practice, the task becomes easier, until we reach a level of proficiency that allows us to do it automatically, almost effortlessly, while hardly being conscious of it. These changes are due to habit. Habits make our brains more efficient, permitting us to direct spare mental energy to processing new and unforeseen data, while letting already familiar processes run their course. They give our brains the necessary down-time or rest.

Habit-formation or learning may be described as a three-step process consisting of a cue, a routine, and a reward, that ends in a reinforcement loop (Duhigg 2012). The cue could be a certain place, time of day, emotional state, or the presence of other people that immediately triggers the succeeding routine. The routine, in turn, could be a physical or a mental event. The reward is the goal or end of the routine, and the satisfaction it brings helps the brain retain the habit-forming procedure for future use. For example, most office workers have breaks during the day, which they use to take some drinks and snacks. Almost always, these break-time activities are constituted by habits. Often, it's the same group of people who, at a given moment, head toward the cafeteria to order the same food and beverages, then leave at approximately the same time, day after day. It's more comfortable that way. It saves everyone time and energy in deciding when to take a breather, how, with whom, and for how long each day. Those decisions may have been taken during the first few days in the job, but afterwards, they have been left to habit. In this particular case, the cue could be the time of day, the smell of coffee wafting through the air, certain stirrings of hunger, or some colleagues knocking on one's door. Any one or a combination of the above would be sufficient to activate the snack routine, with the people involved hardly realizing it. The reward will be, of course, the relaxation, the satisfaction of hunger or thirst, and the enjoyment of the social interaction.

In the past, James described habit-formation in the brain metaphorically as some sort of origami, the art of folding paper which, once creased, tends to remain always in the same way. Nowadays, modern neurological science is able to explain the process in more accurate terms. It has been discovered that even people who suffer severe recent-memory loss or anterograde amnesia are, nevertheless, still able to form habits (Duhigg 2012). Despite damage in their medial temporal lobe, the part of the brain responsible for fresh memories, these individuals are able to navigate through their homes and neighborhoods, for example. When asked to draw a map of their house or block, however, they are unable to produce one. How so? It turns out that those neural pathways corresponding to habits have been created in the basal ganglia, a more primitive part of the brain, which normally controls subconscious behaviors such as breathing and swallowing. As long as the basal ganglia is intact, therefore, people will still be capable of learning or acquiring habits, although the more advanced or rational parts of their brain may be injured.

What makes habits so powerful, such that they are able to proceed even with the individual hardly being conscious of them? Experiments with macaque monkeys reveal that habitual action creates some sort of craving in the subjects, making them anticipate rewards (Schultz 2006). Thus, when despite having performed the set routine on cue, the expected reward is not delivered, a neural pattern corresponding to frustration and anger ensues. If left unattended for an extended period, these negative feelings could even give way to depression. Something similar occurs with human beings. Let's take the habit of physical exercise, for example. For many people, it may have begun on a variety of cues, from having more free time, to stress from work or health reasons. These individuals then start to pick up an established routine. Once this activity is finished, they often experience a very pleasant feeling, due to the rush of endorphins and other neurochemicals, besides an understandable sense of pride and accomplishment. All of these rewards contribute to reinforce the habit loop. Thus, if for one reason or another, such people are unable to perform the exercise routine upon receiving the cue, a deep feeling of unease, restlessness, and anxiety develops. Without them knowing it, they have acquired a craving for the endorphin rush and relaxation that comes at the end of the workout.

So far, we have only considered mainly beneficial habits, such as those that take place during office breaks and in physical workouts. But there are also destructive habits or addictions to alcohol, drugs, gambling, and so forth. From the purely neurophysiological perspective, our brain cannot distinguish a beneficial habit from a destructive one. So it's up to us to deliberate and decide, using the more rational part of the brain, what to do.

Imagine, for instance, that someone has been eating too many sugary and fatty snacks during breaks and has grown overweight. How could he eliminate this habit? Is it possible to undo the neural pathways that have been created in the brain? Barring surgery, it appears that we cannot eliminate old habits, in the sense that those neural connections will always remain with us, but we can override them by developing new ones (Heinze et al. 2009). While retaining the cue and the reward, we will have to change the routine (Duhigg 2012). Let's go back to the break-time habit. Among the several possible cues, one will have to try and find out which is the real behavioral trigger. If it's hunger, he could change the routine by substituting doughnuts with an apple, which is a healthier choice, then still get the same reward of satiation, for example. To one's surprise, it may not even be hunger at all. It could be a mix of tiredness and boredom, in which case one could insert a new routine of going for a short walk, surfing the internet for a few minutes or taking some time out to talk with friends. Of course, none of these options carry additional calories. By persevering in this new routine, chances are that a new habit will be rewired in one's brain, strong enough to overcome the previous one that led to excess poundage. It may be tough in the beginning, but it can certainly work out, since the mechanism employed, the habit loop, is basically the same.

In more deeply ingrained habits such as alcoholism, for instance, there is always the danger of backsliding into one's former ways, even after years of being sober. This often occurs at some particularly stressful moment in one's life caused by severe illness, death of a loved one, the break-up of a relationship, or a serious professional setback. It shouldn't surprise us because as we know, those neural connections have been hard-wired in one's brain and cannot be removed except through surgery. That's why in Alcoholics Anonymous programs there is a reference to belief in God or in a higher power. It has been discovered, however, that what's important is not so much the nature or identity of God or the object of one's belief that matters, but the fact of believing that change can happen (Traphagan 2005). And such a kind of belief is far easier to achieve and sustain if one belongs to a community (Duhigg 2012).

The technology of habit-formation based on pragmatism, therefore, provides us with a potent tool with which to modify behavior in accordance with one's preferences and desires in a way that brings us closer to our ideal of happiness.

* * *

What goes on in the mind or the psychology of happiness cannot be detached from how the human brain works. For this reason, we set out to explore the anatomy and physiology of the brain without losing sight of its importance for an interdisciplinary approach as the one we endeavor to follow.

From the perspective of brain science, happiness may be analyzed at three different levels. The first concerns an understanding of happiness based on pleasures (both physical and mental) and the feeling of joy, which is very closely bound to the heritable, dispositional trait of extraversion. This has been the preferred focus, among others, of hedonic psychologists. Their studies reveal significant differences in the actual experience of pleasures, on the one hand, and the memory or prediction of them, on the other, and its influence on choices and decision making. Also, they alert us to the variety of cognitive illusions to which we are, to a large extent, helplessly subject.

The ephemeral quality or transience of pleasures and joys prods us to continue to a second level of analysis, of happiness as life satisfaction. Positive psychologists argue that positive affect and experiences of "flow" provide a broader, more comprehensive, and lasting platform from which happiness can be more meaningfully examined.

Nevertheless, they likewise serve us notice regarding the benefits of negative emotions and the illusory nature of a life consisting exclusively of positive emotions.

Despite the understandable reluctance in advancing a normative ideal of happiness, sooner or later it becomes clear that this is, in fact, inescapable, as we cannot entirely avoid an evaluative judgment of what qualifies as true satisfaction for human beings. This challenge has been met by psychologists concentrating on the development of human potential, through their various accounts of a eudaimonic life based on "personal expressiveness," "psychological wellbeing," and "self-determination." The emphasis now lies on flourishing or full-functioning, rather than the mere attainment of joys and pleasures or the fulfillment of desires. Albeit inadvertently, proposals from evolutionary psychology referring to happiness as "fitness" or a "synthesis," rather than a deliberate goal or objective, may also be classified as versions of a normative ideal. Whether we like it or not, human activity is directed toward this stage or end, for the benefit of the species, ultimately. Again, we are informed of the variety of ways in which our minds lead us to happiness, largely despite our conscious choices.

The aforementioned considerations regarding the psychology of happiness have not stopped human beings from investigating and developing biotechnological shortcuts. These comprise the ingestion of pharmacological substances such as betablockers, which act on memory, and SSRIs, which affect moods. Alternatively, behavior could also be modeled following certain principles of pragmatism in respect of the cues, routines, and rewards of habit-formation.

REFERENCES

Aamondt, S. and Wang, S. 2008. *Welcome to your brain*. London: Rider.
Argyle, M. 2009. *The psychology of happiness*. London/New York: Routledge.
Berridge, K. C. and Kringelbach, M. L. 2008. "Affective neuroscience of pleasure: Reward in humans and other animals," *Psychopharmacology*, 199: 457–480.

Bloom, P. 2010. *How pleasure works: The new science of why we like what we like.* New York: W. W. Norton and Co.

Brickman, P., Coates, D. and Janoff-Bulman, R. 1978. "Lottery winners and accident victims: Is happiness relative?" *Journal of Personality and Social Psychology*, 36(8): 917–927.

Carmon, Z. and Ariely, D. 2000. "Focusing on the foregone: how value can appear so different to buyers and sellers," *Journal of Consumer Research*, 27 (December): 360–369.

Csikszentmihalyi, M. 1990. *Flow: The psychology of optimal experience.* New York: Harper and Row.

    1997. *Finding flow: The psychology of engagement with everyday life.* New York: Basic Books.

Duhigg, C. 2012. *The power of habit.* New York: Random House.

Geirland, J. 1996. "Go with the flow," *Wired Magazine*, September, Issue 4.09, (www.wired.com/wired/archive/4.09/czik_pr.html, accessed November 12, 2013).

Gilbert, D. 2006. *Stumbling on happiness.* New York: Vintage.

Gruber, J. 2013. "The scientific study of positive emotion" (http://edge.org/panel/ headcon-13-part-ii, accessed November 21, 2013).

Heinze, H. J., Heldmann, M., Voges, J., Hinrichs, H., Marco-Pallares, J., Hopf, J. M., Müller, U. J., Galazky, I., Sturm, V., Bogerts, B. and Münte, T. F. 2009. "Counteracting incentive sensitization in severe alcohol dependence using deep brain stimulation of the nucleus accumbens: Clinical and basic science aspects," *Frontiers in Human Neuroscience*, 3: 22.

Hochman, D. 2013. "Mindfulness: Getting its share of attention," *New York Times*, November 1.

Hossain, T. and List, J. A. 2012. "The behavioralist visits the factory: Increasing productivity using simple framing manipulations," *Management Science*, INFORMS, 58(12): 2151–2167.

James, W. 1975. *Pragmatism: A new name for some old ways of thinking.* Cambridge, MA: Harvard University Press.

    1981. *Principles of psychology.* Cambridge, MA: Harvard University Press.

Kahneman, D. 2000a. "Experienced utility and objective utility: A moment-based approach," in Kahneman, D. and Tversky, A., (eds.), *Choices, values and frames.* Cambridge: Cambridge University Press, pp. 673–692.

    2000b. "Evaluation by moments: Past and future," in Kahneman, D. and Tversky, A., (eds.), *Choices, values and frames.* Cambridge: Cambridge University Press, pp. 693–708.

Kahneman, D., Diener, E. and Schwartz, N. 1999. *Well-being: The foundations of hedonic psychology*. New York: Russell Sage Foundation.

Kahneman, D., Knetsch, J. L., and Thaler, R. H. 2009. "Experimental tests of the endowment effect and the Coase theorem," in Khalil, E. L. (ed.), *The new behavioral economics*, vol. 3. *Tastes for endowment, identity and the emotions. Elgar reference collection. International library of critical writings in economics, vol. 238.* Cheltenham, UK and Northampton, MA: Edward Elgar, pp. 119–142.

Kenny, A. and Kenny, C. 2006. *Life, liberty and the pursuit of utility*. Exeter: Imprint Academic.

Murphy, K. 2013. "Jump-starter kits for the mind," *New York Times*, October 28.

Myers, D. G. 2002. *The pursuit of happiness*. New York: HarperCollins.

Neal, D. T., Wood, W. and Quinn, J. M. 2006. "Habits – a repeat performance," *Current Directions in Psychological Science*, 15, 4: 198–202.

Nettle, D. 2005. *Happiness: The science behind your smile*. Oxford/New York: Oxford University Press.

President's Council on Bioethics 2003. *Beyond therapy: Biotechnology and the pursuit of happiness*. New York: Harper Perennial.

Rodriguez, T. 2013. "Negative emotions are key to well-being," *Scientific American*, April 11.

Ryan, R. M. and Deci, E. L. 2000a. "On happiness and human potentials: A review of research on hedonic and eudaimonic well-being," *Annual Review of Psychology*, 52: 141–166.

2000b. "Self-determination theory and the facilitation of intrinsic motivation, social development, and well-being," *American Psychologist*, 55(1): 68–78.

Ryff, C. D. 1989. "Happiness is everything, or is it? Explorations on the meaning of psychological well-being," *Journal of Personality and Social Psychology*, 57: 1069–1081.

Ryff, C. D. and Keyes, C. L. M. 1995. "The structure of psychological well-being revisited," *Journal of Personality and Social Psychology*, 69(4): 719–727.

Schacter, D. 2001. *The seven sins of memory: How the mind forgets and remembers*. New York: Houghton Mifflin.

Schultz, W. 2006. "Behavioral theories and the neurophysiology of reward," *Annual Review of Psychology*, 57: 87–115.

Scitovsky, T. 2002. "My own criticism of The joyless economy," in Easterlin, R. (ed.), *Happiness in economics*. Cheltenham, UK/Northampton, MA: Edward Elgar, pp. 55–65.

Seligman, M. E. P. 2002. *Authentic happiness*. New York: Free Press.

2011. *Flourish*. New York: Free Press.

Thaler, R. 1980. "Toward a positive theory of consumer choice," *Journal of Economic Behavior and Organization*, 1: 39–60.

The Economist 2013. "Schumpeter: The mindfulness business," November 16.

Traphagan, J. W. 2005. "Multidimensional measurement of religiousness/spirituality for use in health research in cross-cultural perspective," *Research on Aging*, 27: 387–419.

Tversky, A. and Griffin, D. 2000. "Endowments and contrast in judgments of wellbeing," in Kahneman, D. and Tversky, A. (eds.), *Choices, values, and frames*. Cambridge: Cambridge University Press, pp. 709–725.

Verplanken, B. and Wood, W. 2006. "Interventions to break and create consumer habits," *Journal of Public Policy and Marketing*, 25(1): 90–103.

Ward, A. F. 2013. "The neuroscience of everybody's favorite topic," *Scientific American*, July 16.

Waterman, A. S. 1993. "Two conceptions of happiness: Contrasts of personal expressiveness (eudaimonia) and hedonic enjoyment," *Journal of Personality and Social Psychology*, 64(4): 678–691.

5   Working on happiness

At times we come across a description of the ideal state of the economy as a "Goldilocks economy": that is, one neither "too hot," nor "too cold," but "just right." In simplest terms, macroeconomic temperature here is regulated mainly through two levers, one controlling employment, and the other, inflation. Politicians and economic managers generally aim for a balance between the two, such that everyone seeking work can find it, thus ensuring a steady source of income to cover people's needs and keep the country's productivity moving ahead, but without causing the engine to "overheat," registering high rates of inflation, either. High inflation rates indicate a situation in which the economy is swamped by excess liquidity, with too much money chasing the same goods, making prices climb in a spiral and people lose purchasing power. Therefore, although employment and inflation have contrary effects, the two extremes of high unemployment rates and a galloping inflation are, equally, recipes for economic and social unrest that are best avoided. This explains the insistence on finding an equilibrium or balance. Similarly, negative consequences can also be expected for the happiness or subjective wellbeing of individuals, when the two macroeconomic indicators of unemployment and inflation rates run amok. However, as we shall discover later, the strain caused on happiness by each one does not exactly play out in accordance with that predicted by neoclassical economic principles.

Following the principal lines of research established by Frey and Stutzer (2002), we shall first consider the effects of employment, then later, of inflation, on happiness. With regard to the former, we shall investigate why unemployment exerts a downward pressure on happiness, not only for those who themselves are out of work, but also for those who, nonetheless, manage to keep their jobs. Next, we shall inquire about the different factors that contribute to (or, at least, are highly correlated with) superior levels of satisfaction in the workplace. Afterwards, we will take a close look at the connection between happiness and leisure, insofar as it refers to something taken to be the opposite of work or employment. And finally, we shall describe the various ways in which high rates of inflation detract from happiness.

HAPPINESS AND EMPLOYMENT

Strange as it may seem, there is a lingering doubt within academic circles regarding the voluntariness of unemployment (Frey and Stutzer 2002). On the one hand is the Keynesian view, according to which, given the costliness of being unemployed, it certainly must be involuntary (or otherwise, the result of a completely "irrational" choice). If this is so, then it makes all sense for government, or whoever is in charge of the general welfare, to intervene by raising aggregate demand for goods and services within a territory. That way, more labor would have to be contracted to meet the demand, and unemployment levels would subsequently fall. Perhaps an extreme, but nevertheless coherent application of this reasoning is the National Rural Employment Guarantee Act in India (National Portal Content Management Team 2011), the first ever law that guarantees waged employment on an unprecedented, massive scale. Implemented by the Indian Ministry of Rural Development, the law seeks to enhance the livelihood of rural households by providing at least 100 days of guaranteed wages a year to adult members, who volunteer to do unskilled manual work. In line with its secondary objective of natural resource management and sustainable development, most mandated tasks involve efforts to combat deforestation and soil erosion, as well as to alleviate the effects of drought or flooding in villages. At the same time, this directive is also meant to strengthen grassroots democracy, and increase transparency and accountability in governance.

Alternatively, new classical macroeconomic theory suggests that unemployment is voluntary and that government should leave it alone, for any other remedy the state may promote could actually be worse than the disease it seeks to cure (Frey and Stutzer 2002). For instance, in the midst of the 1930s Depression, Friedrich Hayek and Joseph Schumpeter were said to have inveighed against efforts to combat the economic doldrums by printing money, since that would leave "the work of depressions undone" (Krugman 2014). In these circumstances, people are supposed to find the option of work and the wages offered unattractive, compared to the possibility of simply receiving unemployment benefits and engaging in leisure. In any case, the short-term disequilibrium caused by involuntary unemployment should largely sort itself out, as soon as both individuals and firms carry out finer adjustments. Government initiatives to raise demand for labor would only result in higher inflation rates which punish everyone in the end. Therefore, the state should learn to respect people's choices, including those of the unemployed, who are more than capable of looking after their own wellbeing or happiness.

The question of which of the two schools of thought is right is by no means moot. It bears heavily on the policies governments ought to have pursued in response to the global financial crisis that began in 2007–2008, for instance. Should governments spend and stimulate demand, despite getting deeper in debt, or should they, instead, drastically cut spending, to keep public finances in line through austerity programs? Obviously, one cannot do both at the same time. The stimulus of deficitary spending would be in accord with a Keynesian view of unemployment, while austerity would be more in keeping with the new classical macroeconomic perspective.

Championing the cause of austerity and fiscal responsibility were Harvard economists Carmen Reinhart and Kenneth Rogoff. In their paper "Growth in a time of debt" (Reinhart and Rogoff 2010), they identified a critical threshold or tipping point for government indebtedness, 90 percent of GDP, beyond which economic growth drops off sharply. Similar conclusions were drawn from reports by the International Monetary Fund (Kumar and Woo 2010) and the Bank for International Settlements (Cecchetti, Mohanty, and Zampolli

2011), as well as from the work of Alberto Alesina and Silvia Ardagna (2009) on "expansionary austerity." However, when University of Massachusetts economists Herndon, Ash, and Pollin (2013) tried to replicate the results of the Reinhart–Rogoff study, they found it impossible. What's more, they discovered that, purportedly, Reinhart and Rogoff had omitted some data, used some dubious statistical methods, and made a coding error on their Excel spreadsheets. Once all this was taken into account, although one could detect some correlation between high debt and slow growth, nevertheless, there was no indication at all of a 90 percent threshold, nor was the direction of causation between the two variables clear. In other words, one could not tell from the available data whether it was the high level of debt that slowed down growth or whether it was the other way around, as had occurred indeed in Japan in the early 1990s, when the country got deeply mired in debt after growth had collapsed (Krugman 2013a).

In a reply, Reinhart and Rogoff (2013) acknowledged the spreadsheet coding error, which led them to miscalculate the post–World War II growth rates of highly indebted countries. However, they continued to dispute the charges of "selective exclusion" of relevant data and the "unconventional weighting" of statistics. They also reiterated their view that, with respect to the negative correlation between debt and growth, causality actually ran in both directions.

In short, with respect to the exact nature of the link between the level of public debt and the degree of economic growth, the science is not yet settled. The policy choice between stimulus and austerity in face of the financial crisis, therefore, was not a purely technical and necessary economic decision, but a political one, with serious ethical undertones. Krugman claims that at the height of the global financial crisis, between August and September 2008, US Federal Reserve officials continued to be obsessed with inflation, mentioning it 773 times in their meetings, compared to only 54 mentions for unemployment and 23 for systemic risks – a situation similar to crying "Fire!" while engulfed in a flood (Krugman 2014). What is really best for a country and what do its people, after having been properly informed, truly want? Is it economic growth now at all costs, never mind the debt and the future, or is it embracing austerity and balancing books while still possible, even if it means cutting social spending and high unemployment? And among the ethical repercussions to be considered is the effect of either option not only on the state of the economy, but above all, on people's wellbeing and happiness. To this matter we now turn.

THE UNHAPPINESS OF THE UNEMPLOYED

It is not exactly shocking, but still, some may find it counterintuitive, that the unemployed self-report much lower levels of happiness than the employed, while controlling for factors such as income and education (Frey and Stutzer 2002; Frey 2008). Similar results are obtained from both cross-sectional and longitudinal studies (Warr 2007). In particular, an Irish study that distinguishes among several categories of the employed, unemployed, and inactive (homemakers, retired, students, disabled, and so forth) came up with the following ranking of life satisfaction in descending order: self-employed, full-time employed, retired, students, part-time employed, homemakers, disabled, in government training scheme, not working/not seeking work, unemployed (Brereton, Clinch, and Ferreira 2008). The unemployed always turn up at the bottom. Moreover, the category of employment doesn't seem to matter much to the level of self-reported happiness, when compared to the mere fact of actually being employed. It is not the kind of work one does, but work itself that uplifts the spirit. Thus, a British study reveals that unemployment exerts the greatest downward pressure on individual wellbeing, even more than divorce or separation (Clark and Oswald 1994).

What is it with being unemployed that brings in the doldrums? By "unemployed" we understand, in the strictest of terms, individuals without jobs who are seeking one or would like to have one (Warr 2007). Frankly, it is hard to determine whether or not to include those who may be looking for a job, although they really do not want one (they do so only to comply with requirements to claim unemployment benefits, for instance). This is one of the controversies surrounding Spain's Rural Employment Act (*Plan de Fomento del Empleo Agrario*, or PFEA, formerly known as *Plan de Empleo Rural*, or PER) (Diputación de Granada 2013). According to this law, rural workers who have worked for a minimum of 20 days a year would be entitled to 6 months' worth of unemployment benefits and a contributory pension, within certain conditions of age and family income. Critics claim that instead of boosting farmwork, all this does is to encourage fraud or even facilitate some covert form of vote buying by the ruling parties in the Spanish regions of Andalusia and Extremadura.

Frey and Stutzer (2002) indicate two explanatory factors for unemployment misery: individual, psychological costs and social costs. Included among the individual, psychological costs of unemployment are higher incidences of depression, anxiety disorders, loss of self-esteem, strained personal relationships (domestic abuse, separation, divorce, extra-marital relationships), and substance addiction, as well as increased rates of suicides and mortality in general, due to poorer health. This could be explained partly by the frustration experienced by a person actively looking for work, yet unable to find it. The stronger the personal commitment to employment or paid work, the greater the distress (Warr 2007); although role preference also matters (Ross, Mirowski, and Huber 1983). That's why wives who preferred domestic activities were actually more prone to depression upon having a job, than those who preferred employment outside the home. Various studies also reveal that unemployment generally bears more heavily on men than on women, and on the more educated than on the less (Frey and Stutzer 2002). Even part-time employment has a significant negative correlation with life satisfaction for males, whereas for females, nonesuch appears (Brereton, Clinch, and Ferreira 2008). This may be due to the greater expectations of men to be working outside the home than women, and the higher opportunity costs or forgone income normally associated with superior educational attainment.

When differentiated into age groups, the negative correlation between happiness and unemployment yields an inverted U-shaped graph: it hurts most at the middle ages, between 30 and 49 years old, and less at the extremes, before the age of 30 and past the age of 50 (Frey and Stutzer 2002; Frey 2008). This could be understood through a combination of the factors previously mentioned, concerning societal expectations and opportunity costs. Until the age of 30, people could be easily excused from not working because they are still receiving an education. And after the age of 50, again they may be excused, because – at least in some countries with generous welfare states – they may soon be eligible for an early retirement. Nonesuch applies to those caught in the ages in between. Moreover, it often occurs that during those middle years, the financial burdens related to building a family weigh heaviest. Hence, the unhappiness that comes from being unemployed is more acute.

In the United States, although 75 percent of individuals plan to continue working after retirement, only less than 20 percent actually do, and many retire even earlier, due to ill health, dissatisfaction with their job, or the realization that they have accumulated a big enough nest egg (Greenhouse 2014). That doesn't mean that they all do so voluntarily, however. Quite a number simply leave the workforce after having been laid off and upon finding it practically impossible to get another job, due to some form of age-discrimination. All told, there still is a net increase in the number of Americans past 65 years of age who continue working, from 12 percent two decades ago to 18.9 percent in 2014, citing reasons such as good enough health, less taxing jobs, and having to make up for recent stock market losses. In a related survey among 1,502 individuals, the AARP (formerly the American Association of Retired Persons) mentions "enjoyment," at 31 percent, as the top motive why senior citizens remain in the workforce, closely followed by "extra money," at 30 percent, "to have something interesting to do," at 21 percent, "to be physically active," at 14 percent, "to be mentally active," at 11 percent, and "for self-support," at 10 percent.

It has also been discovered that those who are unemployed for the first time take a much harder hit than those who have been through it before (Frey and Stutzer 2002). Apparently, experience helps to alleviate some of the pain from unemployment. The duration of unemployment also matters. Longitudinal studies show significant distress during the first 6 months, after which it stabilizes until the first year, then improves a little until the second year (Warr 2007). Two forms of adaptation may enter into play: a constructive adaptation, by which individuals develop interests outside the labor market, and a resigned adaptation, by which they reduce aspirations and emotional investment in employment. Nonetheless, there is also a difference depending on who, when, and for how long one suffers a bout of unemployment, particularly a long-term one. The 2008 financial crisis hit young American males especially hard for several reasons (Peck 2010). Fewer were college educated compared to the women in their cohort, and they were concentrated in industries in decline, such as manufacturing, or in the construction sector, which is highly cyclical. By contrast, it was much easier for women to find jobs in the more resilient service sector. Besides the practical impossibility of recovering lost earning power in their lifetimes, unemployed males also take a hard blow to their self-esteem and identity, easily falling into substance abuse and grave difficulties in personal relationships. In the four decades beginning 1970 to 2010, the median earnings of men fell by 19 percent, and those with only a high school diploma, by 41 percent. By contrast, women have practically regained all the jobs they lost during this recent recession, compared to just 75 percent of men (Coontz 2014).

Likewise, being unemployed at a time when unemployment rates are high, as in Spain between 2009 and 2014, with more than 25 percent, seemingly eases its sting. The same occurs when more members of the household, such as one's spouse, are also unemployed. People then tend to see themselves as innocent victims of the bad state of the economy, rather than personally responsible for their unenviable fate, because of incompetence or poor work attitudes, for example.

It may be worth considering, at this point, whether it is unemployment that drives down happiness, or it is unhappiness (in terms of low self-worth or poor mental wellbeing) that hinders employment instead (Frey 2008). Neither effect can be discounted, although evidence seems to suggest greater causation from the side of unemployment toward unhappiness (Winkelmann and Winkelmann 1998; Marks and Fleming 1999).

As for the social costs of unemployment, these include becoming an outcast, the loss of a sense of place or belonging, and suffering stigma, granted the singular importance of work in the modern world (Frey and Stutzer 2002). It wasn't always like this, however. In previous times, from the ancient Greeks well down to the last remnants of aristocratic societies, it wasn't work, but not having to work, that was deemed desirable and in keeping with the best expression of human dignity (Kenny and Kenny 2006). Nowadays, however, not only the value of a life before others, but also one's own sense of self-worth depends heavily on the work one performs, whether or not it is prestigious, and how much one earns. Much has already been said in previous chapters with regard to how income and social comparison affect happiness; yet work introduces certain interesting modifications. For instance, work is seen as an expression of dignity and therefore a net contributor to the happiness of adults, but not of children. On the contrary, child labor is considered unbecoming and even an affront to human dignity, because children are supposed to be learning at school, rather than earning a living. So probably it is not work itself that is objectionable, but work insofar as it deprives children of the chance to receive a proper education. Whether or not that is possible, given the socioeconomic conditions of the child's family, is, of course, an altogether different issue. There may be some cases in which we should probably just keep an open mind to a child's being initiated to some form of livelihood early in life, in order to be able to contribute to the support of the family. After all, how many minors in affluent societies take on jobs delivering newspapers or packing supermarket bags, only to have more spending money during weekends at the shopping malls?

In the case of adults, perhaps the lack of work leads to unhappiness, not so much for the loss of income, but due to social exclusion (Kenny and Kenny 2006). Indeed, in many industrialized societies such as the United States and Europe, high levels of per capita income now coexist with equally high rates of unemployment. In the 1950s and 1960s, people may have had lower incomes, but it was easier for them to find work. Social exclusion, however, is an ill that money alone cannot remedy.

As if to emphasize the social nature of human beings, we are told that even those lucky enough to keep their jobs also suffer distress, when unemployment rates are high and they are surrounded by the jobless (Frey and Stutzer 2002). There are several reasons for this. One is that they themselves may feel threatened. If the depressed state of the economy continues, their jobs may be the next to go. Another cause is the so-called survivor guilt, due to which they somehow feel responsible for their former colleagues losing their jobs. A third is a mixture of pity and disdain for the jobless. They certainly feel sympathy for those out of work, but at the same time, they cannot help but think that they now have to work double-time, in order to pay for the latter's unemployment benefits. It is fairly easy to cast the unemployed as freeloaders, receiving money and aid despite not doing anything productive. Lastly, high unemployment rates usually cause a surge in criminality and social disorders, thereby adding to the worries and the tension, even of those fortunate enough to be working.

Much of the social cost attributed to unemployment depends on the strength of the social norm for work (Frey and Stutzer 2002; Frey 2008). It is certainly not the same to be out of work in the Gaza strip, where the social norm for work is low and even abysmal, or in Japan, where it is extremely high. After all, *karoshi*, the term for "death from overwork," is Japanese. It is estimated that around 10,000 Japanese workers die from "work-related cardiovascular disease" yearly, apart from a record-breaking number of suicides (around twenty-one per 100,000 people, according to the OECD), many of which are related to stress from overwork. There exists in Japanese society a very strong compulsion toward high-quality work, which unfortunately is often confused with excessively long working hours. For instance, it is fairly normal for school teachers to clock in 13 hours a day (Hutcheson 2007). Rather than desire for money, Japanese workers seem to be driven by a combination of social pressures ("face time" and an overbearing respect for hierarchy) and a sense of pride in work. For this reason, giving tips to service workers is not practiced at all and is considered insulting, in stark contrast to countries such as the United States, where the amount even figures in restaurant bills, for example. Neither is the experience of joblessness comparable between an ethnic Roma, accustomed to a culture of dependence, and a person belonging to the dominant ethnicity of a European country in which the Roma are found. The latter is more likely to believe in the principle of self-reliance.

Those out of work tend to shun the company of the employed due to an understandable sense of shame. Instead, they band together and frequent the same places, adding credence to the saying that "misery loves company." For purposes of getting a job, however, such behavior is indeed odd, because what they should do is the exact opposite. Rather than retreating to their cocoons with fellow unemployed, they ought to go out more and engage with all sorts of people, especially those with jobs. The wider and more varied their social networks, the easier it would be for them to find work.

THE HAPPINESS OF THE EMPLOYED

Although on the whole, the employed are significantly happier than the unemployed, realism requires that we at least acknowledge that working is not all fun and games. Work may also produce its share of costs or negative outcomes by way of various stress factors, some job-specific, others organization-specific (Gavin and Mason 2004). Among the job-specific stressors are long working hours, heavy workloads, conflicting or ambiguous orders from superiors, and work–family conflicts. Among the organization-specific stressors, we may count job insecurity, interpersonal conflicts, major changes in work conditions, such as the installation of new technology, and perceived injustices, especially those related to pay in the workplace.

Of particular interest are the stressors arising from technological change, often wrought in the name of enhancing worker productivity. Indeed, ever since the industrial revolution, mechanization has steadily reduced the need for most kinds of manual labor. Consisting mainly in reductionist techniques, it simplifies, standardizes, measures, monitors, and controls job performance. At the same time, however, mechanization tends to minimize the unique contribution of workers to the realization of tasks and isolate them from each other. Even worse, it may promote conditions for zero-sum competitions among workers in the same firm. Despite economic benefits for the firm, efforts to increase worker productivity, therefore, do not invariably add to employee wellbeing, satisfaction, or happiness. This occurs when such efforts thwart the attainment of the employees' wider, personal goals. Such jobs have come to be known by the not very polite term of "bullshit jobs" (Graeber 2013), insofar as they are generally perceived to be outrageously meaningless kinds of employment, tolerated by the desperate exclusively for the money. They come largely as the result of applying industrial line-worker productivity principles to the lower end of the service sector, giving rise to mind-numbingly repetitive tasks. Think of making photocopies, taking round-the-clock routine customer service calls or doing night shifts in fast-food deliveries. These are dumbed-down tasks that are perhaps best carried out by machines.

The combined impact of stressors could be such that people even opt to forgo work opportunities presented, as occurred with autoworkers in Detroit, in face of plant closures and factory relocations (Uchitelle 2007). Many decided to accept company buyouts which included a huge lump sum of separation pay or early retirement, pensions, health insurance, education benefits, and job replacement assistance instead of continuing to work, albeit in a different post or at a different factory. Age, health, and family circumstances undoubtedly played a huge role in these decisions. But at the same time, there were lots of complaints from workers about the alternative jobs offered: they entailed a loss in rank or seniority, tasks were hollowed out to the point that hard-earned skills had become superfluous, returning to the assembly line had just become too demanding and stressful, valuable social circles were broken up with the transfers, and shoddy treatment from the new bosses had turned out to be unbearable.

However, not only blue-collar jobs, but also several white-collar occupations are in danger of disappearing, thanks to the technological disruption caused by an increasing number of ever more powerful computers being hooked on to the internet. Among the most susceptible categories are those of telemarketers, accountants and auditors, retail salespersons, technical writers, real estate agents, and legal workers (Frey and Osborne 2013). This trend follows what transpired during the first great period of industrialization, when the substitution of labor by capital goods destroyed thousands of jobs – think of the weavers being replaced by mechanized looms, triggering the Luddites' protests (Brynjolfsson and McAfee 2014). Although in the end, such forms of innovation may bring about enormous benefits, the huge adjustment problems in terms of displaced and obsolete workers cannot be ignored.

Moreover, even the ranks of highly educated professionals could now fall prey to the "automation of knowledge work" and lose their hitherto secure livelihoods (Krugman 2013b). This could certainly prove to be a threat, not only to mid-level manufacturing and service jobs in general, but also to the economic base of the middle class, which would increasingly be eroded. Society, then, would tend to become more polarized in a "winner takes all" scenario, between a few super-rich entrepreneurs and investors, on the one hand, and a great majority of subsistence wage-earners doing grunt work, on the other. Consider what happened when 15-month-old Instagram was bought by Facebook for $1 billion, the value of which was distributed among its 4,600 workers, and compare that to recently bankrupt Kodak – the Instagram of its day – which at its peak employed 145,000 workers (Brynjolfsson and McAfee 2014).

We shall now refer to the sense of wellbeing and satisfaction experienced within the domain of work. Job satisfaction has been found to be one of the major indicators of overall life satisfaction, alongside satisfaction with one's health, housing, and the environment (Frey and Stutzer 2002). And within the domain or life-space of work, we can further specify different aspects or facets, such as income, insofar as they impact satisfaction. Although it is helpful for analytical purposes to distinguish between general, overall happiness and work-related happiness, we mustn't forget that the two are inextricably related (Gavin and Mason 2004). Even if values for each one were different and seemingly independent, the truth is that no one can be genuinely happy if he is unhappy at work. This is not only because we spend a lot of time – and increasingly so – at the workplace, but also because of the learning, attachments, and human relations we develop there. It is virtually impossible to work in an organization without imbibing or internalizing its policies. Thus, workplaces need to be attuned not only to considerations of productivity or health, but also to overall wellbeing and satisfaction, granted the interpersonal and holistic qualities of happiness.

What are the sources of satisfaction at work? Job titles themselves seem relevant. In a British study, gardeners, hairdressers, and care assistants were found happiest with their jobs, while bus drivers, postal workers, and assembly-line workers were found least happy (Rose 2003). In the United States, managers and administrators declared themselves most satisfied with their work, in contrast to machine operators and laborers, who were least satisfied (Weaver 1980). But job titles in themselves do not provide much useful information, and the tasks or contents associated with the same title may vary widely. It would be more advisable, therefore, to examine the features that make certain jobs generally desirable. And considering that not all individuals are happy or unhappy to the same degree even with the same jobs, it would also be worthwhile to inquire which personal characteristics allow them to flourish in a particular job.

The premise, therefore, is that although there are certain objective, environmental features to a job which, on the whole, make them attractive, individuals themselves contribute some personal characteristics to transform work into a satisfying experience (Warr 2007). Among the objective environmental features are: availability of money, physical security, valued social position, supportive supervision, career outlook, equity, opportunity for personal control, opportunity for skill use, externally generated goals, variety, environmental clarity, and contact with others. "Availability of money" refers to wage or salary level, and "physical security," to the absence of danger and presence of good working conditions, such as ergonomically designed equipment and safe levels of temperature and noise. A "valued social position" relates to whether the job is white-collar or blue-collar, whether it enjoys high or low prestige and whether it is viewed mainly as a job (taken out of economic necessity), a career (focusing on future advancement), or a calling or profession (affording personal fulfillment through service to the community). "Supportive supervision" indicates management style – the extent to which it goes beyond the merely transactional, "carrots and sticks" exchange to the transformational kind of leadership, which inspires better performance and elevates morale. "Career outlook" means opportunity for progress in activities, roles, and positions within the same or across different organizations, while "equity" denotes fairness, in both the way the organization treats its employees (distributive justice) and the way employees deal with the organization (contributive justice). "Opportunity for personal control" measures influence or discretion and ultimately freedom to determine one's own actions, whereas "opportunity for skill use" is the degree to which the workplace encourages or inhibits the development of physical and mental abilities. "Externally generated goals" signify challenges that arise in the course of work and "variety," the range of tasks one is expected to perform, in contrast to monotony and repetition. "Environmental clarity" or "predictability" reveals the ability to plan and prepare for the future, because goals and expectations are set. And finally, "contact with others" points to interpersonal relationships that reduce loneliness and lend various forms of support.

On the other hand, included among the subjective, personal characteristics are the judgments individuals make in particular situations, their baseline happiness, demography, and relevant personality traits or dispositions (Warr 2007). Judgments are subject to opinions and pressures from other people (contagion), such as the way in which individuals process information and appraise situations (comparing oneself to others). Baseline happiness alludes to the consistency of satisfaction levels across time and place. Demography encompasses gradations of happiness not only through sex, age, or race, but also through culture (East or West) and occupational status (part time or full time, temporary or permanent work contract). Lastly, personality refers to the way the five major inherited traits condition the degree of workplace satisfaction: neuroticism is associated with anxiety, depression, hostility, and moodiness; extraversion, with sociability and assertiveness; openness to experience, with an artistic or an intellectual orientation; agreeableness, with cooperativeness and trustworthiness; and conscientiousness, with proactivity and self-discipline. Happiness at the workplace results from a conjunction or the interactive fit between these two sets of factors: the objective, environmental features and the subjective, personal characteristics.

In this regard, it is fascinating to try and understand people's perceptions of manual *vis-à-vis* intellectual work, and their preference for one over the other (Crawford 2009). For the most part, manual work is considered dirty and grueling, lowly paid, unprestigious, and not requiring any special degrees or preparation. By contrast, intellectual work is cast as clean, distinguished, lucrative, and difficult, in the sense that only a gifted few can do it. However, there are certain kinds of purportedly intellectual activities, such as writing abstracts for academic journal articles, that are so dependent on procedures and protocols that they have become alienating. There is practically no room for a humanly distinctive contribution in terms of creativity or genius. One works in isolation and suffers from a complete disconnect between personal efforts and the finished, anonymous product. On the other hand, it is possible to find some kinds of manual work, such as that of a vintage motorcycle mechanic, for instance, which encourage one to hone all sorts of skills and abilities, and where the connection between one's efforts and the results are immediate. At times, it may even be as absorbing as neurosurgery, and if successful, perhaps equally satisfying. Moreover, it allows one to form part of the community of vintage motorcycle enthusiasts and gain some well-deserved prestige. Certainly, it could even pay more than abstract-writing.

Environmental features do not affect job satisfaction in the same way, nor is there a linear relationship between them. Instead, Warr (2007) proposes a more nuanced relationship, based on the manner in which vitamins affect the health of human beings (the "vitamin analogy"). Certainly, all vitamins are important to human health, such that deficiencies may lead to disease. But that doesn't mean that every additional dosage consumed of a particular vitamin gives rise to a proportional health benefit indefinitely. Rather, there's a level of dosage for some vitamins in which benefits plateau or taper off, and for others, there's even a dose in which any additional ingestion of vitamins becomes harmful.

Thus, we could speak of environmental features which produce a "constant effect" (CE) on job satisfaction, such as availability of money, physical security, valued social position, supportive supervision, career outlook, and equity; and others which, past a certain level, are more likely to produce an "additional decrement" (AD) or even become "toxic," such as opportunity for personal control, opportunity for skill use, externally generated goals, variety, environmental clarity, and contact with others. Indeed, there may be an amount of money, for example, the marginal utility of which to job satisfaction already equals zero. Similarly, it could occur that too much variety in the tasks involved in a job, for instance, make the job unbearable. As can be gleaned from the above, CE features indicate characteristics extrinsic to work, and AD features, intrinsic ones.

Hence, in analyzing job satisfaction, it is useful to distinguish between two related aspects: a job's extrinsic features, which result in extrinsic motivations in the worker, and its intrinsic features, which give rise to intrinsic motivations (Frey and Stutzer 2002). The extrinsic features form the background conditions of work, such as pay and fringe benefits, the ambient conditions in which it is carried out, job security, social status, and so forth. These are the external rewards ("carrots") and threats or punishments ("sticks") used by managers to achieve worker compliance. The improper use of these "carrots and sticks" leads to all sorts of unsavory results. Besides being addictive, they can dampen motivation, lower performance, suffocate creativity, discourage good behavior, promote cheating, and foster short-term thinking (Pink 2009). In the origins of the US banking crisis in 2007, for example, mortgage brokers were paid for the number of the loans they sold, regardless of the likelihood that such loans were ever going to be repaid.

The intrinsic features, on the other hand, refer to the actual performance of the work itself. They become a source of motivation insofar as they provide workers with a chance to exercise personal control and to utilize and develop their knowledge and skills in a variety of tasks. Intrinsic motivations are enhanced when workers are subject to supportive, rather than controlling forms of supervision, and when the job offers opportunities for meaningful personal relationships. Instead of mere compliance, intrinsic motivations require initiative, engagement, and commitment.

Daniel Pink (2009) summarizes these intrinsic motivations under the headings of autonomy, mastery, and purpose. Autonomy or self-direction means the ability to decide which tasks are to be completed, when, how, and with whom. For instance, since the 1950s, 3M employees have spent 15 percent of their time on whatever projects they wish, serendipitously developing blockbuster products such as "post-its." More recently, by allowing engineers to work on any project they choose for about a day a week, Google has been able to come up with products such as "G-mail" and "Google News." Similarly, successful educational institutions such as Montessori schools fundamentally let kids follow their natural curiosity in self-directed activities, rather than spoon feeding them with pre-packaged information.

Mastery implies the desire to improve performance simply because one likes to; because one revels and takes pride in excellent work. Even progress along the path to mastery is in itself already rewarding, not only actually reaching the destination (Amabile and Kramer 2011). The urge for mastery is what leads people to invest valuable free time in playing musical instruments or engaging in hobbies, for example. This same principle prods millions of people to contribute high-quality work to open-source software projects, such as Linux, Apache, and Wikipedia, while deriving enjoyment and satisfaction.

And purpose indicates the will to contribute – through work – to make the world a better place, to be at the service of something bigger than oneself, to be part of a transcendent whole. In fact, it has been shown that by introducing context and purpose to tasks, people perform better, despite the absence of monetary rewards (Grant 2008, 2013). Perhaps that's because it becomes easier for them to find meaning in their work, as is the case – for instance – of the employees of Mozilla, the creator of the open-source web browser Firefox. The company's declared mission is to promote choice and innovation on the internet. These types could be better described as "purpose-maximizers" than "profit-maximizers."

For rudimentary mechanical and algorithmic functions, extrinsic motivations may be enough to get the job done, and the more external rewards offered, in principle, the better the performance. This worked quite well with industrial economy jobs. For instance, changing from hourly wages to piece-rate pay in a huge manufacturing company was shown to increase productivity by 44 percent (Lazear 2000). But as soon as the slightest cognitive or creative skills are involved, as is characteristic of the more valuable twenty-first-century jobs, not only do extrinsic motivations prove insufficient, but they also turn out to be counterproductive. That is, the greater the external rewards, the less of the desired result is achieved, given certain circumstances. Such was the conclusion in a series of experiments involving motor (typing letters) and cognitive (concentration, problem-solving, creativity) skills and performance-contingent incentives replicated in rural India and at MIT (Ariely et al. 2005). Contrary to what was expected, those who received the highest level of financial incentives performed worst of all.

Why does this happen? In first place, it's important to acknowledge both types of motivations, as well as their usefulness for particular kinds of work and particular workers. Certainly, people do not work for external motivations such as money alone, but also pay attention to other factors, such as intrinsic motivations. To some extent, this position goes against the one espoused by Kohn (1999), although originally formulated in an educational setting, rather than the workplace. According to Kohn (1999), giving students external rewards such as gold stars or praise for learning invariably hurts them in the end. For him, such external motivations are no better than bribes. Although this may be true most of the time for students in school, it is not the same for people at the workplace. In general, external motivations are necessary in order to get a job done, but they are not the only ones, nor are they the most important for peak performance.

This line of thinking revisits what Maslow (1954) and Herzberg (1966) had already affirmed before. Maslow (1954) spoke of a hierarchy of needs, where lower-order needs concerning physiology and safety ought to be satisfied first, before proceeding to attend to higher-order needs, such as love and belonging, esteem, and self-actualization. Herzberg (1966), in turn, proposed a dual theory consisting of "hygienic" factors and motivators. "Hygienic factors," such as a reasonable salary and job security, affect performance only by decreasing motivation, when deficient. In other words, their lack causes poor performance. It is the other set of "motivational factors," such as achievement, recognition, responsibility, advancement, and the work itself, that spur performance on. These are what we have referred to so far as intrinsic motivations.

In more contemporary language, Pink (2009) interprets these "hygienic factors" in terms of conditions of fairness. Provide workers with a sufficient level of external incentives and motivations; pay them well enough, in accordance with the market and the demands of a decent lifestyle, so that they don't feel cheated. In fact, as we learn from third-party dictator games, most people are willing to give up their own gains and rewards, if only to punish someone perceived to be unfair or uncooperative (Fehr and Fischbacher 2004). Only when they feel secure about these matters can they concentrate and focus on doing the job well, which is what they would really like to do. Besides, for some people, it may not even be the money itself, in terms of what it can buy, that is important. Rather, money or pay is just a signal, a way of keeping score, of how much one is valued relative to others. It points to something deeper, then, such as a legitimate pride and self-satisfaction with the results of one's efforts and contributions.

But this shouldn't lead us to think that by simply raising external, monetary incentives, we get superior performance, especially if the job requires something more than elementary motor skills. People dislike being bribed; they resent being manipulated like rats in a cage, being promised more money if they improve their performance. This goes against their sense of self-worth and professionalism. Moreover, increasing pay contingent upon performance could sometimes induce only greater stress, anxiety, and fear. This phenomenon is often described as "choking under pressure" (Baumeister 1984) and has been documented in several instances. Elevated monetary stakes have been found to be detrimental to performance in both highly practical, automatic tasks and those which require a great amount of insight and creativity. This is because, in the first case, money makes one more self-conscious or self-aware, while the job is best done by going with the force of habit; and in the second case, because economic rewards narrow one's focus of attention, when a more comprehensive view of the situation is needed in order to solve the problems at hand. That's why more pay does not always guarantee that professional athletes will perform better. These empirical results tend to confirm in humans what was posited by the "Yerkes–Dodson law" (1908), according to which there is an optimal level of arousal for executing tasks, and any deviation from it results in poorer performance (Neiss 1988). Huge amounts of money create a motivation that goes beyond this threshold of optimal arousal, consequently impairing performance.

Another occasion on which increased incentives, especially of the monetary kind, do not result in enhanced performance is when the task involved depends more on an innate ability or natural gift, than on effort and strategy. No amount of prizes will ever make someone who is tone-deaf win a singing contest, for instance. So much for the effects of extrinsic and intrinsic motivations on job performance.

But how do extrinsic and intrinsic motivations impact job satisfaction or happiness at work? Initially, one may think that they are accumulative: that is, intrinsic motivations build on extrinsic ones, or the other way around; in any case, they all add up to one's work satisfaction. However, a growing body of research indicates that this is not entirely correct. In several circumstances, extrinsic motivations are inimical to intrinsic motivations; they "crowd them out" (Frey and Jegen 2001). Faced with a dearth of blood donors, it has been found that paying for blood reduces and could even totally eliminate the willingness to donate, apart from resulting in blood of poorer quality (Titmuss 1970). This is because such an act is borne more from a sense of altruism, something which is seriously undermined by the introduction of payments. Likewise, it has been discovered that students soliciting donations door to door actually visited fewer houses and collected smaller sums when paid a small commission, than when they did it for free (Gneezy and Rustichini 2000a). Also, establishing a fine for collecting children late from daycare precisely promotes such kind of behavior in parents, even doubling its incidence, compared to when one simply appeals to their sense of responsibility (Gneezy and Rustichini 2000b). The fine ended up being perceived by the parents in Haifa as a price for the extra service of waiting, and as a price, it seemed to them just fine. In such cases, when external motivations in the form of money are introduced, they squelch the worker's intrinsic motivations, and in consequence, his job satisfaction. A job's intrinsic features as origins of intrinsic motivations satisfy an individual's deeper needs and longings more effectively; they contribute a greater share to subjective wellbeing at work than extrinsic motivations.

Having outlined the effects of extrinsic and intrinsic motivations on job performance and job satisfaction, respectively, we may now ask how the two are related, if at all. Studies reveal that work performance is positively correlated with work satisfaction, with causation probably moving in both directions (Frey and Stutzer 2002). But higher work satisfaction by itself does not necessarily translate into greater profits for the firm, at least directly. It could very well happen that, because of high-level performance, workers experience superior job satisfaction. Yet greater satisfaction with a job does not entail that the job be particularly useful or profitable for the company. It could be an auxiliary or a marginal job, such as one that results in sparkling clean toilets or fantastic cafeteria food, for example (if cleaners and kitchen staff were intrinsically motivated). Also, people who enjoy themselves at work do not necessarily perform the more difficult jobs which, nevertheless, are still required.

More interesting would be to trace the connection between job satisfaction and job performance via the so-called organization citizenship behaviors (OCBs) (Organ 1988). OCBs refer to discretionary tasks not included in job descriptions or evaluations, but which workers nonetheless carry out gratuitously. Although legally non-enforceable, thanks to these behaviors, production in the firm goes on smoothly and it becomes easier for workers to flourish. They may not be particularly relevant to the organization's core competences or functions. Think of holding the door while waiting for a colleague carrying a pile of office materials to pass through, for example. Doing this does not make sense according to strict economic rationality; but in real life, it would be difficult to collaborate with someone who does not bother to perform this small act of service. Besides acts of altruism, other OCBs involve sportsmanship (taking small irritants or difficulties in one's stride), courtesy or respectfulness, conscientiousness ("going the extra mile") and civic virtue (engagement in philanthropic activities).

We are told that people with high levels of job satisfaction are more inclined to display OCBs, demonstrating pro-social attitudes and engaging in extra-role conduct (Frey and Stutzer 2002). Perhaps this just goes to show that *homo sapiens* cannot be reduced to the abstraction of *homo economicus*, and that even in firms or businesses, it is the former, not the latter, that truly counts. In other words, human beings are never really purely self-seeking individuals; rather, they have an unrenounceable relational or social dimension because of which they also care for the good of the group.

Probably the strongest proof in support of the greater importance of intrinsic motivations over extrinsic motivations in work-related happiness is the existence and expansion of the third sector economy, associated with volunteering, foundations, philanthropic or charity organizations, not-for-profits, and non-governmental organizations (NGOs). The growing number of people doing serious, high-quality work for free in these organizations is the counterfactual impossible to dismiss, against the dictum that people work, above all, for money. Instead, we have to admit that voluntary, charity work in itself is a source of intense satisfaction and fulfillment for many people (Frey and Stutzer 2002).

HAPPINESS AND LEISURE

That happiness and work do actually mix quite well may give us second thoughts about the link between happiness and leisure. After all, leisure is commonly understood as what work is not, precisely.

So the finding that leisure and free time are positively correlated with happiness should lead us to reconsider the true nature of leisure (Frey and Stutzer 2002). Firstly, leisure does not consist in simply being idle. Unless one were sick or extremely tired, that would be boring. So leisure is, indeed, compatible with carrying out some form of activity, physical or mental. What sets leisure apart from work could, in fact, be one of two things: either the activity in question is unpaid or it is unproductive. (In principle, we exclude being paid for performing unproductive activities, but you never know.) If unpaid, then it is just a matter of applying what has already been said above, about volunteering and other forms of non-remunerated or non-income-generating jobs. If unproductive, then it begs the question of what those activities might be – sports, watching television, listening to music, holiday tours, play, practicing musical instruments, hobbies, art, and so forth – and why we find them enjoyable.

Leisure, therefore, is what generally qualifies as unpaid and unproductive activity which, nevertheless, we find enjoyable and satisfying: that is, contributive to wellbeing and happiness. Besides being unpaid and unproductive, we could venture a host of positive characteristics of leisure as well. Many of them have already been dealt with previously: among others, regular aerobic and endurance-building exercise, the consumption of high culture and fine art, engaging activities that generate "flow," and meaningful actions that manifest autonomy, mastery, and sense of purpose. In other words, although people apparently avoid activity and challenges, there's nothing farther from the truth (Frey and Stutzer 2002). We all like challenges, we love to learn and improve, we wish to perform and show off, even if we only have ourselves as audiences. What we don't like is to be overstretched, to be forced beyond our capabilities, to experience failure. That's why watching too much television can make one feel even more depressed and it also explains why team sports are, on the whole, more fun than individual ones.

In the end, just like in work, what seems to matter in leisure is the strength of intrinsic motivations. Neither money earned nor results produced count for much, as long as one is fully engaged and functioning in a freely chosen activity. Leisure, because we pursue it for itself, makes us happy. It conforms to the model of an "autotelic" activity.

Given the astonishing rate at which both incomes and productivity have risen, it is indeed paradoxical that people spend even less time now on leisure than before. Toward the middle of the past century, Keynes (1963) predicted that by 2030, the majority of people would have to work only 15 hours a week to cover their needs. It was expected, therefore, that they would be dedicating more time to leisure. But of course, we know that none of that has actually happened. On the contrary, there has been a growing trend for people to go beyond 40 to 60 and even 80 hours a week, just to earn more (Schor 1991; Peiperl and Jones 2001; Crouter et al. 2001). In short, people seem to have fallen into the trap of "overearning," deliberately forgoing leisure to work and earn well beyond their necessities (Hsee et al. 2013).

In experimental contexts, researchers have found that both high and low earners succumb to this tendency of "mindless accumulation," working until they have grown tired, rather than stopping when they have had enough. Apart from needlessly enduring the pain of extra work and passing on the pleasure of leisure themselves, overearners can also diminish the happiness of people around them. They spend less time with family and exert great pressure on peers to follow their example. Herein lies the perversity of the practice of "face-time" at work in many Asian cultures. Even from the purely economic perspective, overearning is wasteful, inasmuch as it consumes resources that could otherwise be conserved or used for other purposes. Still within controlled conditions, however, it has been discovered that setting an "earning cap" and providing enjoyable and meaningful leisure activities besides idleness can help curb overearning, and positively contribute to the happiness of workers and their immediate circle.

HAPPINESS AND INFLATION: HAVING MORE MONEY, YET FEELING WORSE

In earlier chapters we have seen the non-linear relationship between income and happiness. There's a certain point beyond which additional income no longer increases individual subjective wellbeing. What we haven't imagined is a situation in which, despite having more money, one actually feels more miserable. This happens in the case of high currency inflation. How so?

Economists often distinguish two kinds of inflation: the anticipated one, for which people can prepare and adjust accordingly, and the unanticipated one, which usually comes as a shock (Frey and Stutzer 2002; Frey 2008). While a low and predictable inflation rate, say, between 1 and 5 percent a year, is normally considered manageable, an upward spiraling inflation rate is perceived as a major threat to economic wellbeing and sociopolitical stability. Although the nominal value of income increases – that is, people actually have more money – its purchasing power falls rapidly. The rise in income is not able to keep up with that of prices and the cost of living. People, as a result, feel poorer, despite the system being awash with money (or rather, perhaps because of it). The reason for this phenomenon comes under several, already familiar names, such as "loss aversion" and the "endowment effect." This means that, as a rule, people are more sensitive to losses (of purchasing power, in this case) than to illusory gains (in nominal income).

The negative effects of runaway inflation causing a drop in happiness (Di Tella, MacCulloch, and Oswald 2001) are varied. The first are tremendous price hikes. In countries suffering from hyperinflation, supermarkets hire personnel to add zeroes to the price tags of goods on the shelves, even several times a day. This creates a lot of economic insecurity, as both buyers and producers never really know how much their goods and incomes are worth, in the face of rapid currency depreciation. As a result, people spend as soon as they earn, for money has ceased to be a reliable store of value, investments are put off, and prime necessities become scarce in the market, all of which further feed the inflation monster. Social chaos and violence then ensue, with shops and banks being ransacked. National pride, reflected in the value and stability of the currency, also suffers a huge loss. In this aspect, however, not all countries and cultures react in the same way. Germany and Great Britain, for instance, have historically displayed greater aversion to high inflation rates than France and Argentina.

In mainstream neoclassical economic thinking, unemployment and inflation form a binary system from which to choose a remedy, when macroeconomic sailing gets rough. It's like picking your poison, knowing you just have to bite the bullet. That may still be the case from a purely economic perspective. One may just have to bear with high inflation, if one wishes to combat unemployment. Or tolerate high unemployment rates, if one wants to tame a galloping inflation. You cannot have it both ways. From the viewpoint of modern happiness studies, however, this is no longer an accurate account of the situation. Inflation rates and unemployment rates do not affect people's sense of wellbeing equally. In fact, it has been calculated that a percentage point increase in the unemployment rate could be compensated only by a much higher 1.7 percentage point decrease in the inflation rate (Frey and Stutzer 2002; Frey 2008). That is, people suffer significantly more from a rise in unemployment than from a proportional decrease in inflation. This may certainly have to do with how work, or its lack, affects human beings intimately at their core, in a manner quite different from the way in which currency depreciation does.

* * *

Crucial to understanding the impact of work on happiness is determining whether such work or employment is voluntary or not. We have examined the two rival schools of thought and their respective implications for the proper role of government (intervention or *laissez-faire*) and policy of choice (stimulus or austerity) regarding employment, within the context of the crisis affecting the developed world toward the end of the first decade of the new millennium.

We moved on to consider the unhappiness of the unemployed compared to those who have work, a finding consistent in both cross-section as well as longitudinal studies, while controlling for income and education, and regardless of employment category. There are considerable individual and social costs attached to unemployment which vary according to demographics. We have also seen how work is closely associated nowadays with the notion of human dignity.

Although the employed are much happier than those without jobs, we cannot ignore the fact that work also entails its own stressors, some job-specific, others, organization-specific. In analyzing the domain of work (in contrast to overall happiness or life satisfaction), we could distinguish certain job features which either contribute to or detract from individual satisfaction. These job features, in turn, could be objective and environmental or subjective and personal. The relation between them, insofar as it impacts job satisfaction, is best explained through the vitamin analogy.

Apart from job features, satisfaction at work could likewise be understood as a function of the motivations present. In this respect, we differentiate between extrinsic motivations and intrinsic motivations (autonomy, mastery, purpose). Each kind of motivation has a distinctive effect on performance and satisfaction, depending on the type of job involved. We have also discovered a peculiar "crowding out" relation, instead of an accumulative one, between extrinsic and intrinsic motivations.

The happiness of the employed does not rule out that happiness could also be found in leisure. Such a statement begs the question of what leisure truly consists in. Rather than simple idleness, it seems that leisure indicates a kind of activity which, although unpaid or unproductive, nevertheless allows for intrinsic motivations to develop and to flourish.

Lastly, we have discussed how inflation relates not only to unemployment, but to happiness as well. Much depends on the kind of inflation that takes place. There are a host of disutilities that can be expected from a spiraling inflation rate which consequently diminish happiness. Behavioral economics accounts for the drop in happiness associated with inflation in a manner different from that of mainstream neoclassical economics.

REFERENCES

Alesina, A. and Ardagna, S. 2009. "Large changes in fiscal policy: Taxes versus spending" (http://scholar.harvard.edu/files/alesina/files/largechangesinfiscalpolicy_october_2009.pdf, accessed December 26, 2013).

Amabile, T. and Kramer, S. 2011. *The progress principle. Using small wins to ignite joy, engagement, and creativity at work*. Boston: Harvard Business Review Press.

Ariely, D., Gneezy, U., Loewenstein, G. and Mazar, N. 2005. "Large stakes and big mistakes," *Federal Reserve Bank of Boston Working Papers*, no. 05–11.

Baumeister, R. F. 1984. "Choking under pressure: Self-consciousness and paradoxical effects of incentives on skillful performance," *Journal of Personality and Social Psychology*, 46: 610–620.

Brereton, F., Clinch, J. P. and Ferreira, S. 2008. "Employment and life-satisfaction: Insights from Ireland," *Economic and Social Review*, 39 (3): 207–234.

Brynjolfsson, E. and McAfee, A. 2014. *The second machine age: Work, progress, and prosperity in a time of brilliant technologies*. New York: W. W. Norton.

Cecchetti, S., Mohanty, M. and Zampolli, F. 2011. "The real effects of debt," *BIS Working Papers*, no. 352, September.

Clark, A. and Oswald, A. 1994. "Unhappiness and unemployment," *Economic Journal*, 104 (424): 648–659.

Coontz, S. 2014. "How can we help men? By helping women," *New York Times*, January 11.

Crawford, M. B. 2009. *Shop class as soulcraft: An inquiry into the value of work*. New York: Penguin.

Crouter, A., Bumpus, M., Head, M. and McHale, S. 2001. "Implications of overwork and overload for the quality of men's family relationships," *Journal of Marriage and Family*, 63: 404–416.

Diputación de Granada 2013. *Programa de Fomento de Empleo Agrario* (http://pfea.dipgra.es/pfea, accessed January 7, 2014).

Di Tella, R., MacCulloch, R. and Oswald, A. 2001. "Preferences over inflation and unemployment: Evidence from surveys of happiness," *American Economic Review*, 91 (1): 335–341.

Fehr, E. and Fischbacher, U. 2004. "Third-party punishment and social norms," *Evolution and Human Behavior*, 25: 63–87.

Frey, B. 2008. *Happiness: A revolution in economics*. Cambridge, MA/London: The MIT Press.

Frey, B. and Jegen, R. 2001. "Motivation crowding theory," *Journal of Economic Surveys*, 15: 589–611.

Frey, B. and Stutzer, A. 2002. *Happiness and economics. How the economy and institutions affect well-being*. Princeton, NJ/Oxford: Princeton University Press.

Frey, C. B. and Osborne, M. 2013. *The future of employment: How susceptible are jobs to computerisation?* (oxfordmartin.ox.ac.uk/publications/view/1314, accessed March 18, 2014).

Gavin, J. H. and Mason, R. O. 2004. "The virtuous organization: The value of happiness in the workplace," *Organizational Dynamics*, 33 (4): 379–392.

Gneezy, U. and Rustichini, A. 2000a. "Pay enough or don't pay at all," *Quarterly Journal of Economics*, 115: 791–810.

2000b. "A fine is a price," *Journal of Legal Studies*, 29: 1–18.

Graeber, D. 2013. "On the phenomenon of bullshit jobs," *Strike! Magazine*, August 17.

Grant, A. 2008. "Does intrinsic motivation fuel the prosocial fire? Motivational synergy in predicting persistence, performance, and productivity," *Journal of Applied Psychology*, 93 (1): 48–58.

2013. *Give and take: A revolutionary approach to success*. New York: Viking.

Greenhouse, S. 2014. "The gray jobs enigma," *New York Times*, March 12.

Herndon, T., Ash, M. and Pollin, R. 2013. "Does high public debt consistently stifle economic growth? A critique of Reinhart and Rogoff," *PERI Working Papers*, no. 322, April.

Herzberg, F. 1966. *Work and the nature of man*. Cleveland, OH: World Publishing.

Hsee, C. K., Zhang, J., Cai, C. F. and Zhang, S. 2013. "Overearning," *Psychological Science*, 24: 852–859.

Hutcheson, J. V. H. 2007. "All work and no play," *Mercatornet*, May 30 (www.mercatornet.com/articles/view/all_work_and_no_play, accessed January 10, 2013).

Kenny, A. and Kenny, C. 2006. *Life, liberty and the pursuit of utility*. Exeter: Imprint Academic.

Keynes, J. M. 1963. "Economic possibilities for our grandchildren," in Keynes, J. M. (ed.), *Essays in persuasion*. New York: W. W. Norton, pp. 358–373.

Kohn, A. 1999. *Punished by rewards*. Boston, MA: Houghton Mifflin.

Krugman, P. 2013a. "The Excel depression," *New York Times*, April 18.

2013b. "Sympathy for the Luddites," *New York Times*, June 13.

2014. "The inflation obsession," *New York Times*, March 2.

Kumar, M. and Woo, J. 2010. "Public debt and growth," *IMF Working Papers*, July.

Lazear, E. P. 2000. "Performance pay and productivity," *American Economic Review*, 90: 1346–1361.

Marks, G. and Fleming, N. 1999. "Influences and consequences of well-being among Australian young people: 1980–1995," *Social Indicators Research*, 46 (3): 301–323.

Maslow, A. 1954. *Motivation and personality*. New York: Harper.

National Portal Content Management Team 2011. "National Rural Employment Guarantee Act" (www.archive.india.gov.in/sectors/rural/index.php?id=12, accessed December 25, 2013).

Neiss, R. 1988. "Reconceptualizing arousal: Psychological states in motor performance," *Psychological Bulletin*, 103: 345–366.

Organ, D. W. 1988. *Organizational citizenship behavior: The good soldier syndrome*. Lexington, MA: Lexington Books.

Peck, D. 2010. "How a new jobless era will transform America," *The Atlantic*, March 1.

Peiperl, M. and Jones, B. 2001. "Workaholics and overworkers: Productivity or pathology?" *Group and Organization Management*, 26: 369–393.

Pink, D. 2009: *Drive: The surprising truth about what motivates us*. New York: Penguin.

Reinhart, C. and Rogoff, K. 2010. "Growth in a time of debt," *NBER Working Paper Series*, no. 15639.

2013. "Debt, growth and the austerity debate," *New York Times*, April 25.

Rose, M. 2003. "Good deal, bad deal? Job satisfaction in occupations," *Work, Employment and Society*, 17: 503–530.

Ross, C. E., Mirowski, J. and Huber, J. 1983. "Dividing work, sharing work, and in-between: Marriage patterns and depression," *American Sociological Review*, 48: 809–823.

Schor, J. 1991. *The overworked American: The unexpected decline of leisure*. New York: Basic Books.

Titmuss, R. M. 1970. *The gift relationship*. London: Allen and Unwin.

Uchitelle, L. 2007. "The end of the line as Detroit workers know it," *New York Times*, April 1.

Warr, P. 2007. *Work, happiness and unhappiness*. Hillsdale, NJ/ London: Lawrence Erlbaum Associates.

Weaver, C. N. 1980. "Job satisfaction in the United States in the 1970s," *Journal of Applied Psychology*, 65: 364–367.

Winkelmann, L. and Winkelmann, R. 1998. "Why are the unemployed so unhappy? Evidence from panel data," *Economica*, 65 (257): 1–15.

Yerkes, R. M. and Dodson, J. D. 1908. "The relationship of strength of stimulus to rapidity of habit-formation," *Journal of Comparative Neurology of Psychology*, 18: 459–482.

6   Happiness, politics, and religion

Now and at the hour of our death

THE ROLE OF INSTITUTIONS

Our investigation on happiness has thus far revealed that it is pre-eminently a subjective value, in the sense that it represents, perhaps, an individual's most prized aspiration or possession in life. We have examined the different ways in which happiness depends on a person's self-awareness, income, consumption decisions, neurological functionings, work, and perceived wealth, among other things. All these factors have in common that they are private or exclusionary. They refer to things, characteristics, or events that are, strictly speaking, one's own and therefore cannot be shared. Of course, one is free to give away one's money or to solicit someone else's collaboration to complete a task. But in the first case, it's no longer for one to decide how that money is spent, and in the second, whatever the other person does, logically, one ceases to do. In other words, it seems as if happiness were some form of "private property" from which others are excluded. But is that really the case?

On the one hand, we have also learned how happiness is never truly achieved in isolation and that it depends essentially on others. Just to stress the fact of how harmful isolation can be, we are told that most prisoners in solitary confinement develop severe physical and mental disorders, ranging from dizziness and headaches through digestive problems and paranoia to self-mutilation and suicide (Grassian 1983). Beyond a certain level, it's not so much absolute income but relative income that matters. Our choices and desires, pleasures and satisfactions, even hormonal levels – not to mention workplace contentment and subjective purchasing power – are all influenced by other people, by what they have and what they do. It has even been claimed that happiness, like an emotional contagion, spreads through up to three degrees in social networks, with effects lasting up to a year (Fowler and Christakis 2008). We understand this, given the inescapable relational or social dimension constitutive of human beings. Thus, while there's no question that happiness is definitely one's own, it may nevertheless occur that it can be shared; that other people can participate in one's happiness. It could even be the case that other people are, in fact, necessary for one to attain happiness. This sharing dynamic in happiness is made possible through what are commonly called "institutions." For moral progress to take place, we do not merely depend on good intentions and force of will, but we establish laws that constrain our choices and create social institutions (Bloom 2014).

One approach to institutions is to trace their origins to the interaction between subjective and objective worlds, between the individual and the environment, broadly understood (Ng 2002). Hence, we could think of the joys and pleasures that we feel as arising, in some way, from the purchasing and consumption decisions we undertake within a particular market society. Institutions condition, regulate, and may even determine both worlds, insofar as they establish how society is organized. Oftentimes, institutions are construed too narrowly, as referring only to generally accepted rules or procedures. However, a more careful reckoning indicates that it is virtually impossible not to consider idiosyncratic values, customs, and traditions at the same time. They constitute the necessary material element, without which formal rules and procedures would be vacuous or empty. Take for granted the widespread belief in most societies that the rich are happier than the poor. As a social norm it would undoubtedly affect, not only the evaluations regarding happiness or life satisfaction coming from third party observers, but also self-reports. With these formal and material aspects taken together, institutions can account for many of the differences in happiness across societies.

In the succeeding pages, we shall consider two types of institutions, a political and a religious one. In particular, we will examine how democracy, first, and religious belief and practice, afterwards, mediate in the happiness of individuals. Within democracies, constitutions often represent the "basic law of the land," containing the fundamental values, rules, and procedures that are meant to guide collective decision making. Constitutions define the roles that politics, markets, bureaucracy, and civil society actors play, the rights and responsibilities belonging to citizens, and the competencies of the different levels and branches of government, among others. Religious institutions, on the other hand, normally concern belief systems, codes of conduct, and highly symbolic ritual practices that create deep bonds among their members and with a higher, supernatural force usually referred to as "God."

THE DEMOGRAPHICS OF HAPPINESS

Democracies define a specific kind of state regime and states are constituted ultimately by people or citizens. Hence, in analyzing the impact of institutions such as democratic states on the happiness of individuals, it may be worthwhile to have a look first at the demographics of happiness.

To the best of our knowledge, there are hardly any definitive, uncontested findings in this regard. This is not at all surprising, bearing in mind that demographic indicators are a grab bag of characteristics such as age, sex, ethnicity, civil status, nationality, and so forth. Furthermore, it is also very difficult to disentangle the influence of other factors like psychological traits and prevailing socioeconomic conditions. Nonetheless, this has not stopped researchers from putting forward the results of their studies. Blanchflower and Oswald (2011), for instance, make the following claims regarding the happiness of Americans, based on statistical analyses of data from the US General Social Survey between 1972 and 2008. First, throughout a person's life span, happiness is U-shaped, such that the young and the old are happier than the middle aged. Secondly, women are happier than men. Thirdly, whites, the highly educated, full-time workers, the married, and those earning high incomes report high levels of happiness. Fourthly, the unemployed, those who work at home, the widowed, divorced, and separated, as well as those whose parents divorced before they were 16 years old, report low levels of happiness.

At least as interesting as the claims in themselves are the reasons or causes behind them. Although we cannot look into all the correlations between demographic markers and happiness, however, we could examine some especially significant ones, such age, sex, and civil status. Let us begin with age. According to Blanchflower and Oswald (2011), Americans reach the nadir of happiness, on average, at the age of 40. This corresponds to what is often called the "midlife crisis" (Myers 2002). In the case of males, this is around the time when they realize that they will never fulfill their ambition of becoming company president, for example, that their marriage has long lost its flame or passion, and that their bodies are beginning to show unequivocal signs of wear (silver streaks or loss of hair, a bulging middle, increasingly flaccid muscles, and so forth). They usually react by searching for new life meanings and engaging in a variety of ego-propping activities. In the case of women, it is somehow linked to the onset of menopause. Despite the fact that, in Western countries, the average menopause age is around 50 years, to undergo an early transition, say between 40 and 45 years old, is still fairly normal. The physical consequences of menopause notwithstanding, much of its emotional impact depends on the particular woman's attitude, whether she centers on the liberation from monthly periods and pregnancies, or on the loss of attractiveness or even "femininity." All told, perhaps it is not even age itself, but certain significant life events that occur more or less at that time – child leaving, relocation, occupational shifts, divorce, illness, widowhood, and so forth – that could somehow explain the drop in happiness.

Before reaching midlife, people are on the whole happier, not only because of generally better health, but also because of a widespread and strongly entrenched "youth cult," to which the media unabashedly panders (Frey and Stutzer 2002). At the same time, there's no denying the difficulties and challenges that adolescents and young

adults face, in the form of mood swings, a sense of insecurity, subjec-
tion to parental power, peer pressure, and anxieties about the future,
especially in what refers to work and family. Among those past midlife
and the elderly, despite generally poorer health, lower incomes, and
a greater likelihood of being a widow or widower, superior happiness
levels are again reported. A combination of circumstances may contribute to this (Frey and Stutzer 2002). Due to experience, seniors
tend to have lower expectations and aspirations in life, and consequently, smaller gaps between goals and achievements. Overall, less
frustration ensues, as both demands and stress decline. Further, they
have had sufficient time to adjust to their conditions and limitations,
attaining greater self-acceptance, serenity, or resignation. As for the
unavoidable negative affects or emotions, they have had more chances
to learn to reduce and regulate them. Age seems to smooth out the
abrupt peaks and troughs of emotions; feelings begin to mellow. In
summary, older people are more likely to display personal wisdom
(Clayton 1982). They may take more time in retrieving information,
but that's because they have more and its quality is more nuanced. A
reduction in self-centeredness allows them to be more reflective and
compassionate, and better prepared to face their own physical decline
and eventually, their own death.

Yet there are those who affirm that overall wellbeing or
happiness remains stable throughout one's lifetime; or that different
age groups feel differently regarding specific domains (Myers 2002).
Following the principle that our priorities heavily condition our
wellbeing, it may happen that younger people are happier at work,
while older people value leisure and social activities more. Scientists
usually reach their career peak in their late thirties – those in
abstract, theoretical fields such as physics, a few years before those
in context-sensitive, experimental ones, such as medicine – while for
those in the humanities, age doesn't seem to matter for the quality
of their output (Jones, Reedy, and Weinberg 2014). Younger people
are more concerned about their attractiveness, something to which
older people hardly pay any attention. Older people feel more worried

about loneliness, while younger people simply don't mind spending time alone. While younger people tend to associate happiness with excitement, older people are more likely to do so with peacefulness (Mogliner, Kamvar, and Aaker 2011). Likewise, age-related differences in happiness could be accounted for, purportedly, by traits particular to a given generation. For instance, in the United States, those born after 1980, known as the "generation Y" or "millennials," seem to be less bent toward materialism and financial success, and more toward meaning (purpose, value, and impact on others) and happiness, compared to their "baby boomer" parents (Smith and Aaker 2013). Growing up in the midst of a deep recession may have exerted a strong influence on this generational value shift.

Also, younger boomers tend to be more sensitive to health-related quality-of-life issues than older boomers (Span 2014). In a study among patients with congestive heart disease, it was found that the younger ones, those aged 62 and less, fared worst in the negative physical, psychological (anxiety and depression), and social impacts of their illness, while those over 70 reported an even better quality of life. Considering that older patients are prone to have more co-morbidities (other diseases), have worse functional capacities, and are hospitalized more often, one would not expect these results. It seems that people who, objectively, could do less, nevertheless thought that they lived better-quality lives, because they were able to re-frame their expectations and achievements better. Rather than comparing themselves to their former years, they would look to their peers, for instance. Knowing that things could be worse, they felt grateful just to be alive and do whatever they could. That's why the elderly often resist assistance and change (hearing aids, grab-bars, caregivers, and so forth), even in matters that others recognize as crucial to their safety and wellbeing. It's not necessarily intransigence or denial of reality, but a difference in perception among age cohorts. Despite having more chronic illnesses, the elderly are less mindful of the discomforts of flu and other short-term diseases (Myers 2002). They are less given to complaining.

How about sex? How does it figure in the happiness equation? All along, we've been seeing how sex modulates the repercussions of other components, such as age. But are there pure sex effects on happiness? Research shows that women display higher self-reported happiness than men, although at the same time, women exhibit more frequent and stronger mood swings between positive and negative emotions, resulting in higher incidences of mental disorder (Blanchflower and Oswald 2011; Frey and Stutzer 2002). All sorts of justifications have been offered, from a superior genetic capacity to express happiness, to lower aspiration levels or ambitions, to greater social skills (more cooperative, more empathy). Differences in upbringing have also been cited, as girls are usually allowed to be more emotional than boys.

Nevertheless, the gap between the sexes doesn't seem to be large and may be, in fact, diminishing, at least in the United States and other industrialized countries: women's happiness has declined, both absolutely and relative to men (Stevenson and Wolfers 2009). Important socioeconomic forces seem to be at work. First are the documented macrotrends of decreased social cohesion, increased anxiety and neuroticism, and increased household risk, to which women are more vulnerable. Second are the changing roles of women in society. "Satisfaction at home" becomes contaminated and eventually lowered by "satisfaction at work," in the same way that the correlation between overall happiness and marital happiness becomes lower for working women than for stay-at-home wives. Thirdly, it may just be the case that women have become more confident in being more honest about their true happiness, deflating their previous responses. More controversially, "the changes brought about through the women's movement may have decreased women's happiness" (Stevenson and Wolfers 2009: 28). Together with the increased opportunities for women come greater demands and requirements for happiness. They are subject to a mounting pressure to perform both at home and at work, and eventually, many succumb. As a result, women more and more feel that their life is falling short or not measuring up. Some even say that sex by itself hardly gives us a clue to a person's state of wellbeing, although the sexes may be unequal in social power, in wellbeing they are (Myers 2002).

Be that as it may, we shouldn't forget that human beings – both male and female – necessarily occupy several roles: parent, spouse, sibling, offspring, worker, amateur athlete, community leader, church member, hobbyist, and so forth (Myers 2002). Perhaps without going as far as to assume multiple identities, it would be safe to say that each of these roles may exert a greater impact, positive or negative, on happiness than one's sex. Of course, a person's sex modulates the way in which each of these roles is performed. But it is success in fulfilling the role, rather than one's sex, that matters more for happiness.

For its part, civil status has been found to have a strong correlation, comparable to that of employment status, on individual happiness: married Americans declared themselves happier than singles, and being separated displays a large, negative correlation (Blanchflower and Oswald 2011; Proulx, Helms, and Buehler 2007). In an earlier work, Waite and Gallagher (2000) rank the married as happiest, followed by the widowed, singles, and cohabitors at more or less the same level, then the divorced, and in last place, the separated. This may be due partly to the effects of family structures on income, since marriage and poverty run divergent paths: either marriage is a remedy for poverty or poverty is an obstacle to marriage (Chetty et al. 2014). Civil status also affects the happiness of the next of kin, as is shown in the lower levels reported by individuals who, at the age of 16, lived with only one parent due to divorce (Blanchflower and Oswald 2011). The psychological trauma of parental divorce somehow lingers through the years and decades after the event. What's more, children of divorced parents are more likely to divorce themselves, somehow repeating the cycle. Similarly, children raised in two-parent households tend to be wealthier, given the presence of two potential income earners, and they also fare better on a range of educational, social, and economic outcomes, such as a higher probability of going to college (Reeves 2014).

Nevertheless, some investigators detect the happiness gap between the married and the single to be diminishing; perhaps the important factor not being marriage in itself, but the close relationship (Frey and Stutzer 2002). Yet others (Waite and Gallagher 2000) present a different view, based on the reasoning that married couples, compared to cohabitors, are more likely to invest in each other's "human capital" due to the permanence and long-term nature of their relationship; therefore, they also reap increased returns. Moreover, there are greater opportunities for specialization and division of labor, with concomitant benefits of scale (Becker 1981). This ultimately redounds to the better health (Gardner and Oswald 2004), greater wealth (Chun and Lee 2001), more satisfying sex lives, and higher overall levels of happiness and life satisfaction among married couples (Waite and Gallagher 2000).

Certainly, marriage is not for everyone. For some people, such as those caught in abusive relationships, the experience of marriage may even be the closest they can get to hell. In a German panel study, life satisfaction seems to rise as the year of marriage approaches, then drops after the event, presumably, due to some form of adaptation (Frey 2008). But for a great number, and even the majority of people, marriage may serve to enhance happiness in at least two ways: first, marriage provides a safeguard against loneliness and an insurance against adverse life events, insofar as it implies an enduring, supportive, and intimate relationship; and second, marriage offers additional sources of self-esteem by giving access to potentially fulfilling roles as a spouse and parent (Myers 2002).

Of course, none of this is automatic, and nowadays, social mores in many societies are such that one could obtain many of the benefits of marriage without actually getting married. What's surprising, however, is the persistent advantage of married couples with regard to wellbeing and life satisfaction compared to their functional equivalents. Despite raised expectations in terms of economic security, romance, self-expression, and successful child-rearing, marriage always seems to deliver. We already know that the married are happier than the divorced; but making divorce more available and common hasn't made the divorced happier either (or their children, for that matter). Furthermore, there appears to be a correlation between the number of premarital sexual partners and marital unhappiness, and hence, also with the increased risk of marital rupture. Among teenagers, it's even worse, as promiscuity elevates risks not only of sexually transmitted diseases, unwanted pregnancies, and poverty, but also of sexual violence (especially among males) and, eventually, divorce. The reason for this may not only be a weaker commitment to the institution of marriage, but also a dearth of impulse control and patience, character traits that are beneficial to solid, long-lasting relationships. These precisely are characteristics which married couples may be said to possess in greater abundance.

Whether young or old, male or female, rich or poor, people involved in a stable, loving relationship such as marriage enjoy greater happiness and wellbeing (Myers 2002). Despite wider mood swings, such that emotional highs are higher and lows lower, women report higher happiness levels than their husbands. They also seem to enjoy close relationships more. Sometimes, romantic love – as is typical of marriage – has been described as going through different phases, reminiscent of addictions. It begins with a "big kick," an infatuation; but it needs repetition and nurturing in order to grow and develop. Otherwise, contrary emotions gain strength until love eventually peters out. If romance is taken for granted, it dies. But if romance is fed with sympathetic actions and gestures, one begins to require an increasingly higher dose, to prevent withdrawal symptoms from setting in. Not only is romantic love addictive, but among married people, fidelity, too, is epidemic. Therefore, among the psychological contributors to marital bliss, we find the attunement of kindred minds, heightened sexual warmth and social intimacy, and increased opportunities for equitable giving and receiving of emotional and material favors.

So far we have seen how marriage helps the spouses satisfy each other's deepest needs and longings. But what if the passion or romantic love begins to fail? That is when the complementary side of marriage, consisting in the fulfillment derived from catering to third parties, particularly the couple's children, begins to occupy center stage. It has even been said that joy from the nurture of children is an adaptive measure to the parents' waning passion and interest in each other (Myers 2002). This, of course, need not always be true, and the joys of parenting often sit side by side with those of being a couple. The main reason why being a parent boosts one's happiness is that it lends meaning to life in the long run (Brooks 2008). In the short run, everyone is familiar with the travails of raising children, so much so that minding the kids often turns up as the least pleasurable or enjoyable activity for parents.

We also have to be open to the possibility that it's not having children that makes married people happier, but that happy people are more likely to have children. When viewed from this direction, happiness here means optimism, the psychological trait described in the belief that if one works hard and plays by the rules, he is likely to succeed. Apparently, such optimism is likewise positively correlated to a person's political views, specifically, to those of conservatives in America, as well as to one's degree of religiousness (Brooks 2008). Liberals, again in the American sense of the term, purportedly seem to be too obsessed with inequality and the idea that everything goes wrong; they are more pessimistic, less likely to be religious, less likely to marry, and less likely to have kids. All of this seems to indicate lower happiness levels as well.

In the end, a recipe for a happy marriage and for staying married includes the following: tying the knot after the age of 20; having dated for a long time before marrying; being well educated; counting on a stable income from a good job; living in a small town or farm (cities, by breaking traditions and fracturing families, tend to breed psychiatric illnesses); not having cohabited or gotten pregnant before marriage; and sharing a religious commitment (Myers 2002). The importance of a homogamous relationship, of "like marrying like," for happiness cannot be understated (Stutzer and Frey 2006).

DEMOCRACY AND HAPPINESS

Having surveyed – albeit partly – the demographics of happiness, we shall now direct our attention to the link between democracy and happiness. To be sure, a democracy is not the only state regime possible; nor is it, by far, representative of all political institutions. In fact, there are numerous ways of establishing the connection between politics and happiness (Pacek 2009). For instance, besides the relationship with democracy, one could choose to study correlations with measures of social capital and civic engagement, the role of government, the impact of specific political actors, and the repercussions of concrete state policies, among others. However, it may be safe to say that, insofar as democracy is often touted as the "ideal" or "least bad" form of government, democracies have been, by and large, the preferred object of study, and therefore, the topic in which one can find the most data. Moreover, by selecting the relationship between democracy and happiness as a guide, it would be fairly easy to shed some light on other, similar political institutions and markers.

A straightforward definition of a democracy is that state regime governed in accordance with regularly held, free, and fair elections. "Regularly held" refers to the fact that elections are convened with the periodicity established in the country's constitution, rather than by the caprice or calculation of whoever may be in power through "snap elections," for instance. "Free" means multi-party, with all *bona fide* candidates departing from the same starting line in the race, so to speak. And "fair" indicates that voters are not subjected by candidates to any form of coercion and that results are respected and upheld. It also excludes boycotts, not because the process is trumped, but simply because one has a very slim chance of winning.

Such a "formal" or procedural definition of democracy would have been enough, were it not for the fact that, on occasions, "anti-democratic" factions may turn out victorious. Think of a fundamentalist Islamic or a fascist party winning the highest number of votes in an election, for instance. That is when the need for a "material" complement consisting of liberal values becomes evident. Historically, liberal regimes arose in contrast to autocratic or absolutist regimes, and in due course, they developed the notion of "rule of law." This means that no individual will is above the law, and conversely, that everyone is subject to the law as expression of the sovereign general will. Hence, equality before the law and freedom become enshrined as the foremost liberal values (Zakaria 2003). Therefore, for the purpose of determining its relation to happiness, our understanding of democracy includes both "formal" elements (regularly held, free, and fair elections) and "material" elements (liberal values such as rule of law, equality, and freedom). Without these liberal values, democracy easily degenerates into just another form of tyranny: the tyranny of the majority. Take the case of Pakistan, for example. Although a nominal democracy, within its borders religious minorities – not only Hindus and Christians, but also other non-dominant Muslim sects such as the Shiites and the Ahmadis – live in constant fear (Ahmed 2013).

The first question to deal with is whether people, in general, and citizens, in particular, are happier in democracies than in alternative regimes (Frey and Stutzer 2002). At the very least, in democracies it is possible to inquire about this, and it should be fairly easy to find out, in contrast to autocratic regimes, for instance. Apart from elections, in democracies one could freely conduct surveys and polls in order to gauge the level of satisfaction of the people, based on past experiences as well as future expectations. If the citizenry is content and happy with government, chances are that the individuals or the party in power would enjoy high levels of popularity and get re-elected, or at least, obtain a large share of votes. None of this would occur if people were dissatisfied.

However, there's no guarantee that a successful government, according to some measure, will always win the elections. Think of the British premier Winston Churchill, who, despite leading the country to win the Second World War, nevertheless lost the 1945 general election to the Labor Party. It may not necessarily be because citizens are ungrateful. Rather, most people tend to attribute good results, especially in the economy, not to their political leaders, but to themselves, to their individual efforts. Asymmetrically, dismal outcomes are almost always blamed on the people in government, in line with the "responsibility hypothesis" (Frey and Stutzer 2002). Moreover, oftentimes, it may not even be the actual results or outcomes, but mere perceptions, in whatever direction, that count; hence the importance of the government's media efforts and its spin doctors.

In democratic regimes, politicians have a strong, almost overriding incentive to be responsive to the citizens' needs and desires, whatever these may be ("reaction function") (Frey and Stutzer 2002). In consequence, their decisions and actions generally reflect the will – or "revealed preference" – of the people they serve. Yet several caveats are in order here. First, one does not know whether government truly seeks to maximize or optimize general welfare and wellbeing, or simply wants to create that impression for electoral purposes. Second, granted that government is sincere in doing what's best, nevertheless, the people may not want it. No one likes bitter medicine, although it may be good and necessary. For instance, in response to the economic crisis that began in 2008, the majority of European governments decided to implement austerity programs, which inevitably resulted in the shrinking of the welfare state and the cutting down on social services. From the viewpoint of economic orthodoxy, it was a logical move, given the bloated public debt. But it was also hugely unpopular. So governing parties were caught in a dilemma: whether to adopt a necessary, but unpopular policy of austerity, or to give in to the public's wishes of increased, albeit deficitary spending. Much depended on the confidence the parties in power had over their parliamentary majorities and the closeness of the next elections. Should the government, then, focus on the people's short-term desires or on their long-term and sustainable happiness?

As mentioned earlier, impressions – especially those in retrospect – count more than facts or realities for the people's level of satisfaction with politics (Frey and Stutzer 2002). This is particularly true with regard to macroeconomic conditions, such as unemployment and inflation rates, as we have already seen in the previous chapter. They weigh even more heavily than average income levels. High unemployment and inflation rates can certainly bring the government down or remove the ruling party from power. But an increase in per capita income by itself does not assure victory at the polls; nor is it statistically significant for satisfaction in the positive sense. On the other hand, increased social spending on health, the care of infants and the elderly, unemployment benefits, housing, and so forth unequivocally serves to boost satisfaction levels.

An individual's ideological preference, undoubtedly, also has much to do with the satisfaction experienced over politics (Frey and Stutzer 2002). Right-wing voters, who are generally more worried about inflation than unemployment, are happier under a conservative government, while left-wing voters, who feel more bothered by unemployment than by inflation, would be more content with a progressive party in power.

Recent research by Haidt (2012) reveals to what extent one's ideological options may be predicted by heritable personality traits (McCrae 1996) and innate moral sensibilities. Haidt (2012) identifies six in-born axes which purportedly serve as the foundations of morality. The first is "harm/care," which is related to our status as mammals with a need for attachment and an ability to empathize with the pain or pleasure of others. It underlies the traits of kindness, gentleness, and nurturance, among others. The second is "fairness/cheating," which has to do with reciprocal altruism and serves as the soil in which the notions of justice, rights, and autonomy thrive. The third is "liberty/oppression," which explains feelings of reactance and resentment that bind people together to bring down whoever dominates them and curtails their freedom. The fourth is "loyalty/betrayal," which is linked to our long tribal history and the necessity of forming shifting coalitions among different groups in order to survive. It manifests itself in the attributes of patriotism and self-sacrifice, for instance. The fifth is "authority/subversion," associated with the hierarchical social structure and interactions characteristic of primates. Thanks to this, we develop traits of leadership and followership, alongside respect for authority and traditions. And the sixth is "sanctity (purity)/degradation," responsible for psychological reactions of disgust and contamination, as well as the desire to live in a more noble or sublime and less carnal way.

According to Haidt (2012), these axes form matrices on which depend one's moral "taste buds" as well as one's ideological leanings. He tested this through sixty psychological surveys and experiments posted online (www.YourMorals.org), where over 300,000 people were asked to indicate their political orientation (from "very liberal/left" to "very conservative/right"), then requested to state their degree of agreement/disagreement with a list of statements such as "Compassion for those who are suffering is the most crucial virtue," "People should be loyal to their family members, even when they have done something wrong," and so forth. Based on these results, he claims that liberals or progressives concentrate on just three of the moral foundations, such that if an action does not harm (harm/care), cheat (fairness/cheating) or violate anyone's freedom (liberty/oppression), nobody should be censured or condemned for doing it. The harm/care principle appears to be their overriding concern. Conservatives, on the other hand, seem to have a much wider moral register that takes into account all six foundations; hence their preoccupation with love of country, respect for duly constituted authority, and the integrity of marriage and the family. It is also possible that liberals and conservatives have different perceptions even of the same value, such that justice usually translates as "equality" for the former and "proportionality" for the latter. As for the much smaller group of libertarians – that is, people who define themselves as liberals on social issues but conservatives on economic issues – they display a moral profile more similar to that of liberals. They put little value on loyalty, authority, and sanctity; however, unlike liberals, they score low on "harm/care."

So far we have considered a couple of reasons why people in democratic regimes tend to be happier: the relative ease with which people's preferences are known and the strong incentive for those in power to be responsive to their needs and desires. Taking the Freedom House political rights and civil liberties scores of countries as indicators of their degree of democratization, we find that there are strong positive correlations between these and their happiness levels (Inglehart 2009). However, we also know that in Russia, despite the shift toward democracy and the increase in political and personal freedoms from 1981 to 1995, happiness entered into a free fall. Of course, this phenomenon could be explained partly by the country's drastic economic contraction, with real incomes falling to about 40 percent of their 1980 levels, as well as the social and ideological upheaval brought about by the collapse of the Soviet Union and the communist belief system (Inglehart 2009). But just the same, it serves as proof that greater democracy, by itself, does not produce an increase in happiness; it could even bring or coexist with greater misery. The experience of former communist countries in eastern Europe tells a similar story, with much depending on how smoothly the transition from a totalitarian government and central planning to a democracy and a market economy was carried out. These overall negative results become more troubling when compared to those of China, which despite its unwavering commitment to authoritarianism, managed to register even higher levels of subjective wellbeing than Russia and other countries in eastern Europe during this same period. Delivering rapid economic growth and stability appears to have legitimized the incumbent communist regime in China and produced greater happiness, even in the absence of democracy (Inglehart 2009).

In light of the above, it is worth inquiring whether happiness itself has a greater impact on democracy than the other way around (Inglehart 2009). Indeed, there seems to be some evidence to this effect, inasmuch as a "happy social climate," characterized by high levels of trust, tolerance, and self-expression, creates the ideal conditions for democracy to thrive (Inglehart and Welzel 2005). This may have been, precisely, the problem in the former Soviet Union and satellite countries. Due to the extreme economic downturn and sociopolitical chaos, the majority of its citizens went on "survival mode" and had little use for the liberal self-expression values that democracy, in theory, guaranteed. In other words, they were "too unhappy," to start with, in order to appreciate the self-expression values conducive to democracy's long-term success.

Indeed, empirical inquiries indicate the following as probable sources of dissatisfaction with political institutions (Frey and Stutzer 2002). First of all, major negative political events, such as the murder of a country's leader, bring about immense suffering. A well-documented occurrence was in the Dominican Republic, with President Trujillo's assassination in 1962. Stable governments, on the other hand, as was the case in Denmark, Switzerland, and Norway in the 1990s, give rise to high satisfaction levels. Once more, the direction of causation isn't clear. Tullock (1987) suggests that instead of an unfortunate event triggering dissatisfaction, which he calls a "romantic view," it could be the other way around. Certain factions within the ruling class could simply be taking advantage of the people's dissatisfaction with politics in order to pull off a revolution or *coup d'état* to serve their own interests. This cannot entirely be ruled out in the so-called Arab Spring – think of the Muslim Brotherhood or the military in Egypt – country by country differences notwithstanding. Secondly, unfavorable foreign policy developments could force a country's stress levels to rise, as was experienced by the Israelis between June 1967 and August 1979, when it was officially at war with its neighbors. A third factor would be the loss of trust in government, which can be symptomatic of unhappiness not only with the individuals or the party in power, but also with the way in which politics is conducted in general. Confidence in government has been in steady decline for much of the developed world in recent years and even decades (Desilver 2013). Reasons cited include political inefficacy, inasmuch as politicians are unable to deliver on their electoral promises, and government being taken hostage by special interest groups, thereby increasing the feeling of helplessness and alienation of ordinary citizens. As a result, "occupy movements" by the disaffected have spread like a global wildfire in about 950 cities in eighty-two countries: at Wall Street, to protest government bailouts of large financial institutions, and in Madrid, where the "indignants" demonstrated against people being thrown out of their bank-repossessed homes, among others.

DEMOCRACY AND ECONOMIC GROWTH

Let us now turn to the positive measures that political institutions in general, and democratic regimes in particular, can undertake to promote happiness and life satisfaction among the people. To the degree that per capita income is important, we could inquire whether democracy bolsters economic growth (Frey and Stutzer 2002). To that extent, democracy would then contribute to happiness indirectly, by generating greater wealth.

The empirical and statistical relation between democracy indicators and those of economic development are not as straightforward as we would desire or imagine. Democratic regimes, by granting more protection to political and civil liberties, enable citizens to demand and earn higher wages. However, some studies show that democratization speeds up economic growth in some countries and the weakening of democratic institutions hinders wealth creation in others. The latter may be due to the fact that investments shy away from regimes with a severe democratic deficit, thus putting a brake on growth. Nevertheless, one thing is to have democratic principles enshrined in law, and another, to actually put them into practice. Even regimes that in theory are democratic are not immune to political unrest and violence. Furthermore, their economic policies could be ill-conceived or badly implemented. And all this serves ultimately to put the country's economic development on hold.

In a landmark panel study of around a hundred countries between 1960 and 1990, Barro (1996) shows how the economic growth rate is enhanced by a greater respect for the rule of law, among other things. (We have referred to this earlier as a "liberal value," a "material component" of a functioning democracy.) Yet political freedom, associated with democracy, appears to have only a weak and non-linear effect on growth. In fledgling democracies, the expansion of political rights stimulates economic growth; but once a moderate degree of democracy has already been attained, growth tapers when further political rights are introduced. Inversely, there seems to be a strong positive influence of a country's stage of economic development or standard of living on its propensity to experience democracy.

A few inferences may be drawn from here. Firstly, liberal values, such as the rule of law, seem to have an unequivocal positive effect on economic growth, unlike democracy. Think of Hong Kong, which experienced strong economic growth due to its well-functioning courts and administrations, long before it had a taste of democracy. Secondly, democracy, measured in terms of political freedoms, initially enhances growth, but later reduces it, as more political freedoms become entrenched. Democracy helps reap the low-hanging fruits of the economy. Purely from the perspective of economic growth, therefore, there is such a thing as "excessive democracy" or "excessive political freedom" apparently getting in the way; although we cannot discount the logical expectation that growth slows down at more mature stages of development. There could also be some sort of "decreasing marginal utility" to be derived from democracy. This, of course, begs the question of what we want democracy for: is it as an end in itself or as a means or instrument for economic growth? It also nuances the strength of a democratic prescription as a growth strategy for specific countries. Lastly, there seems to be stronger push from the side of economic growth toward democracy than the other way around. The richer a country becomes, the higher its standard of living, the more likely its people are to demand a democratic form of government. The experience in China in these past few years tends to confirm this finding. Russia, by contrast, began with democ- ratization in the hope of achieving greater economic growth. Its failure to do so has put even its nominally democratic institutions in jeopardy.

DEMOCRACY, RIGHTS, AND FREEDOMS

Democracy, then, displays a complicated and controversial relationship to happiness via economic growth. In earlier chapters we have already studied the effects of income and economic growth on happiness. We shall now focus, then, on another channel through which democracy may influence happiness: that is, through the promotion of different rights and freedoms (Frey and Stutzer 2002). The exercise of rights and freedoms in a democracy makes it easier for citizens' wishes and desires to be known and followed. It also allows them to participate in the decision-making process, experiencing some form of autonomy or self-rule, which in itself is inherently satisfying. Moreover, despite its faults, a democratic government is often perceived as one of superior quality in terms of honesty, effectiveness, efficiency, and trustworthiness (Helliwell and Huang 2008). Together, all these influences help explain the superior happiness levels of citizens in democratic regimes, when a host of other factors (sociodemographic, economic, and cultural) are taken into account (Dorn et al. 2007).

Ever since Berlin (1969), it has been commonplace to distinguish between negative and positive liberties or freedoms. "Negative liberties" are "freedoms from interference" by the state, primarily, and by extension, from interference by any other political actor; while "positive liberties" refer to democratic self-government and human self-realization, above all, through the mastery of passion by reason. In more recent years, Holmes and Sunstein (2002) have applied this same distinction to "rights" – the claims upon taxpayer resources managed by the state, which enable citizens, in the first place, and other assimilated individuals, secondarily, to perform or refrain from performing certain actions. Thus, we could speak of "negative rights" ("freedom from") as "absences of interference" or "immunities" with regard to private property and enterprise, for example, and "positive rights" ("freedom for") as "specific powers" in connection with healthcare, education, and unemployment benefits, for instance. "Negative rights" are especially dear to conservatives, whereas "positive rights" come closer to the hearts of liberals or progressives.

Meanwhile, closely linked to the 1948 United Nations Declaration of Human Rights and European Law, a parallel, "genetic" classification of rights has been offered, consisting of "first generation," "second generation," and "third generation" rights (Vasak 1977). First-generation rights encompass civil and political rights which protect individuals from state abuse and guarantee their freedom to participate in political life and government. Hence, included among these first-generation rights are freedom of religion, freedom of speech, the right to a fair trial, and voting rights, to name a few. After World War II, many states began to acknowledge second-generation rights, ensuring citizens equal treatment in various economic, social, and cultural matters, such as healthcare, housing, education, and employment. As a result, governments commit themselves to respect, and insofar as resources allow, to help and promote the fulfillment of these rights for their citizens. These rights signal an expansion of the welfare state, well beyond the provision of internal and external security and a *laissez-faire* economy. Lastly, third-generation rights are those expressed in many progressive documents of international law as aspirational objectives: the right to self-determination, rights to intergenerational equity and sustainability, the right to preserve and develop one's cultural heritage, and so forth. They are considered instances of "soft law," as the principle of national sovereignty exercised by independent states makes them very difficult to enact and implement.

It is fairly easy to understand from the above how the conquest and consolidation of various kinds of rights contribute to the well-being, satisfaction, and ultimately happiness of individuals. We also know that such developments are possible only within the context of democratic regimes. Even then, not all citizens of democratic states will be equally happy, since their experience will be inflected by their ideological preferences. Economic and social conservatives will be quite content with the first-generation rights, and will hardly push for the second-, and much less, the third-generation ones. Liberals or progressives, on the other hand, won't have a problem with the expansion of the welfare state through the second-generation rights, perhaps not even with the internationalism that the third-generation rights beckon. For them, the first-generation rights seem radically insufficient. In any case, regardless of ideological leanings, a democratic regime at least affords one a chance to bring about a peaceful and orderly change toward a direction more in line with one's preferences.

Another way of analyzing the advantages of democracies for the happiness of individuals lies in the study not only of results or "outcome utilities," but also of processes or "procedural utilities" in decision making (Simon 1978; Sen 1995). Earlier we said that in a democracy, it is easier to discover what people want – the rights and freedoms they cherish, for instance. This refers to a desirable result or "outcome utility." However, we also mentioned that simply having a voice or being consulted as to the direction one thinks government should take is already an inherently satisfying experience. This indicates a process or "procedural utility." "Procedural utilities" explain why people insist on choosing their "lucky number" – as if it mattered, probability-wise – in lotteries, and why they gamble at all, despite the odds heavily stacked against them. Obviously, it's not the prize, but the hope of winning that the great majority of them pay for. Similarly, "procedural utilities" have to do with the intrinsic satisfaction that comes from the performance of or participation in certain activities, which people carry out without much regard for results. Think of voluntary work or amateur sports competitions where it's not uncommon for people to give their very best efforts. In any case, both outcome and procedural utilities should be taken into account when considering the total utility or satisfaction enjoyed by individuals.

We shall now look into outcome and procedural utilities as we examine the effects of direct democracy and federalism in Switzerland (Frey and Stutzer 2002). It is the only country that recognizes the right to direct democracy, be it in the form of referenda or popular initiatives, to all its citizens, over whatever issue and at all levels of government or the state. In popular initiatives, the citizens themselves are the ones who put an issue, either optional or mandatory, on the political agenda, after collecting a minimum number of signatures, while in referenda, the government or legislators directly put the issue to a vote. Frey and Stutzer (2002) have found that direct democracy channels are positively correlated with individual subjective wellbeing or happiness. The reason for this may be that it devolves decision-making power and agenda setting from government and politicians to the citizens themselves. Aside from stimulating grassroots discussion, direct democracy can likewise produce other positive effects, such as a reduction in per capita debt as well as in government expenditures and revenues, while increasing public spending on education and lifting real estate prices, as these regions become more attractive places in which to live. Direct democracy allows for greater participation in government and as close an experience as possible to self-government.

Similarly, federalism, the decentralization of state power and its devolution to lower levels of government, is also positively correlated with increased individual subjective wellbeing and happiness (Frey and Stutzer 2002). This may have to do with the fact that decisions are taken by those who are most affected, by the ones who will actually bear the costs and enjoy the benefits, rather than by some detached politician or faraway bureaucrat who hardly has a stake in the issue. Having one's skin in the game undoubtedly helps one to arrive at a more prudent and realistic decision. Apart from increased participation, a federalist set-up also facilitates the exercise of subsidiarity. It has been shown that the benefits of federalism and local autonomy are felt by everyone, regardless of income, sex, education level, or employment status (Frey and Stutzer 2002). Moreover, it doesn't seem possible to clearly separate the effects of federalism from those of direct democracy on happiness.

The distinction between procedural and outcome utilities with regard to democratic institutions may be detected in the differences in the happiness levels between citizens and foreigners or non-citizens residing in Switzerland (Frey and Stutzer 2002). Both populations enjoy the same outcome utilities, insofar as they live subject to the same laws, for instance. However, citizens, additionally, can enjoy procedural utilities, inasmuch as they have a right to participate in the decision making or electoral process that produces those outcomes. Resident foreigners or non-citizens are excluded from this. Apparently, the mere possession of the right to participate in decision making matters more for individual satisfaction or happiness than the actual exercise of the right. Indeed, from the perspective of the result or outcome, the influence of a single vote may be insignificant. Therefore, when people do participate in the political process instead of engaging in some alternative leisure activity, for example, it should be due to the "procedural utility" or intrinsic satisfaction of fulfilling one's civic duty, expressing one's view, or believing that one is being taken into account on the issues put to the ballot. Unsurprisingly, citizens are said to reap thrice the welfare benefit of foreigners or non-citizens from political processes, most of it from procedural utilities (Frey and Stutzer 2002).

Given the importance of procedural utilities which are distinctive from outcome utilities, politicians ought to be wary of attempts to maximize objective wellbeing or welfare results without taking processes such as popular consultations into account (Frey and Stutzer 2002). This is the main error into which authoritarian regimes, even supposedly benevolent ones, readily fall. They always think that "father knows best" and the dictator, or his cadre of the technocratic elite, resolutely goes ahead establishing political objectives and priorities, without even bothering to listen to the people's voices. They forget about subjective values and the psychological components of wellbeing and satisfaction in politics, which consist chiefly in participation and the exercise of autonomy or self-determination. Therefore, it is not enough simply for public policy to be sound, in the sense of targeting the right objectives, but it should also choose the appropriate means or procedures in order to reach those goals. This usually means providing people with pertinent information and giving them the chance to get involved in the decision-making process as much as possible.

This principle has important repercussions in economic policy making, if happiness is understood to matter (Frey and Stutzer 2002). For instance, poverty should not be defined solely on the basis of disposable income, but also in terms of individual preferences, satisfaction levels, and living standards. Although, objectively speaking, a cement floor may seem a sturdier structure than a dirt floor, it could be the case that home dwellers prefer the latter because it is warmer and more comfortable. The evils of unemployment will not be addressed exclusively by providing greater income, but also by paving the way toward an appropriate job with which to practice self-agency. And the redistribution efforts through the tax policy should not focus so much on absolute incomes as on relative incomes, since individuals derive greater satisfaction from comparing their position to that of others. Because of this, a significantly larger percentage of people from Tanzania consider themselves very rich compared to the general population than in the United States, for example, although their wealth may consist mainly in goats (Kenny and Kenny 2006).

The difference between processes and outcomes, together with the intrinsic value of democratic procedures and their substantial contributions to individual happiness, should serve as cautions to political leaders who wish to establish "gross national happiness" as their government's goal or objective. This has been proposed not only in the remote Himalayan kingdom of Bhutan, but in mainstream industrialized nations as well, such as the United Kingdom, under David Cameron, and France, under Nicolas Sarkozy. In fact, the United Nations even declared March 20, 2013, as the first ever "International Day of Happiness," to underscore the commitment of the 193 member states to the pursuit of happiness as a development goal and a guide to public policy. That's fine if all one wishes is to remind governments everywhere that human development and well-being transcends purely economic growth. But it should not be taken as an excuse to engage in anti-democratic forms of state intervention, manipulation, and paternalism. Bhutan, the movement's poster-child, is a case in point. Far from being Shangri-la, it is one of the poorest countries on earth, with a fourth of its 800,000 people surviving on less than $1.25 a day, and 70 percent of them living without electricity, despite the country exporting hydroelectric power to India (Ryback 2012; Kelly 2012; Revkin 2013). It was also an absolute monarchy until 2008, and although now nominally a parliamentary democracy, that means very little to the disenfranchised ethnic Nepalese, almost a tenth of the total population, living within its borders, who are victims of a policy of "cultural purity or homogeneity." Buddhism continues to be the state religion and citizens are obliged to wear their national dress for special public events. Tobacco and plastic bags are banned, as well as the sale of meat during religious holidays, which can sometimes stretch to as long as a month.

To the degree that happiness depends on how society and the economy are organized, it depends on institutions. Much of what people find satisfying in democratic institutions pertains not only to superior results or outcomes, but also to means or procedures employed. Invariably these democratic processes entail participation, autonomy, and subsidiarity as subjective, psychological components. These powers are often enshrined in state-guaranteed rights and freedoms which reflect a person's dignity as an individual capable of exercising choice.

In fact, dignity manifests itself – among other ways – in the ability to choose or decide over one's own life and life-plan (Kenny and Kenny 2006). For this reason, it is often presumed that the greater the margin for choice, the greater the dignity as well, for that particular decision or action. However, not all choices are of equal standing, and some, such as those referring to one's cultural identity, civil status, job or profession, and social role, come closer to the core of a human being. They also have a much larger bearing on individual happiness, than, say, the football or basketball team one decides to support. Among these more significant choices is that of political participation – perhaps the defining trait of citizenship. In democratic regimes, the exercise of citizenship consists in "governing and being governed in turn," and this capacity to choose one's leaders as well as the laws under which one lives is precisely what grants legitimacy to both.

In the same way that slavery or unjust discrimination is an affront, so the recognition of equal rights and freedoms of individuals is an indicator or measure of human dignity. This acknowledgment impacts happiness not only because it determines what society permits or allows people to do, but also because it affects how they see themselves, their self-image (Kenny and Kenny 2006). Oftentimes, an individual's perception of his skills, abilities, and rights (or lack thereof) is linked to the social status of his group, defined in terms of ethnicity or religion, for instance. Based on this premise, it won't be surprising to find low levels of happiness among indentured servants or women in some remote areas of Ethiopia and Peru, who think that their husbands are entitled to beat them up, if they don't do the housework properly (Kenny and Kenny 2006).

Apart from the recognition of rights within democratic regimes, education and urbanization also seem to favor the cause of human dignity, to an even greater extent than an increase in income. This is consistent with the positive effects of education (primary and secondary levels especially at initial stages of development) and city living on human development and empowerment in general. Arguably, the causal relationship seems to run from dignity to economic growth, rather than the other way around. In fact, a more rapid economic growth has sometimes been associated with greater authoritarianism instead of democracy. Moreover, the positive correlation between income and democracy seems to disappear when one controls for historical determinants of economic and political development in certain countries (Acemoglu et al. 2005).

Thus far we have analyzed the relationship between happiness and democracy, in general, and direct democracy and federalism in Switzerland, in particular. We have seen that democracy may be valued either as a means or an instrument, or in itself – that is, intrinsically. As a means, democracy does not seem to have a straightforward effect on economic growth; rather, the correlation seems stronger from economic growth toward democracy. However, democracy is more effective than other regimes in bringing about the desired outcome of an alignment between political decisions and the preferences of citizens. In itself, democracy fosters the recognition of various rights and freedoms, which uphold human dignity. While the acknowledgment of dignity may exert a positive influence on economic growth, economic growth by itself cannot guarantee greater respect for human dignity. These rights and freedoms, in turn, enhance the procedural utilities of participation and autonomy (free choice), which are positively correlated with life satisfaction and happiness.

RELIGION: BELIEF AND PRACTICE

It is often taken for granted that Europeans no longer believe in God or go to church. In fact, they don't even consider themselves to be religious at all. It is a foregone conclusion, therefore, that Europe – unlike the rest of the world – is a very much secularized continent. However, the European Values Study (2005) presents a much more nuanced picture. In half of the surveyed countries, the majority of the population, sometimes an overwhelming majority, found the statement "There is a personal God" as the one which comes closest to their belief; while in the remaining countries, the statement "There is some God, spirit or life force" was chosen. Certainly, there are a significant number of agnostics in a few countries, given that the statement "I don't know if there is a God, spirit or life force" was second choice for France and the Russian Federation. But the atheistic option, "There is no God, spirit or life force," always came in last. This is true even in France, which has the highest percentage of non-believers, where it was chosen by 15 percent of the population. Believers, therefore, still vastly outnumber non-believers, despite an important variance in the objects of their belief.

The same study affords an equally varied panorama for religious practice. Although in most countries, the majority of the population never attends religious services, in ten, the majority of the population attends religious services once a week. On the aggregate, half of all Europeans pray or meditate at least once a week, and even in a country known for its liberal tradition, such as the Netherlands, one fourth of its inhabitants attends church. So despite the decrease in church attendance and religious practice over the years, a considerable number of Europeans still engage in religion, albeit with varying frequency.

Relatively new is the category of Europeans who consider themselves religious, three out of four, although they do not necessarily belong to an institutional church or attend services. Their position may be described as that of "believing without belonging" (Davie 1994); in lieu of an organized church, each individual is said to follow a fluid, eclectic approach to religious beliefs and practices. Sociologists call this "cafeteria religion" or "church-free spirituality," as if to emphasize the role of free choice and individuality. This is a major growing trend throughout the whole continent, not only in the more secular northwest (Scandinavian countries), but also in the more religious southeast (Mediterranean countries).

In line with the experience of most industrialized nations, religion in Europe is increasingly decoupled not only from an institutional church but also from God. For this reason it is worth inquiring separately about the importance of God in one's life. On a scale from 1 (not at all important) to 10 (very important), the European Values Study (2005) reveals that the Irish, Portuguese, Romanians, Poles, and Turks give God the highest points, while the Norwegians, Swedes, Danes, Estonians, and Czechs relegate God close to the bottom of their priorities. It is interesting to note that the countries whose people consider God important are also the ones with relatively higher population growth rates. So although no one can guarantee that the next generation will hold the same beliefs as their parents, chances are that there will be more people who find God important than those who do not in the future, given the relevance of education and upbringing in the home on this matter.

RELIGION AND HAPPINESS

Despite the growing literature on the sociology of religion, on the one hand, and on happiness and economics, on the other, the relationship between religion and happiness, at least in Europe as a whole, is still very much an open question. Contradictory findings may be attributed to methodological differences and, above all, to an inadequate theoretical base from which to understand the relationship between religion and happiness (Lewis and Cruise 2006). Making use of the 1972–1996 General Social Survey in the United States, Ferriss (2002) found happiness to be associated with the frequency of attendance at religious services, denominational preference, and doctrinal preference. Brooks (2008) concurs with the finding that in the United States, religious participation is positively correlated with high levels of happiness. However, Snoep (2007), comparing data from the 2000 World Values Survey in the United States, the Netherlands, and Denmark, found that, unlike in the United States, there is no significant individual-level correlation between religiosity and happiness for the Netherlands and Denmark. This has led some people to think that religion affects happiness differently, depending on which side of the Atlantic one resides. In European countries such as the Netherlands and Denmark, where the welfare state is huge, people do not have as strong a need for the social support that organized churches provide as in the United States, where the welfare state is minimal. In some sense, therefore, Europeans seem to view the welfare state as a substitute for a church, as a source of security and comfort, if not as an object of faith and belief unto itself. In Hegelian terms, the welfare state is the God that has established his dwelling-place among men.

Gundlach and Opfinger (2011), in another study using international data from the World Values Survey for 1982, 1900, 1995, and 2000, also focused on the relationship between personal wellbeing and religiosity. Their results support the view that happiness and religiosity are related in a U-shaped pattern. People with both higher religiosity and lower religiosity report high happiness levels.

According to Gundlach and Opfinger (2011), the U-shaped pattern for religion and happiness might be due to the so-called: religious people are happier if they live in a religious society, and so are atheists, if they live in a society in which religion does not play an important role.

Indeed, for certain groups of people, religion produces a fair amount of unhappiness, insofar as it is associated with feelings of guilt (Hood 1992), anxiety, and fear of death (Pressman et al. 1992). Moreover, religion can create difficult interpersonal tensions, as when one lives in a religious minority or when religious precepts clash with one's preferences, as in the case of an arranged marriage, for instance. That some religions subject their members to a tyrannical control is also widely known. In any case, the worst-off in society are those who are neither religious nor atheistic, those who live within the shadows of religion by being nominally religious but without engaging in its practice; even the Gospels condemn them for being "lukewarm" (Douthat 2014).

In the succeeding pages, we would like to focus on the relation between religion, on the one hand, and happiness, on the other, particularly in Europe. More specifically, we would like to see whether people who profess religious belief and engage in religious practices are happier than those who do not. For this we shall analyze data for twenty-four European countries from the first three waves (2002/2003, 2004, and 2006) of the European Social Survey (ESS 2010) (Cuñado and Sison 2011).

As is customary, the survey determines happiness levels by asking the question, "How happy are you?," to which individuals respond on a scale from 1 to 10, where "1" stands for "not happy at all" and "10" for "completely happy." Two groups of variables function as indicators of religion. The first group, comprising three variables, represents "religious belief": belonging to a particular religion or denomination; religion or denomination to which one belongs at present (1: Roman Catholic, 2: Protestant, 3: Eastern Orthodox, 4: Other Christian denominations, 5: Jewish, 6: Islam, 7: Eastern religions,

8: Other non-Christian religions); and the question, "How religious are you?" (0: not at all religious...10: Very religious). The second group of variables indicates "religious practice." They consist of the following: "How often attend religious services apart from special occasions?" (1: every day, 2: more than once a week, 3: at least once a month, 4: only on special holy days, 5: less often, 6: never); and "How often do you pray apart from religious services?" (1: every day, 2: more than once a week, 3: at least once a month, 4: only on special holy days, 5: less often, 6: never). In addition to religion and happiness variables, the ESS likewise contains a large number of socioeconomic indicators, such as gender, age, health, income, employment status, and education, which can be used as control variables.

Statistical analyses show a number of interesting results. Firstly, belonging to a religion seems to have a significant effect on happiness, such that those who do report higher levels of happiness than those who do not. Second, the particular religion or denomination to which an individual belongs also appears to have a significant effect on happiness. Protestants, those belonging to other Christian religions, and Roman Catholics report higher happiness levels, whereas Orthodox Christians and followers of Eastern religions register the lowest levels. Third, there seems to be a positive relationship between how religious a person is and happiness: the more religious a person, the happier. However, those who consider themselves to be "not at all religious" (0) have comparable levels of happiness to those who give themselves a "5" in the scale of religiosity, confirming the U-shaped curve mentioned earlier. Thus far the findings for "religious belief." Fourth, as far as religious practice is concerned, the frequency of attendance at services is likewise positively correlated with happiness. For example, those who attend religious services every day say they are happier than those who never attend. Fifth, still in the realm of religious practice, we find that the frequency of prayer is positively correlated with happiness, such that those who pray every day report higher levels of happiness than those who never pray. Sixth and lastly, we discover that frequency of attendance in services is more relevant than frequency of prayer in the self-reported happiness levels.

Many of these results concur with those of Soydemir, Bastida, and Gonzalez (2004) for a group of middle-aged Mexican Americans: the religiously involved and regular attendees of religious services assess themselves to be healthier and happier than those who are not involved and who attend services sporadically, if at all. However, the incremental reward on happiness also seems to taper off as frequency of attendance rises.

These findings may be discussed from the perspective of both the psychology of religion and the sociology of religion. Regarding the psychology of religion, Nielsen (1998) provides us with three possible explanations for the positive link between religion and happiness. Although based on correlations rather than causation, they could nevertheless indicate pathways through which religion affects happiness. The first refers to social support. Generally, people are happier when they find themselves in a supportive environment and religion offers a lot of this. In fact, according to the psychology of religion literature, the beneficial influence of religion on happiness is strongest among those groups of people in most need of support, such as the elderly, those who suffer poor health, and those who are single. Prayer, among other things, promotes social connection and gives one strength by preventing cognitive depletion and loss of self-control (Friese and Wanke 2014). What's more, religion allows people to feel themselves closer to God, who could also be viewed as a valuable source of support. Economics literature expresses this same idea, inasmuch as religion could serve as insurance during negative shocks (Chen, Chiang, and So 2003; Lelkes 2006), a source of both direct (e.g., education) and indirect social benefits (e.g., health, work), and an object of "social self-interest" (Glaeser et al. 2000; Finke and Stark 1998).

Secondly, people with firm beliefs and an orientation in life, those who have a sense of what is important, also tend to be happier

(Ellison 1991). Religion supplies people with precisely this kind of firm beliefs. It is even supposed that religious practice raises happiness by strengthening beliefs. This aspect of religion may also have to do with the greater success, in terms of membership, of conservative churches compared to liberal ones (Kelley 1972). Not only are conservative churches stricter and more demanding in terms of morals and practice, but they also offer greater certitude in beliefs. Furthermore, when government becomes more restrictive of religion, it only serves to heighten the impact of personal religiosity on life satisfaction (Elliot and Hayward 2009). Thirdly, religion itself may contribute to happiness by triggering positive experiences, such as a feeling of being in contact with God (transcendence) or in contact with others, among believers and practitioners (Pollner 1989).

How do these explanations from the psychology of religion compare with the statistical results? They undoubtedly support findings (1) "Those who belong to a religion report higher levels of happiness than those who do not," (3) "The more religious a person, the happier," (4) "The frequency of attendance at services is positively correlated with happiness," and (5) "The frequency of prayer is positively correlated with happiness." However, they are not necessarily helpful in explaining findings (2) "The religion or denomination to which the individual belongs has a significant effect on happiness" and (6) "Frequency of attendance in services is more relevant than frequency of prayer in the self-reported happiness levels."

Regarding finding (2), which refers to the varying correlations between particular religions or denominations and self-reported happiness, the above-cited psychology of religion literature seems to imply that Protestant religions provide greater social support, firmer beliefs, and more positive religious experiences – or any combination among these three factors – than Eastern Orthodox religions, for example. However, it is difficult to find evidence for this. Moreover, the lumping together, for survey purposes, of the wide variety of Protestant religions, other Christian religions, and Eastern Orthodox churches, for instance, does not allow one to calibrate the social support, firm beliefs, and religious experiences associated with each one of these denominations.

As for finding (6), which suggests that frequency of attendance at services is more significant than frequency of prayer for happiness, neither is there a straightforward explanation from the psychology of religion literature. On the one hand, attendance at services could provide more social support than prayer, which could be done individually. But attendance at religious services does not necessarily imply firmer beliefs or more positive religious experiences than individual prayer. (Some religions may simply emphasize private prayer more than community worship.) Again, it is impossible to tell with the available data. To further explain this finding, one would have to tease out the individual effects of social support, firm beliefs, and religious experience from their cumulative effects on happiness, for attendance at services, and for prayer. But once more, unfortunately, that cannot be done with the information at hand.

Furthermore, there seem to be other dimensions to both religious belief and religious practice than those considered by the ESS. Here is where the inputs from the sociology of religion prove helpful. The sociology of religion offers insights to better understand the underlying notions of religious belief and religious practice, and the tensions between them. It also sheds light on the relationship between the individual and the group – again from the viewpoint of religion – through the mediating institutions of the church, the state, and the market.

What could be meant by "religious belief" in this context? Starting out with the British experience (Davie 1994), and later on extending it to the rest of Europe and America (Berger, Davie, and Fokas 2008), Davie suggests that "religious belief" mainly refers to feelings, experiences, and the numinous, such as could be associated with the New Age movement, for example. It does not refer primarily to creedal statements with precise and specific contents. It is a profession in an "ordinary God" (Abercrombie et al. 1970), not a God "who can change the course of heaven and earth" (Davie 1994: 1).

Philosophically, this corresponds to the God of Deism. This is a God who, after creating heaven and earth, in practice, left human beings to their own resources alone and in charge. Although nominally Christian, it represents, above all, a non-institutional religiosity, one that is privatized, invisible, and implicit. It comes by other names, such as "popular," "common," "customary," "folk," "civic," or "civil" religion. It is not the absence of belief, but individual patchworks or quilts of belief. Therefore, apart from the categories of belief and unbelief, the degrees of religiosity and institutional religions considered by the ESS, it would also be interesting to look into a wider range of non-institutional religiosity and test it for happiness.

And how are we to understand "religious practice?" Again, for Davie (1994) and colleagues (Berger, Davie, and Fokas 2008), this "belonging" covers a wide range of behaviors, from religious orthodoxy to ritual participation and an instrumental attachment to religion. It may also be called "vicarious religion," meaning that although an individual does not want to be personally involved with a church, he nonetheless wants the church to be there at the service of other people and society as a whole (Berger, Davie, and Fokas 2008). Similarly, therefore, besides data for frequency of attendance at services and frequency of prayer provided by the ESS, there are other forms of religious practice such as "vicarious religion" that can be analyzed in relation to happiness.

Lastly, there are two prevalent models relating the individual to the group in the religious sphere: the traditional, historic, or established church, and the church seen as the result of a voluntary association in an environment of pluralist competition (Berger, Davie, and Fokas 2008). The first is dominant in Europe, especially in continental Europe, whereas the second could be found mainly in the United States. The traditional church, much like the state, exercises a monopoly over its faithful who do not belong by choice, but by default or obligation. In many countries, it is the "national church" often conceived as a ministry of the state. The church which arises through voluntary adherence, on the other hand, follows the market or consumption-led model. There is no established church and there exists, instead, a functioning "market," in which various churches compete for the faithful. The decline in religious belief and practice, often termed "secularization," has hit the traditional churches more than the churches of voluntary adherence. Take note, however, that the same religion may adopt the traditional mode in one place and the voluntary mode in another.

The status of a religion or a denomination in a specific country – whether traditional or voluntary – affects not only the levels of belief and practice, but also the level of happiness reported. Countries which follow the traditional model of religion will have lower levels of religious belief and practice than those that follow the voluntary model. It is also probable that followers of voluntary religion would report higher levels of happiness than those of traditional religion. But again, unfortunately, this cannot be confirmed with the available data and will have to be left for future work.

As a final remark, therefore, despite the positive correlations obtained between religious belief and practice, on the one hand, and happiness, on the other, these results would have to be nuanced by a better understanding of what both religious belief and religious practice actually mean. Take for granted, within the mainstream Roman Catholic tradition, one cannot easily separate "believing" from "belonging," any more than one could separate belief from practice (Catechism of the Catholic Church 1992). "Belonging" is determined by the sacramental rite of baptism, while "believing" refers, above all, to the church or faith community of which one forms part. In fact, babies, who are quite incapable of utterances of belief, are nevertheless eligible to form part of the church through a profession of faith by their godparents. Neither could the "objects of belief," such as the articles of faith and dogma, be severed from "practice," understood as the celebration of the liturgy or the official church prayer. One simply would not exist without the other. And although there is certainly room for individual, personal prayer within this tradition, it could not be seen as divorced from community practice, but rather, the two are viewed as mutually reinforcing acts of worship. But most important caveats would have to be taken insofar as, in this tradition, religion is not considered as a means to achieve happiness through the fulfillment of psychological and other needs; indeed, religion is not even chosen on the basis of its possible impact on happiness. Rather, religion is chosen, believed, and practiced because it is taken by the individual to be true.

VOLUNTARY PARTICIPATION AND INSTITUTIONS

A recurring theme in our study of the links between institutions and happiness is the importance of voluntary participation. It is a key factor in democracy and represents the general objective that all rights and freedoms seek to guarantee in a variety of spheres, such as the political, civil, socioeconomic, and personal. Its exercise allows one to reap procedural utilities and facilitates ownership or identification with the decisions, results, and outcomes of the established mechanisms of public deliberation. It ensures individuals an experience as close as possible to autonomy or self-government which is intrinsically rewarding. A similar beneficial influence may likewise be found for voluntary participation in the case of religious institutions, for belief as well as for practice. It certainly colors the different advantages identified by the psychology of religion, such as social support, firmness of belief, and the gratifying experience of transcendence. Moreover, it helps explain the differences in happiness among the faithful of traditional, historic, and established or "monopolistic" churches, on the one hand, and those of faith communities which compete in an "open market," so to speak.

The exercise of voluntary participation may be connected to one of the core dimensions of personality, called the "locus of control" (Rotter 1990). People with an external locus of control believe that their own behavior does not matter much, rewards in life are beyond them, and their life is guided by fate, luck or other external circumstances. On the other hand, people with an internal locus of control subscribe to the idea that life is what you make it; it is the outcome of one's own personal decisions and actions. While the effects of locus of control in political institutions and democracy are forthright, it affects religion ambivalently. Belief in a personal and rational God, who rewards good deeds and punishes evil ones, together with the acknowledgment of individual freedom and responsibility indicate an internal locus of control. By contrast, belief in an impersonal god or life-force that holds sway over an individual's life, regardless of what one does, points toward an external locus of control. Those with an internal locus of control are said to be happier and more satisfied than those with an external locus of control. Voluntary participation, consequently, reinforces an internal locus of control, leading to greater happiness.

There could be several ways of measuring voluntary social participation. One consists in determining, for instance, the frequency of getting together with friends, how many neighbors one knows, and how many organizations one takes active part in (Phillips 1967). Such a study reveals that greater voluntary social participation is positively correlated with greater happiness and increased positive affect. Hence, activities with a greater degree of voluntariness, such as getting together with friends, may be found to have a stronger impact than those with a lesser degree of voluntariness, such as knowing one's neighbors. Voluntary social participation also seems to be connected with mental health, although the direction of causation is still unclear. That is, it has yet to be determined whether increased voluntary social participation leads to improved mental health or good mental health leads to greater voluntary social participation. In any case, the positive effects of physical and mental health on happiness (and vice versa) are already fairly settled.

Lastly, the role that voluntary social participation and institutions play in happiness seems to underscore not only the social and relational nature of human beings, but also the social and relational nature of that perfect state to which human beings aspire. This suggests that happiness behaves in a manner characteristic of "common goods": objects of desire or values in which an individual takes part only to the extent that other members of the group take part in them as well. More shall be explained about this in subsequent chapters.

REFERENCES

Abercrombie, N., Baker, J., Brett, S. and Foster, J. 1970. "Superstition and religion: The God of the gaps," in Martin, D. and Hill, M. (eds.), *A sociological yearbook of religion in Britain*, vol. 3. London: SCM, pp. 91–129.

Acemoglu, D., Johnson, S., Robinson, J. and Yared, P. 2005. "Income and democracy," *NBER Working Papers*, no. 11205.

Ahmed, M. A. 2013. "Pakistan's tyrannical majority," *New York Times*, May 10.

Barro, R. J. 1996. "Economic growth in a cross section of countries," *Quarterly Journal of Economics*, 106 (2): 407–443.

Becker, G. 1981. *A treatise on the family*. Cambridge, MA: Harvard University Press.

Berger, P., Davie, G. and Fokas, E. 2008. *Religious America, secular Europe? A theme and variations*. Aldershot, UK and Burlington, VT: Ashgate.

Berlin, I. 1969. *Four essays on liberty*. Oxford: Oxford University Press.

Blanchflower, D. and Oswald, A. 2011. "International happiness: A new view on the measure of performance," *Academy of Management Perspectives*, 25 (1): 6–22.

Bloom, P. 2014. "The war on reason," *The Atlantic*, February 19.

Brooks, A. C. 2008. *Gross national happiness*. New York: Basic Books.

Catechism of the Catholic Church 1992. www.vatican.va/archive/ENG0015/_INDEX.HTM, accessed February 5, 2014.

Chen, C. W. S., Chiang, T. C. and So, M. K. P. 2003. "Asymmetrical reaction to US stock-return news: Evidence from major stock markets based on a double-threshold model," *Journal of Economics and Business*, 55 (5–6): 487–502.

Chetty, R., Hendren, N., Kline, P., Saez, E. and Turner, N. 2014. "Is the United States still a land of opportunity? Recent trends in intergenerational mobility," *NBER Working Papers*, no. 19844.

Chun, H. and Lee, I. 2001. "Why do married men earn more: Productivity or marriage selection?" *Economic Inquiry*, 39 (2): 307–319.

Clayton, V. 1982. "Wisdom and intelligence: The nature and function of knowledge in the later years," *Journal of Aging and Human Development*, 15: 315–323.

Cuñado, J. and Sison, A. J. G. 2011. "How does religious belief and practice affect happiness? A European perspective" (unpublished manuscript).

Davie, G. 1994. *Religion in Britain since 1945: Believing without belonging*. Oxford and Cambridge, MA: Blackwell.

Desilver, D. 2013. "Confidence in government falls in much of the developed world," *Fact Tank*, November 21 (www.pewresearch.org/fact-tank/2013/11/21/confidence-in-government-falls-in-much-of-the-developed-world/, accessed January 25, 2013).

Dorn, D., Fischer, J., Kirchgässner, G. and Sousa-Poza, A. 2007. "Is it culture or democracy? The impact of democracy, income and culture on happiness," *Social Indicators Research*, 82 (3): 505–526.

Douthat, R. 2014. "The Christian penumbra," *New York Times*, March 29.

Elliot, M. R. and Hayward, D. 2009. "Religion and life satisfaction worldwide: The role of government regulation," *Sociology of Religion*, 70 (3): 285–310.

Ellison, C. G. 1991. "Religious involvement and subjective well-being," *Journal of Health and Social Behavior*, 32: 80–99.

European Social Survey 2010. www.europeansocialsurvey.org, accessed November 20, 2010.

European Values Study 2005. www.europeanvaluesstudy.eu/evs/research/themes/religion/, accessed November 20, 2010.

Ferriss, A. L. 2002. "Religion and the quality of life," *Journal of Happiness Studies*, 3: 199–215.

Finke, R. and Stark, R. 1998. "Religious choice and competition," *American Sociological Review*, 63 (5): 761–766.

Fowler, J. H. and Christakis, N. A. 2008. "Dynamic spread of happiness in a large social network: Longitudinal analysis over 20 years in the Framingham heart study," *British Medical Journal*, 337 (a2338): 1–9.

Frey, B. 2008. *Happiness: A revolution in economics*. Cambridge, MA/London: The MIT Press.

Frey, B. and Stutzer, A. 2002. *Happiness and economics: How the economy and institutions affect well-being*. Princeton, NJ/Oxford: Princeton University Press.

Friese, M. and Wanke, M. 2014. "Personal prayer buffers self-control depletion," *Journal of Experimental Social Psychology*, 51: 56–59.

Gardner, J. and Oswald, A. 2004. "How is mortality affected by money, marriage, and stress?," *Journal of Health Economics*, 23: 1181–1207.

Glaeser, E., Laibson, D., Scheinkman, J. and Soutter, C. 2000. "Measuring trust," *Quarterly Journal of Economics*, 65 (3): 811–46.

Grassian, S. 1983. "Psychopathological effects of solitary confinement," *American Journal of Psychiatry*, 140: 1450–1454.

Gundlach, E. and Opfinger, M. 2011. "Religiosity as a determinant of happiness," *German Institute of Global and Area Studies Working Papers*, no. 163, April.

Haidt, J. 2012. *The righteous mind*. New York: Pantheon.

Helliwell, J. and Huang, H. 2008. "How's your government? International evidence linking good government and well-being," *British Journal of Political Science*, 38: 595–619.

Holmes, S. and Sunstein, C. 2002. *The cost of rights*. New York/London: W. W. Norton.

Hood, R. W. 1992. "Sin and guilt in faith traditions: Issues for self-esteem," in Schumaker, J. F. (ed.), *Religion and mental health*. Oxford: Oxford University Press, pp. 110–121.

Inglehart, R. 2009. "Democracy and happiness: What causes what?" in Dutt, A. K. and Radcliff, B. (eds.), *Happiness, economics and politics: Towards a multidisciplinary approach*. Cheltenham, UK/Northampton, MA: Edward Elgar, pp. 256–270.

Inglehart, R. and Welzel, C. 2005. *Modernization, cultural change and democracy*. New York and Cambridge: Cambridge University Press.

Jones, B., Reedy, E. J. and Weinberg, B. A. 2014. "Age and scientific genius," *NBER Working Papers*, no. 19866.

Kelley, M. W. 1972. *Why conservative churches are growing*. New York: Harper and Row.

Kelly, A. 2012. "Gross national happiness in Bhutan: The big idea from a tiny state that could change the world," *The Observer*, December 1.

Kenny, A. and Kenny, C. 2006. *Life, liberty and the pursuit of utility*. Exeter: Imprint Academic.

Lelkes, O. 2006. "Tasting freedom: Happiness, religion and economic transition," *Journal of Economic Behavior and Organization*, 59 (2): 173–194.

Lewis, C. A. and Cruise, S. M. 2006. "Religion and happiness: Consensus, contradictions, comments and concerns," *Mental Health, Religion and Culture*, 9 (3): 213–225.

McCrae, R. R. 1996. "Social consequences of experiential openness," *Psychological Bulletin*, 120 (3): 323–337.

Mogliner, C., Kamvar, S. and Aaker, J. 2011. "The shifting meaning of happiness," *Social Psychological and Personality Science*, 2 (4): 395–402.

Myers, D. 2002. *The pursuit of happiness*. New York: HarperCollins.

Nielsen, M. E. 1998. "An assessment of religious conflicts and their resolutions," *Journal for the Scientific Study of Religion,* 37: 181–190.

Ng, Y. K. 2002. "Economic growth and social welfare: The need for a complete study of happiness," in Easterlin, R. A. (ed.), *Happiness in economics.* Cheltenham, UK/Northampton, MA: Edward Elgar, pp. 66–77.

Pacek, A. 2009. "Politics and happiness: An empirical ledger," in Dutt, A. K. and Radcliff, B. (eds.), *Happiness, economics and politics: Towards a multidisciplinary approach.* Cheltenham, UK/Northampton, MA: Edward Elgar, pp. 231–255.

Phillips, D. L. 1967. "Social participation and happiness," *American Journal of Sociology,* 72 (5): 479–488.

Pollner, M. 1989. "Divine relations, social relations, and well-being," *Journal of Health and Social Behavior,* 30: 92–104.

Pressman, P., Lyons, J. S., Larson, D. B. and Gartner, J. 1992. "Religion, anxiety and fear of death," in Schumaker, J. F. (ed.), *Religion and mental health.* Oxford: Oxford University Press, pp. 98–109.

Proulx, C., Helms, H. and Buehler, C. 2007. "Marital quality and personal wellbeing: A meta-analysis," *Journal of Marriage and Family,* 69 (August): 576–593.

Reeves, R. 2014. "How to save marriage in America," *The Atlantic,* February 13.

Revkin, A. 2013. "Can Bhutan achieve hydropowered happiness?" *New York Times,* December 10.

Rotter, J. B. 1990. "Internal versus external control of reinforcement: A case history of a variable," *American Psychologist,* 45 (4): 489–493.

Ryback, T. W. 2012. "The UN happiness project," *New York Times,* March 28.

Sen, A. 1995. "Rationality and social choice," *American Economic Review,* 85 (1): 1–24.

Simon, H. 1978. "Rationality as a process and product of thought," *American Economic Review,* 68 (2): 1–16.

Smith, E. E. and Aaker, J. L. 2013. "Millennial searchers," *New York Times,* November 30.

Snoep, L. 2007. "Religiousness and happiness in three nations: A research note," *Journal of Happiness Studies,* 9: 207–211.

Soydemir, G. A., Bastida, E. and Gonzalez, G. 2004. "The impact of religiosity on self-assessments of health and happiness: Evidence from the US Southwest," *Applied Economics,* 36: 665–672.

Span, P. 2014. "Generation Y-Me," *New York Times,* January 14.

Stevenson, B. and Wolfers, J. 2009. "The paradox of declining female happiness," *NBER Working Papers,* no. 14969.

Stutzer, A. and Frey, B. 2006. "Does marriage make happy, or do happy people get married?" *Journal of Socio-Economics*, 35: 326–347.

Tullock, G. 1987. *Autocracy*. Dordrecht: Kluwer.

Vasak, K. 1977. "A 30 year struggle: the sustained efforts to give force of law to the Universal Declaration of Human Rights," *UNESCO Courier*, XXX, 11 (November): 28–29, 32.

Waite, N. and Gallagher, M. 2000. *The case for marriage*. New York: Doubleday.

Zakaria, F. 2003. *The future of freedom: Illiberal democracy at home and abroad*. New York/London: W. W. Norton.

7   Aristotelian virtue ethics
The forgotten philosophical tradition on happiness

Having surveyed the major themes of modern happiness research, two main criticisms come to mind. The first is that more than two and a half millennia's worth of philosophical investigations regarding happiness has been nonchalantly cast into oblivion, except, perhaps, for a few token references to Aristotle or Bentham. The second, largely as a consequence of the above, is the willful omission of virtue and its decisive role in the achievement of happiness.

Thanks to the excellent work of McMahon (2006), we can, in good conscience, excuse ourselves from the formidable challenge of explaining in detail the most significant contributions of each author and period to the philosophical understanding of happiness. McMahon (2006) elaborates an intellectual exploration – almost hegelian in breadth and depth – of the different conceptions of happiness, deftly interweaving strands of ethical, philosophical, political, and religious thought, set against a shifting and sometimes convulsive background of Western history. It would be sufficient for our purpose to outline the three main divisions he suggests: "tragic happiness," "perpetual felicity," and "the right to happiness," corresponding to ancient Greece, medieval Christendom, and the Enlightenment, respectively.

Ever since the time of Hesiod, happiness has been conceived as "tragic." This is so not only because, in the worldview of the ancient Greeks, suffering is widespread, almost as a permanent condition of humankind, but also because happiness is entirely beyond our control. Human wisdom, therefore, consists in the acknowledgment and resignation that happiness is a product of chance, the result of a whim of fortune or fate, a gift from frivolous gods (McMahon 2006). Despite reasonable variations, however, a certain consensus can be reached among Greek authors in the following points with regard to happiness (McMahon 2006: 65). First of all, it is objective, not subjective, and it encompasses the whole of one's life, not just disconnected or intermittent moments. Secondly, happiness is less a matter of feeling – pleasure and the senses do not deserve to be trusted – than of rational development. Thirdly, as the end or purpose (*telos*) of human life, it could only be attained through constant effort and discipline: it is virtue's reward, resulting from the harmony or balance among the various powers and faculties of the soul.

The ideal of "perpetual felicity" summarizes the notion of happiness within the medieval Judeo-Christian tradition, cognizant of its debts to Greco-Roman philosophy. This signals the abandonment of the temporal or worldly conception of happiness, dominant in the previous times. A more surprising change, however, is the espousal of suffering and, in particular, of martyrdom, as the one true path leading to the eternal goal. Hence the paradoxical proposals of finding pleasure in pain, joy in sorrow, life in death, and happiness in sadness (McMahon 2006).

It is difficult to find a more eloquent example of this than the passion or martyrdom of Sts. Perpetua and Felicity in the arena of Carthage. Vibia Perpetua was a liberally educated Roman noble who was still nursing a child and she was accompanied, among others, by Felicity, a servant, who herself had just given birth to a son, when they were both condemned to fight with gladiators and be fed to wild beasts for refusing to offer sacrifices to the emperor: "Now dawned the day of their victory, and they went forth from the prison into the amphitheater as it were to heaven, cheerful and bright of countenance; if they trembled at all, it was for joy, not for fear. Perpetua [...] glorious of presence, as a true spouse of Christ and darling of God; [...] Felicity likewise, rejoicing" (Shewring 1996).

Aquinas (*Summa Contra Gentiles*, book 3, chapter 48) unequivocally affirms that perfect happiness is not available in this life for the *homo viator* or wayfarer; it could only be achieved after death, with Christ in heaven. Without denying what the ancients taught about happiness as the supreme good and final end, or the role of virtue as its principal means or guide, the medieval schoolmen nonetheless believed that ultimately, happiness, like grace, is a divine gift which is out of proportion to all human striving (McMahon 2006).

Before the transition to the modern age, came the renaissance and the reformation, each of which introduced a slight twist in the understanding of happiness (McMahon 2006). By and large, during the renaissance period, the rediscovery of the classical world served to confirm its supportive and complementary character to Christianity's revealed truths. The reformation, on the other hand, triggered a shift in the locus of authority, from the institutional Church to the realm of individual conscience.

In the culture of the Enlightenment, happiness ceases to be "tragic" or a "divine gift." Instead, it becomes, above all, an entitlement or right grounded on human reason, consciousness, and freedom (McMahon 2006). Essentially, happiness consists in pleasure and good feeling, as Bentham (2000) defends. Or, as the physician and materialist philosopher La Mettrie (1987) declares more radically, it lies in a kind of pleasure without limit, one in which all stops have effectively been pulled. Of course, the condition for this is that all links between happiness, on the one hand, and truth, reason, nature, virtue, and even God, on the other, be actually severed. Since happiness is no longer a reward reserved for virtue and good behavior, anyone and everyone could now aspire to it and even demand it. It has become the sole "moral obligation" against which success or failure in life is to be measured. There is no reason for anyone not to be happy, here and now. Flowing from the individual's right to happiness is the right to change or remove whatever obstacle that may stand in the way.

In the succeeding pages, we shall turn to virtue, the other major casualty of modern happiness studies' neglect. We are certainly aware that virtue, even only in its particular relation to happiness, already covers a scope wide enough to merit its own intellectual history (Annas 1993). However, our intention here is going to be far more modest. It is to show how much Aristotelian virtue has to offer by way of explanatory power to a great number of issues that continue to befuddle even the best of modern happiness research. It is interesting to note that Aquinas (*Summa Theologiae*, part I, question 62, article 1) does not regard Aristotle's views regarding happiness to be wrong, but simply incomplete, due to the fact that he was not yet aware of divine revelation. To be sure, although Aristotle had no notice of the "beatific vision" (seeing God as He is), he did indeed entertain the possibility of happiness as contemplation (*theoria*) even in this world. Our wager is that Aristotle wasn't wide off the mark either in most of the things he said regarding virtue in relation to happiness (*eudaimonia*). What does Aristotle's architecture of happiness look like? What is virtue's role within it?

POLITICS, ECONOMY, AND ETHICS

"Politics" in Aristotle could mean at least three different things. It could refer to a kind of life (*Nicomachean Ethics*, henceforth NE, 1095b), a qualifier for the virtues of justice (NE 1129b) and prudence (NE 1140b), or a body of knowledge (NE 1094a). We shall focus primarily on this last definition. As a body of knowledge or discipline, its object is none other than happiness (*eudaimonia*), the supreme human good and final end of all other goods (NE 1094b). Precisely because of the superiority of its object, politics deserves to be called the highest ruling discipline, that which governs or controls all other bodies of knowledge (NE 1094a–b). Aristotle defines the good as "that at which everything aims" (NE 1094a); the end of an appetite, desire, inclination or tendency; that which satisfies them. He also tells us that all goods can be classified into two: those pursued in themselves and those pursued for the sake of another (NE 1094a). Happiness belongs to the first of these. In fact, among the various goods pursued in themselves, happiness is the highest, because everything else is pursued only insofar as it leads to happiness (while happiness leads to nothing beyond itself). Similarly, happiness is described as being complete and self-sufficient (NE 1097b): as a good, it lacks nothing; it encompasses all other goods.

Apart from these formal characteristics, Aristotle informs us about the "content" of happiness as well. It is not a mere object of knowledge (*gnosis*), but also of action (*praxis*); in particular, it consists in "living or doing well" (NE 1095a), in accordance with the proper function of human beings, which is rational activity (NE 1098a). Aristotle considers reason to be the highest of all human powers, and happiness, therefore, cannot be anything other than reason functioning at its best. "Virtue" (*arete*) is the expression he uses to indicate excellence in human functioning (NE 1098a). Thus, happiness is linked to the exercise of the most perfect virtue in human beings, that of contemplation (*theoria*) (NE 1177a). Immediately after, however, Aristotle tones down his teaching, acknowledging that, perhaps, such a life of contemplation is more proper to the gods than to human beings (NE 1177b).

Without entirely discounting the possibility of contemplation for happiness, Aristotle, nevertheless, tries a different tack. He shifts from an "intellectualist" account of happiness to a "comprehensive" one (Nagel 1972). Starting off from his account of human nature as that of a "political animal" (the *Politics*, henceforth Pltcs, 1253a) – that is, an animal that lives in the *polis* or state and makes use of words or speech (*logos*) – he recasts happiness within the more accessible context of a political community. For Aristotle, political communities (*poleis*, the plural form of *polis*) – together with families and villages – are "natural" societies on account of their end or purpose (Pltcs 1252b). Families take care of the day-to-day needs for survival, while villages, which come about from the union of several families living in the same place, attend to the necessities beyond the daily ones. But only political communities are big and complex enough to provide all the means necessary for a full, flourishing life. That is why political communities are regarded as "perfect," because they are "self-sufficient" for the end that they seek, which is happiness (*eudaimonia*) (Pltcs 1253a).

From this point onwards, Aristotle's investigation revolves around the best form of government, always based on the assumption that this is what would make happiness possible (NE 1181b, Pltcs 1260b). He explores the different forms of government or regimes, classified according to how property is owned (constitutions): whether citizens should have everything in common, or nothing in common, or some things in common and others, not (Pltcs 1261a). He surveys a number of theoretical as well as historical regimes, analyzing their accomplishments and weaknesses (Pltcs 1261a–1274b). Only then does he put forward his own proposal, establishing a clear division between regimes at the service of the common good and those at the service of private, individual goods (Pltcs 1278b–1287b, NE 1160b–1161a). He further subdivides the regimes of the common good depending on the number of rulers, calling them "monarchies," if there is but one, "aristocracies," if there are a few, and "republics" (politeiai), if everyone rules. Similarly, regimes serving private, individual goods are subdivided into "tyrannies," in the case of a single ruler who seeks power above all, "oligarchies," in the case of several rulers who primarily seek wealth, and "democracies," when everybody rules in pursuit of each one's own pleasure.

He then continues to study the events that are most likely to lead to the preservation and destruction of each kind of regime (Pltcs 1301a–1316a). Upon reaching this stage, Aristotle explains that, although in theory, monarchies are the best regimes, in practice – which is what in the end counts – a "mixed constitutional regime," a cross or hybrid between oligarchies and democracies, is preferable (Pltcs 1295a–1300b). He reasons out that, in such a regime, there will be a dominant middle class, with enough property to procure for itself sufficient pleasures without coveting the property of others, but not so much that it could afford to ignore public deliberations regarding what is just in laws and customs. Above all, such a middle class would control and temper society's extremes, thereby guaranteeing political stability.

Having established the political community as context and the "mixed constitutional regime" as the best form of government in practice, Aristotle now inquires about other necessary elements for happiness. Two complementary accounts are found. One lists food, arts, arms, revenue, religion, and decision-making power over the public interest and justice (Pltcs 1328b); while another enumerates external goods, goods of the body, and goods of the soul, also known as excellences or virtues (Pltcs 1323a). This second one also indicates the order or hierarchy to be observed. External and bodily goods are to be sought as means or conditions for the goods of the soul and the virtues: "the best life, both for individuals and states, is the life of excellence, when excellence has external goods enough for the performance of good actions" (Pltcs 1324a). In other words, for happiness to be achieved, we need, on the one hand, material resources (external and bodily goods), and on the other, non-material powers (internal goods of the soul, excellences, or virtues); bearing in mind that material resources are instruments at the service of the non-material powers.

With regard to material resources, Aristotle states: "the happy person is a human being, and so will need external prosperity also; for his nature is not self-sufficient for study, but he needs a healthy body, and needs to have food and the other services provided" (NE 1178b). Likewise, he adds: "happiness evidently also needs external goods [. . .] since we cannot, or cannot easily, do fine actions if we lack resources" (NE 1099a). Yet he also recognizes that a moderate amount of material goods is sufficient: "we can do fine actions even if we do not rule earth and sea; for even from moderate resources we can do the actions expressing virtue. [. . .] It is enough if moderate resources are provided; for the life of someone whose activity expresses virtue will be happy" (NE 1179a). For material resources belong to that class of goods pursued not in themselves but for the sake of others; and their purpose is to allow us to perform virtuous actions and acquire the goods of the soul: "it is for the sake of the soul that goods external and goods of the body are desirable at all" (Pltcs 1323b).

Granted that happiness rests on material resources and non-material powers of the soul, there ought to be two other disciplines corresponding to each one of the above; these, in turn, are subordinated to politics. For Aristotle, these are economy (*oikono-mia*), related to external, bodily goods, and ethics (*ethike*), related to internal goods of the soul or virtues. We shall now explain each one of these branches of knowledge as it contributes to the overall political goal of happiness.

Aristotle relates that economy originated in the family, as "household management" (Pltcs 1253b). Thus, his treatise on economy begins with a survey of the different parts and relationships necessary for a complete household:

> the first and fewest possible parts of a family are master and slave, husband and wife, father and children. We have therefore to consider what each of these three relations is and ought to be: – I mean the relation of master and servant, the marriage relation (the conjunction of man and wife has no name of its own), and thirdly, the paternal relation (this also has no proper name).   *(Pltcs 1253b)*

In the first place, marriage, which binds husbands and wives to each other, is needed to ensure the birth and education of children, and to provide the state with citizens. Moreover, as a stable and exclusive relationship, marriage assures both husband and wife mutual help in the face of life's difficulties. Next, reflecting a general belief that children belong to the father, the second relation is called "paternal." Certainly, no child is born without a mother. However, what she represents is, at most, a passive principle in the generation, something like the soil or the "matter." In a paternalistic and patriarchal society, the offspring belong to the male. It is he who contributes the active principle, the seed or the "form." Finally, one could ask why the third relation of master and servant is essential to economy. The reason is that slaves constitute a very valuable form of property – broadly understood to encompass all material things indispensable for the good life. However, there are different kinds of property: some living, others lifeless. "And so, in the arrangement of the family, a slave is a living possession, [...] and the servant is himself an instrument for instruments" (Pltcs 1253b). Slaves, therefore, almost like livestock, are a form of living property no family could do without. Their partic- ular usefulness lies in carrying out their master's will (Pltcs 1254a). Another division in property is between "instruments of production (*poiesis*)" and "instruments of action (*praxis*)" (Pltcs 1254a). Instru- ments of production yield something else, like the weaving loom or shuttle yields cloth; while instruments of action yield nothing more than their use, as when a garment is worn or a bed is slept on. Once again, Aristotle defends the superiority of action over production.

Also crucial to Aristotle's understanding of economy is the dis- tinction between the art of wealth usage (economy proper) and the art of wealth acquisition or chrematistics (Pltcs 1253b). In both, he acknowledges the difference between a natural and a non-natural form. Let's begin with the art of acquiring and producing wealth or chrematistics. Natural chrematistics pertains to the provision of "such things necessary to life, and useful for the community of the family or state, as can be stored" (Pltcs 1256b), whereas non-natural chrematistics refers to the supply of "riches and property [which] have no limit" (Pltcs 1267a). Natural chrematistics is premised on the belief that the kind and amount of property needed for a life of happiness has boundaries or limits. Beyond this, the accumulation of material things is more of an obstacle than a help. Non-natural chrematistics, on the other hand, presupposes that "more is always better"; hence, there should be no end in amassing wealth and posses- sions. An example of non-natural chrematistics is retail trade, which allows one to multiply riches in the form of money or coins. However, as Aristotle argues:

> coined money is a mere sham, a thing not natural, but conven- tional only, because, if users substitute another commodity for it, it is worthless, and because it is not useful as a means to any of the necessities of life, and, indeed, he who is rich in coin may often be in want of necessary food. But how can that be wealth of which a man may have great abundance and yet perish with hunger?
>
> *(Pltcs 1257b)*

Continuing his criticism of non-natural chrematistics, Aristotle indicates that "in the first community, indeed, which is the family, this art is obviously of no use, but it begins to be useful when the society increases. For the members of the family originally had all things in common" (Pltcs 1257b). Non-natural chrematistics develops when families grow and society becomes more complex, making the widespread use of money almost inevitable: "when the inhabitants of one country became more dependent on those of another, and they imported what they needed, and exported what they had too much of, money necessarily came into use" (Pltcs 1257a). Together with the rise of these new activities comes the need to create larger organizations, first as extensions of the family and later on as "economic friendships" (Pltcs 1280b).

Let us now return to the second art, that of wealth usage or economy proper. Aristotle teaches that wealth usage is superior to chrematistics, because the acquisition or production of wealth only ought to be carried out with a view to its use and enjoyment. Certainly, without resources, there would be nothing for economy to administer. Hence, the importance of chrematistics, concerned with the production and provision of material means. Yet, chrematistics as such is only a secondary function for the household manager. His main duty is "to order the things which nature supplies – he may be compared to the weaver who has not to make but to use wool, and to know, too, what sort of wool is good and serviceable or bad an unserviceable" (Pltcs 1258a). Economy, therefore, deals more directly with the use of material resources and property than with their procurement and production. The latter activities Aristotle entrusts to nature: "the means of life must be provided beforehand by nature; for the business of nature is to furnish food to that which is born, and the food of the offspring is always what remains over that from which it is produced" (Pltcs 1258a).

Aristotle goes on to offer examples of the natural and the non-natural forms of wealth usage or economy proper. In the first case, he speaks of shoes: if they are worn, one makes a proper use, but if used for exchange, it's an improper use, "for a shoe is not made to be an object of barter" (Pltcs 1257a). The proper use of material possession recognizes a limit that makes it honorable; whereas an improper use is void of limit and, so, justly censurable. To illustrate the unnatural use of wealth Aristotle turns to "usury, which makes a gain out of money itself [...] For money was intended to be used in exchange, but not to increase at interest" (Pltcs 1258b).

It is important to realize that the difference between the natural and the non-natural in both the acquisition and the use of wealth depends on the interior dispositions of human beings, not on the material things themselves (Pltcs 1257b–1258a). Unbridled desires of wealth and pleasure lead human beings to engage in non-natural forms of acquiring and using material possessions. Thus, their efforts to attain happiness or flourishing become self-defeating. However, such failure is the fault not of material things themselves, but of the individual's untutored desires or vices.

After this brief sketch of Aristotle's overarching political theory, we may inquire how organizations such as firms fit in. Although he does not mention firms explicitly, we can find allusions to them in the "family connections, brotherhoods, common sacrifices and amusements" (Pltcs 1280b) that draw human beings together. Unlike families, villages, and states, firms are "artificial" societies; they don't arise directly from human nature. Rather, firms come about through voluntary bonds of "friendship" – we would now say "contracts" – agreed upon by citizens. Also, they are called "imperfect" societies because they do not suffice for happiness or the good life. Firms are examples of "intermediate bodies or associations" situated between families and the state. As such, they are not meant to substitute families in the provision of daily needs, or political communities as the locus of full flourishing. Their purpose is limited to supplying some of the necessary means – specific goods and services – for the good life that families in themselves are unable to provide (Pltcs 1280b).

In particular, how do firms, as a class of intermediate groups, connect with the state? Founded on voluntary and contingent agreements, they are nevertheless vital to the welfare of society, thanks to the goods and services they produce and supply. Not that any concrete business organization – "Acme and Co.," for example – is itself necessary; but the bread-making function, for instance, that it performs may be deemed essential.

There exists a reciprocal relationship between the state and intermediate groups such as firms, known by the name of "subsidiarity" (Pontifical Council for Justice and Peace 2004: 186–187). This means that although both the state and intermediate groups have their own objectives and spheres of action, nevertheless, they owe each other mutual respect and assistance ("solidarity"). Specifically, the state's role with regard to intermediate associations has a double dimension. On the one hand, it is incumbent upon the state, as the superior-order society, to positively help, support, and assist lesser-order intermediate bodies, among which firms are included. On the other hand, phrased negatively, the state should refrain from substituting or absorbing these intermediate groups and appropriating their functions. By encouraging the growth and development of intermediate associations as private initiatives, the state contributes to a healthy pluralism and diversity in society. A well-governed state is one that delegates to these intermediate groups tasks they could carry out more effectively, since they are in closer contact with the people and know their needs and desires better. By acting thus, the state makes a more rational and efficient use of resources, focusing on matters such as defense, foreign relations, the administration of justice, and so forth, that are of its exclusive competence. Subsidiarity acts as a safeguard against various forms of statism, such as centralization, bureaucratization, welfarism, and paternalism. Most important, it protects against a self-serving state, ensuring that the state serves citizens instead.

Insofar as business organizations participate in the production of goods and services for the benefit of society, they operate within the realm of chrematistics. In particular, firms are meant to help or complement families and nature in providing the material resources necessary for happiness or the good life. Thus, business activity falls into the category of non-natural chrematistics. In this sense, businesses are called upon to fulfill a very important, but nonetheless subordinate role in economy, which "attends more to men than to the acquisition of inanimate things, and to human excellence more than to the excellence of property which we call wealth, and to the excellence of freemen more than to the excellence of slaves" (Pltcs 1259b). For, as we have seen, the main purpose of economy is to facilitate the development of human excellence and the virtues by creating favorable material conditions for their practice. Only by the hand of the virtues will the material resources provided by economy help people to attain their ultimate objective of happiness and full flourishing.

In summary, business firms belong to the realm of economy as a class of artificial, intermediate bodies. Their purpose is the non-natural acquisition or provision of material goods. Having chrematistics as their function, business firms and corporations are subject to economy proper, the use of material goods. For their correct functioning, however, economic activities and institutions turn to ethics. A good economy is one which establishes favorable material conditions for the practice of the virtues. And together, material goods and virtues enable citizens to attain happiness or a flourishing life in the state, which is the ultimate objective of politics.

THE ANALOGY OF THE VIRTUES

The time has come to explain the role of ethics and its object, the non-material powers of the soul or the virtues, in happiness (Annas 2011). Initially, Aristotelian virtues are often defined in terms of "character traits." As a result, virtues end up being identified almost exclusively with them. Character traits, however, do not exhaust the realm of the virtues; they are mere parts that should not be mistaken for the whole. Etymologically, "virtue" comes from the Latin word *virtus*, which in turn originates from "vis," meaning "force," "power," or "strength." *Virtus* is the Latin translation of what was, originally, a Greek concept, *arete*, which stands for "what is best" or "excellence" in human beings. "Virtue," then, means "what is best in human beings" or "human excellence."

Although virtue, as "excellence," may apply primarily to character, nevertheless, it also refers to other human capacities or dispositions for action, such as habits (NE 1103a). A virtuous character, in fact, comes from the cultivation of virtuous habits. Virtuous habits themselves result from the repeated performance of virtuous actions, and virtuous actions, in turn, arise from one's having nurtured virtuous inclinations or tendencies. Virtuous inclinations and tendencies are precisely those that are in accordance with human nature and its final end or happiness. Therefore, apart from character and character traits, a conscientious reading of Aristotle reveals that virtues as "excellences" also designate, analogously, inclinations and tendencies, actions, habits, and, indeed, even lives taken as a whole. Virtues are what Hursthouse (2013) calls "multi-track dispositions" attributable to a "certain sort of person with a certain complex mindset." We shall now expound on how the virtues as "excellences" may be present in each of these capacities or dispositions.

Virtues in actions

Aristotelian ethics is distinctively premised on a "proper human function" (*ergon*) in which everyone by nature engages. This consists in "some sort of life of action of the [part of the soul] that has reason" (NE 1098a). Such human function, specifically, expresses reason. Human excellence or virtue, therefore, resides in fulfilling this function in accordance with reason finely and well: "the human good turns out to be the soul's activity that expresses virtue" (NE 1098a).

These human actions are also called voluntary actions. (Involuntary acts are those which occur due to some irrational force of nature, in which people are involved as merely passive subjects. Voluntary actions proceed from an internal principle in the agent (appetite, feeling, desire, or will), accompanied by knowledge of purpose and the means to attain it. The agent performs these actions intentionally and deliberately (NE 1111a). Only voluntary actions, then, are truly human actions. They are capable of binding agents, such that they become objects of value judgments: of praise, if good, or of blame, if evil. Virtues are good voluntary actions. Their moral valence comes from a triple source: the object of the action, the end or intention with which the agent carries it out, and the circumstances in which it is performed. The moral goodness, excellence, or virtue of voluntary actions requires the integrity of all three, and any defect or flaw would render them evil.

Virtues in habits

Habits develop from the repetition of voluntary actions (NE 1103a). Every action leaves a trace or mark. This by-product is called "habit": a stable disposition or manner of being, doing, acting, or behaving. Habits enable people to perform more actions of a certain kind and to perform them better, not only from the objective viewpoint of the actions themselves, but also from the subjective viewpoint, in terms of the agent's "skill," pleasure or satisfaction. Just like "automatic mechanisms," habits allow agents to direct thoughts and energies to other concerns, giving them greater freedom of action.

Aristotle differentiates habits, which are free and changeable, from natural conditions, which are innate and permanent. Unlike natural conditions, where capacities precede activities, in habits, the activities themselves create capacities. The creation of a capacity and the exercise of an activity require each other; they occur simultaneously and become mutually reinforcing. A purely sequential mode of thinking is not appropriate in understanding the dynamics of habits. Habits comprise an integrated feedback loop that increases human potential. They are produced when human beings – by choice, counting on nature – perform voluntary actions, and those voluntary actions, once finished, leave traces or modifications that agents retain. Those modifications are stable dispositions to further actions in a specific manner, toward a certain goal or direction. They are called "habits," for they vest human nature with new, improved, and reinforced tendencies. Thus, habits constitute a "second nature" for human beings.

Both good and bad habits arise from the repetition of actions (NE 1103b). But in the same way that only the right sorts of action produce craft expertise, only good actions produce good habits. How are we to distinguish the right from the wrong sort of habituation? First and foremost, to acquire proper habituation, "actions should express correct reason" (NE 1103b). Individual actions whose repetition constitutes a habit should be done in accordance with reason; not in the abstract, but as what is opportune in each particular case, as expert doctors or navigators decide in practice. Secondly, right habituation equally shuns excess and defect (NE 1104a). Thirdly, proper habituation comes from an individual's experiencing pleasure or pain in the appropriate kind of action (NE 1104b). In summary, with respect to a good habit, "virtue is a state that decides, [consisting] in a mean, the mean relative to us, which is defined by reference to reason, i.e., to the reason by reference to which the intelligent person would define it. It is a mean between two vices, one of excess and one of deficiency" (NE 1107a).

Virtues in character

Just as a habit unifies many different acts of a person, character integrates diverse habits into a whole. Character accounts for the various habits a person possesses and the degree of perfection or development of each one. At first, there may be some confusion whether virtue of character is a feeling, a capacity, or a state of the soul or mind. By feelings, Aristotle understands "appetite, anger, fear, confidence, envy, joy, love, hate, longing, jealousy, pity, in general, whatever implies pleasure or pain" (NE 1105a). But he quickly disqualifies them as virtue of character, for one is neither praised nor blamed for merely experiencing feelings, since they arise by nature, without choice or consent. And virtues – like vices – are character traits for which one is rightly praised or blamed, precisely because they are products of his own volition. In virtues one plays an active role, while with feelings, one is passive.

Aristotle's reasons for precluding capacities from the virtues of character are similar (NE 1106a). Virtue of character is acquired; it cannot be a natural capacity. The disqualification of innate feelings and capacities underscores the difference between a person's natural temperament or *pathos*, and his acquired character or *ethos*. *Pathos* refers to an innate, spontaneous, and pre-moral personality. This is sometimes confusingly called "natural virtue." *Ethos*, on the other hand, results from deliberate and intentional acts, and as such is matter for moral responsibility. The transformation from *pathos* to *ethos*, from natural temperament to acquired character, occurs through a lifelong process of learning and practice through which a person constantly reforms his character.

Aristotle arrives at character states, then, as the proper genus for virtue by elimination (NE 1106a). Virtue of character is a good state that causes its possessor to perform his specific function well (NE 1106a). It is valued both for its instrumental or extrinsic worth (it enables one to perform his function well) as for its absolute or intrinsic worth (it makes one a good human being). The right character state, like the good habit, lies in a mean. However, virtue of character is not a numerical mean in respect of an object, but one relative to agents. Virtue of character is an intermediate state that eschews both the superfluous and the deficient (NE 1106b).

Aristotle clarifies further the relation between virtue of character as a mean and the extremes. Firstly, virtue is contrary to either one of the extremes (NE 1108b). However, the extremes are more opposed to each other than to the mean (NE 1108b). In certain cases, due to the object of the character state itself or our own natural tendency, one extreme is more opposed to the mean than the other. For example, cowardice, the vice of excess, is more opposed to the virtue of bravery than rashness, the vice of deficiency. Similarly, granted our greater natural tendency towards pleasure, intemperance or the vice of excess is more opposed to the mean of temperance than insensibility, the vice of deficiency.

How do we acquire virtues of character? For Aristotle, hitting the mark between two vices entails hard work and is, thus, praiseworthy (NE 1109a). Nevertheless, he offers some bits of advice. Since virtue of character lies in the mean, Aristotle admonishes us, first, to avoid the more opposed extreme (NE 1109a). With regard to courage, for example, it would be better to err on the side of rashness (excess) than on cowardice (defect), because cowardice is the more contrary extreme. Secondly, he suggests that one avoid the easier extreme, depending on his natural inclination or drift (NE 1109b). Aristotle also warns that we should be extremely careful with pleasures (NE 1109b). Indeed, the tendency for the majority is towards intemperance rather than insensibility.

As a final note, Aristotle tells us that rules do not give exact and detailed guidance. This is due not to any defect in the rules, but to the very nature of their objects. Virtues of character deal with concrete, contingent actions and feelings that cannot be covered by general, theoretical accounts (NE 1109b). He remits us ultimately to the perception of a virtuous person, who alone is the competent judge. What matters most in ethics is the kind of person one is, such that right actions, habits, and character are defined in reference to the virtuous person (Hartman 2013). Indeed, having virtue of character is not so much a matter of feeling or acting, as doing so "at the right times, about the right things, towards the right people, for the right end, and in the right way, [that] is, the intermediate and best condition, and this is proper virtue" (NE 1106b). Thus, hitting the mark could only be achieved heuristically. That is why Aristotle says that virtue of character depends on contingent and subjective conditions: "this is not one, and is not the same for everyone" (NE 1106a). Beyond actions or feelings of baseness (NE 1107a), it is up to each one to discover the appropriate virtuous character state. Thus, people of virtuous character are all virtuous in their own particular ways.

Virtues in lifestyles

Despite the terminological agreement that "doing well" and "living well" are the same as "being happy," not everyone coincides on what this kind of life entails. Thus, Aristotle explores four different lifestyles vying for happiness (*eudaimonia*). Firstly, he considers a life centered on wealth or money (NE 1096a). Aristotle does not have a positive judgment of this life because money belongs to things desirable only instrumentally; and a basic condition for a life of happiness is that it be in relation to something good in itself, to the supreme good and final end for human beings (Skidelsky 2009). The value of money, however, lies in its usefulness in exchange for some other object. Money, therefore, represents a means, not an end. However, as we have already seen, Aristotle's contempt for material wealth is not absolute; albeit "external," he still considers it a "good." He recognizes that a certain prosperity is necessary for happiness (NE 1099a–b).

The next contender for happiness is a life dedicated to pleasure or bodily gratification (NE 1095b). Aristotle attributes this choice to the majority of the population, to "the most vulgar," to those without proper education. Neither does this option convince him, for such a life is "completely slavish" and more proper to "grazing animals" than to human beings. Not that Aristotle doubts the appeal of pleasure. But endowed with reason, humans should aspire for higher things than mere sensorial satisfaction. Similarly, Aristotle ascribes this choice to many people in positions of power who behave as slaves of self-gratification.

The third option is a life of action, a political life dedicated to the pursuit of honor (NE 1095b). A political life seems reserved to a cultivated few in society. However, Aristotle does not agree with this choice either. For although honor is certainly more elevated than pleasure, it "appears to be too superficial to be what we are seeking, since it seems to depend more on those who honor than on the one who is honored, whereas we intuitively believe that the good is something of our own and hard to take from us" (NE 1095b). The most satisfying kind of life ought to be one's own doing. But honor is something we receive from others. For Aristotle, this is too big a risk. Furthermore, honor is rendered for a reason. One should, then, investigate the grounds for praise. We seek to be honored not just by anyone, but by people who know us; and we seek to be honored by intelligent people, rather than by the foolish. What we seek, therefore, is to be honored for our virtue (NE 1095b).

What kind of lifestyle is, in absolute terms, the best? For Aristotle, it is a life of contemplation or study (*theoria*), insofar as it represents the highest form of virtue for human beings (NE 1177a). Aristotle enumerates some distinctive features of a life of contemplative virtue. Firstly, it is a self-contained activity, one that includes its own end (NE 1098b). Secondly, a life of virtue is pleasant in itself, for being pleased is a condition of the soul included in its own proper activity (NE 1099a). And thirdly, a life of virtue is in accordance with reason and sound judgment (NE 1099a). Indeed, reason is man's superior faculty, and in a life of contemplative virtue, it revolves around the noblest objects, the immutable and eternal realities (NE 1100b).

The note on the stability, continuity, or permanence of a life of contemplative virtue is mainly in response to the issue that happiness requires a complete life, one no longer subject to reversals of fortune (NE 1100a). Rather than conclude that we have to wait until death to definitively pronounce one happy, we simply say that virtue is the stable and controlling element in a life of happiness (NE 1100b). Thus, true happiness (*eudaimonia*) consists in a life of contemplative virtue. Due to its nobility, self-sufficiency, pleasantness, and continuity, Aristotle describes it as a life inclusive of all good, certainly more proper to the gods than to human beings (NE 1177b).

Thus far we have given an account of the Aristotelian architecture of happiness (*eudaimonia*). It is the proper object of politics, and thus, it could only be achieved within the context of a complete – with families, villages, and a myriad of intermediate institutions – and well-governed political community. Subordinated to politics, however, are two equally necessary disciplines. One is economy, concerned with the administration (including the production, acquisition, and use) of material resources necessary to the good life. And the other is ethics, which looks to the development of the goods of the soul or the virtues, present in different levels of human agency. Economy, however, ought to be subject to ethics, since the limits to the acquisition and use of material objects are not found in the things themselves, but in virtuous dispositions. In other words, without the virtues, no abundance of material resources could ever lead to happiness. It could even do more harm than good.

YESTERDAY'S ANSWERS TO TODAY'S QUESTIONS

We shall now proceed to show how the Aristotelian account of *eudaimonia* helps respond to most of the pressing issues raised within modern happiness studies in the previous chapters. Our purpose here is certainly not to discredit the valuable gains achieved by welfare economics and hedonic psychology, among other branches of knowledge, through their own methods and procedures, in clarifying the true nature of happiness. Rather, it is to show how much more can be accomplished in present-day happiness research, if only we were to recover – at the very least – inputs from the Aristotelian strands of a much broader and deeper philosophical tradition of investigation.

In Chapter 1, we introduced "individual subjective wellbeing" as the object of study for a new group of scientific disciplines, collectively known as modern happiness studies. We immediately referred to its distinctive features of being "quantitative" and "empirical," while explaining the appropriateness and advantages of such an approach compared to the ones previously employed. However, we also indicated a range of problems encountered in measurement, which understandably carried over to correlations with other known quantities, such as income. The empirical or "experiential" characteristic of happiness reinforces Aristotle's intuition of *eudaimonia* as something practical (*praxis*), an activity performed by an individual in accordance with reason; living or doing well (NE 1095a, 1098a). That is, insofar as it is a good, an end, or an object of desire, happiness is not to be confused at all with universal and abstract ideas, as Aristotle's teacher, Plato, was said to have defended. Unlike Plato, Aristotle denied the separate existence of a world of ideas; and the only world he knew, the only one that truly interested him, was this world of individual and concrete realities. If happiness were real, therefore, it had to be found in the here and now, in this world which human beings inhabit. The goal or aim that Aristotelian politics pursues as a practical form of knowledge (and by extension, ethics and economics as well, as disciplines subordinated to politics) is not simply to elaborate a theory, but to effect a change in this worldly state of things. Happiness, mainly, is not a matter to be thought about, but one to be lived and experienced by real individuals of flesh and blood.

To say that the only real world is this material one is not the same as to affirm that only what is material is real. Aristotle obviously acknowledged the existence of non-material realities such as the soul (*psyche*) or life-giving principle. In fact, happiness (*eudaimonia*) itself is not material, strictly speaking, although it definitely has material manifestations and conditions. (Similarly, neither the heart-beat nor breathing in itself is the cause, but only a sign of life.) Hence, happiness cannot be reduced to the intensity of electrical impulses in some regions of the brain or to the concentration of certain hormones in a person's bloodstream, for example. At most, these physical phenomena are just indicators of something else which itself is not physical and, therefore, is not directly measurable either.

This confusion between cause and effect, between a non-material reality and its physical or material sign, is the root of many problems besieging modern happiness studies. That the material alone is directly affected by "quantity," meaning that only it has "extension" or "parts alongside parts," seems to have been forgotten. As Aristotle (*The Categories*, book 6) clarifies, material things are divided into the "continuous," when contiguous parts bear a relative position to each other, as in the case of lines, planes, surfaces, solids, and so forth, and the "discrete," when there is no way to show these relative positions because parts do not even have a lasting existence, such as in the case of numbers and time, among other things. We can see that none of these applies directly to happiness. If ever we use "parts," "quantities," and "numbers" to speak of happiness, we do so only by way of comparison, metaphorically or analogously, as if happiness were a material thing or had a body, which obviously it does not. Unfortunately, the use of polls and scales assigning relative values and numbers to happiness tends to overlook this inherent limitation.

Granted that happiness is not material (it has no color, shape, size, smell, sound, taste, or texture) or quantitative (it has no real parts, continuous or discrete), except indirectly, in the strictest of terms, it cannot be measured. Aristotle again offers some guidance in this issue through some considerations regarding the purpose of measurement. After establishing politics as a rational activity, he adds that it is not, however, an exact science (NE 1094b). But this lack of accuracy should not be taken to detract from the excellence of politics, because the same degree of precision or exactness (akribeia) could not be expected in all sorts of discussions. It should be sufficient in each case for scientific knowledge to adequately capture whatever amount of clarity the subject matter itself allowed, no more, no less.

Therefore, research in politics – and, by inclusion, investigations regarding happiness – should be quite content to arrive at a broad outline of the truth, "since we argue from and about what holds good usually [but not universally]" (NE 1094b). In other words, we ought to be satisfied drawing more or less generalizable conclusions rather than laws or strict and fast rules from propositions. For as Aristotle himself reasons out, "the educated person seeks exactness in each area to the extent that the nature of the subject allows; for apparently it is just as mistaken to demand demonstrations from a rhetorician as to accept [merely] persuasive arguments from a mathematician" (NE 1094b). However, accepting the limitations on precision need not imply a renunciation of measurement itself, or of its usefulness for some particular purpose. Therefore, it's not that modern happiness studies has to do away with measurements; but it needs to bear in mind, while dealing with those numbers, that it is not engaged in physics.

Apart from precision in measurement, another source of tension in modern happiness studies springs from the dichotomy between the objective (broadly economic) and the subjective (broadly psychological) approaches (Kraut 1979). The insistence on the objective arises in response to the demands of rationality: happiness cannot just be whatever one pleases, but should instead have a common basis in universal human experience. The emphasis on the subjective, on the other hand, relates to the requirement of individual freedom: regardless of what other people or society as a whole may say, one ought to have a determining role in one's own happiness. Aristotle assumes the logic of both perspectives by putting forward the virtuous, prudent person as the authoritative judge of whether or not one is truly happy. The verdict of the virtuous person alone strikes the proper balance between the objective prerequisite of rationality and rootedness in human nature, and the subjective need for individual freedom (Sizer 2010). But where does the virtue of prudence come from?

Like all virtues, prudence is not innate; but once gained, it seems to be a natural state. This misleads many to think that it is impossible to acquire virtue, because to become prudent – for example – one must first do prudent actions. Yet prudent actions could only be done by one who is already prudent! This circularity makes us think that either one is already by nature prudent (and therefore, performs prudent actions) or one is not. And being incapable by nature of prudent actions, no amount of habituation will ever make one prudent.

Aristotle offers some clarifications which, besides undoing this paradox, also serve to establish the limits of the craft analogy in the virtues. In the crafts, one may produce something that conforms to a certain expertise only in appearance. The object could have been produced "by chance or by following someone else's instructions" (NE 1105a): that is, without accompanying knowledge. Furthermore, "the products of a craft determine by their own character whether they have been produced well; and so it suffices that they are in the right state when they have been produced" (NE 1105b). Craft products have an objective goodness or excellence without need of reference to the craftsman.

But there is no such thing as an objectively virtuous action in itself considered, independently of the person who performs it. A virtuous act could never be separated from the virtuous habit that it emerges from, or ultimately, from the virtuous person who possesses the habit. There is a feedback loop along the full range of human dispositions that are analogues of virtue. For an action to be virtuous, it has to be performed as a virtuous person would, and this entails three conditions: knowledge or advertence that one is doing a virtuous act; the will or decision to do the virtuous act for itself, not for any other purpose; and lastly, the presence of a habit – that "firm and unchanging state" – from which the virtuous act proceeds (NE 1105a). Insofar as virtuous actions do not occur in a void but in concrete situations, prudence will always be necessary.

The insistence not only on the external, objective conditions surrounding a virtuous act, but also on its internal, subjective conditions is indeed very important. Virtue cannot be confined to what is merely apparent, what is only superficially good (NE 1106a). Virtue demands integrity; a complete, thorough, and integral goodness. Therefore, rather than any form of partial goodness or excellence, "the virtue of a human being will likewise be the state that makes a human being good and makes him perform his function well" (NE 1106a). The virtue of prudence produces an alignment among right thinking or perception, right desire, and right action; it creates harmony among reason, sensibility or emotions, and behavior. Thus, we can distinguish among one who is weak-willed (akrasia) and acts against his better judgment, another who simply practices self-control or is continent (enkrateia), and a third who possesses the virtue of temperance or moderation (NE 1145a–1152a). The first acts contrary to reason, the second experiences desires contrary to his actual behavior, while in the third, desires and behavior are in synch with his character state. Apart from temperance or moderation, the third also displays prudence. Although these three individuals may be performing exactly the same objective actions from the perspective of a neutral, third-party observer, only the third practices virtue. The virtuous, prudent person alone can exercise the proper judgment necessary to tell them apart.

In accordance with Aristotelian thought (NE 1145a), prudence is considered the charioteer that guides and the mother that begets all other virtues; without it, no other genuine virtue would be possible.

This is due to a two-step reasoning. Firstly, all virtues essentially involve practical, normative knowledge just like prudence, and secondly, knowledge is essentially unified, for to evaluate something is to compare it relative to the value of others. There exists, therefore, a unity among the virtues, such that an individual cannot have one moral virtue without the others (Tellers 1990). This is especially true in the case of prudence: without it, one cannot have any other virtue; but once one has it, one has all the others, albeit in varying degrees.

It is not enough for an individual to seem objectively happy to a neutral, third-party observer to be truly happy in the Aristotelian sense. Such an appearance of happiness may only be the result of a natural inclination or a feeling (sometimes called "natural 'proto'-virtue" or *pathos*), but not of rational choice. Take for instance a baby that resorts to smiling instead of crying to attract the attention of grown-ups. Happiness demands that it be the outcome of virtue, among others. Virtue calls for a correct appreciation of the situation and the practical knowledge of how to proceed. It goes beyond theoretical, abstract, general knowledge and rule following. Thus, all virtuous acts require prudence (*phronesis*) or practical wisdom, the habit of making rational choices accompanied by the right reasons to act in a certain way, given a set of circumstances. Prudence distinctively comes with age and experience, which afford an appropriate perception of what is humanly salient in varying contexts (Hursthouse 2013). The "happy" baby in the example above has none of these. Only the prudent person is able to recognize virtue in others and thereby determine whether the happiness they may display is genuine or not.

Chapter 2 asked quite pointedly, "how much happiness can money buy?" Underlying most of the responses and the accompanying analyses was the idea that happiness and money are, indeed, both goods, but goods of entirely different natures. The Aristotelian suggestion of dividing goods into those sought for themselves and those sought for the sake of others (NE 1094a) again becomes exceedingly helpful in this case. It allows us to distinguish happiness, which is a good in itself, from money, which is a good only insofar as it leads to another as means; for certainly, of what use is money, when there is nothing to buy with it? This instrumental feature of money, income, and other forms of wealth is what makes Aristotle regard a life of moneymaking somewhat "forced," "oppressive," and even "anti-natural" (NE 1096a). Absolutely convinced that money is not choice-worthy in itself, he thinks no one in his right mind would choose it as a path to happiness. Such would be the nerve of Aristotle's contention against what would later be known as "utilitarianism" and all its different forms. These positions not only equate utility with the good, but also hold that happiness consists in simply amassing utilities.

The importance of money, but only as means, is reinforced as well by Aristotle's admonitions to subject chrematistics to economy proper, and his insistence on the need for both activities to be governed by the "natural" kind which recognizes a limit. There is no doubt about the need for material resources – which are goods, after all – to attain happiness (*eudaimonia*); hence, the existence of economy. As we have seen, destitution, the different forms of material, moral, and cultural poverty, together with multidimensional deprivation are all inherently incompatible with happiness. Yet the proper administration of material goods entails, first, their acquisition or provision (chrematistics), and second, their enjoyment or use (economy proper). Furthermore, in order to effectively reach their goal or purpose, these two practices need to respect a "natural" limit, imposed by the amount of material resources necessary for flourishing and the essence of the material resources themselves, respectively. Either limit could only be recognized or established by a person of virtue, because none of them is objectively engraved in stone. No purely scientific, empirical, or descriptive knowledge by itself can ascertain where such limits lie. They are neither universal nor necessary, but particular and contingent to the individual and his circumstances. Hence, these limits are "natural" only in the same way that virtue is an acquired, "secondary nature." Operating within this range of flexibility, a virtuous person alone has mastered the desire of acquisitiveness, so as to procure only what is necessary. Likewise, only he has developed enough discernment, so as to employ things in accordance with their ordained purpose.

This, precisely, is what the virtue of moderation (*sophrosyne*) consists in. Without moderation, both chrematistics and economy tend to go up in a spiral, becoming distractions at the least, if not ending up as completely detrimental to the quest for happiness. Moderation guards against consumerism, which leads to the waste of resources in futile competitions that leave everyone worse off; it helps us control our aspirations and expectations of the future. In the form of sobriety and austerity, moderation enables us to better enjoy the material goods we already possess, staving off hedonic adaptation.

We also saw in Chapter 2 the pernicious effects not only of destitution or deprivation, but also of inequality. Against the latter, Aristotle advocates the promotion of a dominant middle class within a "mixed constitutional regime" as the best form of government in practice (Pltcs 1295a–1300b). He acknowledges the impossibility of absolute equality in socioeconomic terms within the political community. Inasmuch as these are relative terms, there will always be "richer" and "poorer" individuals than the average or mean due to a host of factors, some of them freely chosen, others not, such as the results of the "genetic lottery," for instance. His primary concern, however, is that a broad middle class be the one that governs, instead of the rich or the poor. That's because he sees the rich as prone to neglect the common good, and overly conservative: that is, more inclined to secure and protect their own wealth and privilege. The poor, on the other hand, are equally tempted to put aside the common good by subordinating it to a desire to acquire and accumulate material resources and pleasures, often out of envy. This often leads to very risky and even reckless behaviors that put the stability of the state in danger. To the extent that the middle class is free from the temptations that both extremes suffer, it would be easier for it to steer society through the right course. Less likely to succumb to the self-sufficiency and smugness of the rich and the material ambitions of the poor, a huge middle class would be in a better position to seek the common good of the political community above all. In the measure that the state is governed by a huge middle class, the greater are the chances that the political virtue of justice will prevail and the better will be the prospects of stability.

Chapters 3 and 4 both focused on pleasure, insofar as it influences our choices and desires. Unlike money, pleasure is a good in itself, and it makes perfect sense to pursue pleasure precisely because it is pleasant and for no other ulterior reason. This does not mean, however, that pleasure is the "supreme good" and "final end" – a title reserved for happiness (*eudaimonia*) alone – because it does not encompass or include all other humanly significant goods. This is the nub of Aristotle's argument against "hedonism," which identifies pleasure as the highest possible good. His aristocratic streak shows when he criticizes a life of gratification as a vulgar choice, and his intellectualist leanings when he complains that it does not take reason into account, situating human beings at the same level as farm animals. He likewise takes a gibe at self-interested rulers who use political power to satisfy their own pleasures, instead of furthering the common good.

Aristotle defines pleasures as activities, not processes or "becomings"; they arise when we exercise capacities, not when we come to a certain state, as we approach the completion or end of our nature; they consist in unimpeded activities of a natural state (NE 1153a). Katz (2014) sums this up by saying that pleasures are supervenient "perfections in functionings." That is, human beings are not passive subjects with regard to pleasures; these occur when they perform activities in accordance with nature and fulfill their end without encountering any obstacles. Contrary to what others may suppose, pleasures do not imply any other distinct activities besides these. They alight or "supervene" upon these activities as the "bloom of youth" does on those who are found at the flower of their age, says Aristotle in a rare poetic concession (NE 1174b33). Hence, pleasure may be understood as a supervenient perfection on virtuous activity.

In light of the above, we understand the falsehood behind pharmacologically induced pleasures and their counterproductive effect, especially in the case of addictions, on genuine happiness. They merely raise the threshold of pleasure such that one needs an ever increasing dose in order to reach just the same level of satisfaction. We also see the need for constant effort and training, such as normally takes place in the voluntary development of habits. This is necessary not only in order to attain pleasure correctly, but also to be able to aspire to pleasures of a superior kind. Aristotle would never have approved of getting hooked on to a "pleasure machine" or receiving brain stimulations as a way to reach happiness.

To speak of an activity as pleasurable is never just to give a plain description; it somehow always implies an evaluative judgment or endorsement, because, as we have seen, pleasure is a good. There are different kinds of pleasures, however, and among them exists a hierarchy; not all of them are of equal standing and some are objectively considered better than others. To some degree, therefore, the hierarchy of pleasures reflects the order of capacities or faculties together with their activities or functionings, in accordance with Aristotle's teleological theory of life and flourishing (Katz 2014). Given the limitations of time and energies, human beings cannot help, then, but choose among activities and their corresponding pleasures, bearing in mind, moreover, that some may be incompatible with others (NE 1175b, 1153a; Kraut 2014). These teachings somehow foreshadow the conclusions or outcomes of empirical studies regarding the relative pleasure values of material goods compared to experiences, for instance, and the trade-offs that occur when individuals decide for one class of goods over another, such as a bigger house instead of a shorter commute, more time for aerobic exercise, or more frequent socializing. They also confirm the need that the number of choices ought to be limited; that having more choices is not necessarily better, because having excessive choices often leads to confusion, if not to an outright paralysis.

In order to choose correctly, individuals require proper education and training, especially of desires, preferably beginning in early childhood. This consists in learning to respect the above-mentioned natural hierarchy in the first place, giving priority to the pleasures of virtuous activity over those of eating and drinking or relieving an itch, for instance. Next, although there may be room for some "hedonic calculus," imagining the pleasurable consequences of alternative lines of action based on experience, this cannot be the deciding factor in choice. That's because we can never determine, at any given time, all the consequences or outcomes of alternative actions, in a manner that the logic of "hedonic calculus" demands. This requires nothing short of omniscience. Since this is an impossibility for human beings, a decision-making model patterned after a "physics of pleasure," therefore, becomes untenable.

For this reason, perhaps, individuals time and again fall into the same cognitive and evaluative errors when choosing, despite having been repeatedly forewarned of such dangers. They just can't seem to help it. Understandably, these persistent failures in decision making may lead some modern investigators to think that, although advantageous or "adaptive" from the evolutionary perspective, the idea of happiness is, in fact, unrealistic, an inexistent goal or objective. Having accepted this, a nihilistic in life, in the end, would seem not only "rational," but also more than justifiable.

Hence the need to turn to the judgment of a prudent and virtuous person, because "the good person, insofar as he is good, is the measure of each thing, then what appear pleasures to him will also be pleasures, and what is pleasant will be what he enjoys" (NE 1176a). Only the virtuous person perceives things as they really are, and this carries over to matters referring to pleasures as well. The virtuous person alone would be correctly perceptive of what is salient and valuable among the various options presented, gauging what is beneficial and harmful in each, and choosing what is best: that is, what brings him closest to happiness (*eudaimonia*).

Here we find what could certainly be the biggest pitfall of modern happiness studies in its treatment of pleasures and satisfactions. Although it has acutely detected the difference between raw and cultivated tastes, arguing in favor of the latter and of the need for proper education and training, nevertheless, it has refused to acknowledge – for fear of being considered judgmental and premodern – the crucial role of the moral virtues in choices and decision making. While Aristotle insists on moral virtue and proper cultivation as our guide in following desires and making the right choices, modern happiness studies largely ignores them as irrelevant, overly subjective, or "unscientific," certainly not in keeping with the empirical, quantitative, and objective (in the sense of evident to a "neutral third-party observer") standards of post-Enlightenment knowledge.

Chapter 5 focused primarily on the links between work and happiness. One could say that Aristotle displays as much disinterest for work as he does for moneymaking, because both possess a merely instrumental value. They are hardly worth the concern of the Athenian gentleman to whom he addresses his writings. He is aware, however, of the necessity of work, insofar as it provides the means to acquire the amount and kind of property indispensable for flourishing. We could recall his reference to slaves as a kind of living property whose utility lies in obeying their master's will, in performing the work that their master orders (Pltcs 1254a). Liberating their master from menial tasks not only saves him physical and mental energies, but also affords him greater time for leisurely activities. Thanks to the work of servants or slaves, therefore, their master is able to engage and enjoy freely chosen activities, with no end or purpose other than their own performance.

The highest among these activities is contemplation (*theoria*), and a life of study or contemplation is, in an absolute sense, the best contender for a happy life (*eudaimonia*) (NE 1177a). Such would be possible only for a privileged few (the aristocracy or elite), thanks to the work and privations of many, maybe even of the great majority. But then again, perhaps, a life of study may be in fact "too happy" for human beings to aspire to. It may actually be more "divine" than "human." After all, given his bodily needs, it is virtually impossible for a human being to spend his time dedicated exclusively to contemplation. Hence, he may have to settle for a kind of life which is the "second best," not one of pure contemplation, but one involving "action" (*praxis*).

Having renounced contemplation (*theoria*) (NE 1177a) for practical reasons, Aristotle now proposes action (*praxis*), particularly good action (*eupraxia*) (NE 1140b), as the kind of life that brings human beings happiness (*eudaimonia*). How do the two differ? We can distinguish the two firstly, in their purpose or objective, and secondly, in their subject matter. The purpose of study or contemplation is, simply, to reflect things as they are, to acknowledge them in their being. On the other hand, the purpose of action is to effect change in the state of things.

Hence, contemplation applies to matters which are "universal" – that is, unchanging regardless of time and place – and "necessary," meaning they cannot be otherwise. A prime example of contemplation, therefore, is the study of mathematics, which deals with objects that remain the same regardless of circumstances and whose relations are bound by necessity. For example, two plus two equals four, whatever, wherever, and whenever one may be counting; it would remain as such even if one were not around to count, in fact. Action, for its part, applies to things that are "particular," or specific to a time and place, and "contingent," meaning they could be one way or another. Political action, which the eponymous branch of knowledge governs, would be the perfect example. Although there may be a few general rules, such as the preference for the common good over the individual good, everyone agrees that these are insufficient for practice. Instead, one has to exercise "political prudence," keenly observing the ever-changing possibilities and opportunities that each concrete situation offers. Political action requires a lot of improvisation, since events hardly ever follow a pre-defined script. We should not confuse this flexibility with relativism or the mentality that "anything goes," however, because those few general rules still apply with regard to the overall objective. According to Aristotle, therefore, in the case of human beings, action (*praxis*) seems to be more fitting than contemplation (*theoria*) for happiness (*eudaimonia*); although, at the same time, people should take advantage of as many opportunities for contemplation as they may encounter.

In Aristotle's writings, work may be related to property in still another way, when non-living property is divided into "instruments of production (*poiesis*)" and "instruments of action (*praxis*)" (Pltcs 1254a). This classification comes closer to our modern idea of work, which is largely identified with production. The notice Aristotle gives regarding the superiority of action over production rests, once again, on the means–end relationship between the two. For instance, the purpose of producing a piece of cloth is that it be transformed into a garment which in turn is worn (action), and the reason why a bed is made is for someone to sleep on it (again, ironically, action). This is consistent with his views regarding the superiority of ethics over economy, of economy proper over chrematistics, and of a life of pleasure over one of moneymaking.

Work or production (*poiesis*) and action (*praxis*) are the ways through which human beings cause other things to come into existence. Essentially, they correspond to what is expressed in most modern languages by the words "making" (*poiesis*) and "doing" (*praxis*). When an individual works and produces something, he usually makes a tangible object that exists independently, one that can be observed by others. Take, for instance, a piece of cloth or a bed. By contrast, when an individual does something, the result or outcome inheres in him and is inseparable from him. Consider the actions of wearing a garment or sleeping, which cannot be understood without the subject or the agent.

An example of making would be the practice of the crafts. What is important is the external object or handicraft, not the artisan. Originally, all kinds of work belonged to this manual category.

In handicrafts, rules are external to the artisan and production procedures could be written down and codified in the form of instructions. Whoever masters these rules acquires the art or habit of craftsmanship. In theory, anyone who strictly follows this set of guidelines or instructions could be guaranteed the same results. Because of this, handicrafts could be mass-produced.

Doing, on the other hand, centers on the subjective outcome. It denotes an activity that begins and ends in the agent himself, not in an external object. Therefore, the individual is, at the same time, the agent and the patient of his own doing. For instance, if an individual repeatedly performs acts of generosity such as alms giving, he develops the habit of generosity. The main result of doing is not an artifact, but an operative habit or virtue, if the habit is good. In doing, unlike in making, rules are internal to the agent. The generous person alone, as such, knows how exactly to perform genuine acts of generosity. Such rules cannot be codified, as in making and the crafts. And in the measure that, through doing, one acquires virtues, he engages in a dynamic of self-perfection. Doing is guided above all by the habit of prudence or practical wisdom (*phronesis*) (NE 1145a).

We cannot sufficiently stress, however, that for Aristotle, making (*poiesis*) and doing (*praxis*) are activities meant to be carried out by two different groups of people: slaves and individuals engaged in production, on the one hand, and freemen or members of the aristocratic or leisured class, on the other. Inasmuch as happiness (*eudaimonia*) depends on doing and the virtues one develops, rather than making and the arts, it is beyond the reach of the majority of individuals in the political community. In reality, women and children, like servants and foreigners, are all equally excluded, albeit for different reasons. Therefore, only a select few could aspire to reach happiness, despite the fact that in order to do this, they rely on the work and productive efforts of many others.

Modern happiness research informs us that, in work as well as in leisure, the key factor for personal satisfaction is that it be voluntary or freely chosen. All other features of the activity (or lack of it), such as whether it is manual or intellectual, individual or group, the objective or environmental conditions, the fit with subjective or personal characteristics, even the pay and so forth, are merely secondary. What is indeed important is the "intrinsic motivation" that accompanies it. The whole notion of "intrinsic motivation" bears a striking resemblance to the conditions that Aristotle lays down for *praxis*: a self-contained or self-referential activity (it bears its own end) that is fully engrossing (one's capacities rise to meet the challenges), done in accordance with reason and accompanied by a distinctive pleasure. In the presence of intrinsic motivation, extrinsic motivation becomes nothing else but a nuisance and distraction, hence its "crowding out" or corruptive effect.

However, the theory of intrinsic motivation introduces a very significant twist or corrective to Aristotelian teaching, insofar as it is applicable not only to "doing" (*praxis*), but also to "making" (*poiesis*), production or work. Whereas Aristotle was quite incapable of making sense of the expression "intellectual work" with his existing mental categories, thanks to intrinsic motivation we are now able to extend the "doing" or *praxis* dimension even to activities mainly in the province of "making" or *poiesis*. In fact, we could even affirm that all work or productive activity bears both a *praxis* and a *poiesis* dimension, if not simultaneously, at least successively. Take, for instance, a child who learns to play the piano. At first, piano playing is *poiesis*, valued for its consequence of pleasing the child's mother; but later on, it can turn into *praxis*, when the child begins to enjoy piano playing in itself (Hartman 2013).

Whenever we engage in work, we actually produce two results or outcomes: one covered by *poiesis* or the objective dimension, which is the external thing, and the other covered by *praxis* or the subjective dimension, which is the internal perfective habit or virtue. To cite an example, an intrinsically motivated cleaner not only produces sparkling clean restrooms (the objective dimension or *poiesis*), but also acquires the virtue proper to an expert cleaner, which is that of service to others (the subjective or *praxis* dimension).

Praxis, therefore, ceases to be the exclusive reserve of a privileged elite and becomes accessible to everyone in the political community, including manual workers. Even better and more radical, perhaps, is that happiness (*eudaimonia*), which depends directly on *praxis*, now begins to fall within everyone's reach. Only from this perspective could we understand how work can become inherently satisfying – by acquiring an ethical dimension (*praxis*) which, although superior to its economic value (*poiesis*), nevertheless could also contribute to it (Hinchliffe 2004).

Chapter 6 centered on the role institutions such as democratic regimes and religion play in happiness. Aristotle reminds us that happiness (*eudaimonia*) itself is the proper object of politics, considered the pinnacle of all forms of knowledge (NE 1094a–b). Subject to politics are, in their order of importance, ethics, concerned with internal goods of the soul, and economy, which deals with external goods relating to the body. Aristotle likewise underscores the fact that politics is a practical form of knowledge (*praxis*) and not an abstract or theoretical one (*theoria*), if only to mark out the distance that separates him from Plato. Indeed, the supreme human good or happiness is not a platonic "idea," which some exceptionally enlightened individual contemplates and later on transmits to other lesser members of the political community for its realization or execution. Rather than a universal and necessary "master-plan," happiness is the outcome of joint deliberation and decision among "political animals" (Pltcs 1253a): that is, individuals endowed with freedom and reason, and thereby capable of engaging in meaningful and mutually enriching dialogue with each other. Happiness is a practical task that results from the combined and coordinated efforts of everyone in the political community.

Besides the hierarchy among the different bodies of knowledge, Aristotle also posits another hierarchy among political structures. Hence, he speaks first of natural communities, such as the political community, the village, and the family (Pltcs 1252b), in descending order of importance, and secondly, of what we call in contrast "artificial communities" or "intermediate associations" (Pltcs 1280b), among which we count economic organizations such as the modern-day firm. Aristotle takes pains in explaining how each of these bodies has its own function or purpose, justifying a corresponding place within the general political architecture. Furthermore, he specifies how happiness (*eudaimonia*) can be achieved only in certain forms of government, where the common good is given priority over the individual good, ultimately opting for the "mixed constitutional regime" (Pltcs 1295a–1300b) for practical reasons. Whether or not this "mixed constitutional regime" corresponds to the "liberal democracies" in Chapter 5 is an open question that we leave to political theorists and historians. Similarly, whether the religion to which Aristotle refers as a necessary element of happiness (Pltcs 1328b) is the same as the religious beliefs and practices analyzed previously is an issue that we shall leave unsettled. That's because Aristotle seems to have thought, above all, of a "state religion" and of the "gods of the state," in a manner that now sounds almost completely anachronistic and, thus, would hardly be applicable to today's mainstream religious beliefs and practices.

However, the main relevance of institutions, be they political or religious, seems to lie in the fact that happiness (*eudaimonia*) is a "common good," which entails the participation of all members of the political community for its fulfillment. We are already familiar with the Aristotelian definition of the good as "that at which everything aims" (NE 1094a), the end which satisfies an appetite, desire, inclination, or tendency. What, then, is the "common good"? It is the good of the *polis*, which is "finer and more divine" (NE 1094b) than individual goods. We also know that it is a good pursued in itself, lacking nothing (NE 1097a). Therefore, among the goods pursued in themselves, happiness (*eudaimonia*) or flourishing stands out as most choiceworthy, complete, and self-sufficient (NE 1097b). Yet this self-sufficiency does not mean living an isolated life, but sharing a good life in common, with family, friends, and fellow-citizens in the political community (NE 1097b). Happiness (*eudaimonia*), the supreme human good, also turns out to be the common good of the political community.

As we have seen, the common good Aristotle proposes is concrete, contingent, and specific to a political community; it is certainly not the platonic idea of the good (NE 1096a–b). As Smith suggests:

> the common good is the good of all members of a political community once these members have actualized their disposition to live in common. They organize themselves in view of the good which political life can provide them; they enjoy the advantages of life in common. And these advantages can vary from one period of time to another, and also from one place to another.
>
> *(Smith 1995: 63)*

These lines emphasize certain defining features of happiness (*eudaimonia*) as a form of *praxis*. As an action or activity, it seeks to introduce a modification or change in the current state of things. It deals with individual, particular realities which vary according to time and place. And most important, it has to do with the actualization of internal dispositions among the members of the political community, in clear allusion to the development of virtues or good habits. Indeed, these interior dispositions or virtues, more than any form of external rule-following, represent the crucial factor for the successful result or outcome of *praxis*. In this case, virtues are put forward as the controlling element that allows members of the political community, given favorable material conditions, to achieve nothing less than happiness (*eudaimonia*).

How do individuals in the political community participate in the common good? They share or take part in the common good through the conscientious exercise of citizenship, of its rights as well as its duties. For Aristotle, the *polis* is a whole made up of citizens, who are its parts (Pltcs 1274b). "A citizen in the strictest sense," then, is he who "shares in the administration of justice and in offices" (Pltcs 1275a). Hence, the essential task of citizens is to decide on what is good and just in the political community, and to effectively put it into practice. Although many people in a *polis* may actually participate in deliberating and deciding on the common good, only citizens do so by right: that is, by means of a legally protected and guaranteed power (Pltcs 1275b).

For this reason, citizens alone may be said to engage in autonomy or self-governance, insofar as they create the same laws by which they freely promise to abide. Federalism and the mechanisms of direct democracy are mere channels through which the rights of citizenship could be more effectively exercised, in a subsidiary and solidarious manner. The common good results from the joint deliberation, decision, and action of citizens, all of which perfect their freedom. In this case, freedom is no longer to be understood as an infantile "doing whatever one pleases," but in its mature version as self-rule in accordance with one's social nature and reason.

In Chapter 6, dealing with institutions, we broached the possibility that happiness (*eudaimonia*), without ceasing to be one's own, can as a matter of fact be shared with others. Now we realize that, because it is a common good, if it is not shared by all relevant members of the political community, it does not qualify to be called happiness at all. There have been several insinuations to this effect throughout modern happiness research: for instance, when it was suggested that happiness is some sort of "public good," characterized by non-rivalrous and non-excludable consumption. Think of the happiness-boosting effects coming from low-crime and unpolluted neighborhoods; well-maintained parks, roads, and sidewalks; quality education; and healthcare for all.

The Aristotelian notion of a common good actually goes even beyond this. Happiness is an activity (*praxis*) in which one can engage only to the extent that everybody else engages in it as well, and as corollary, one's engagement or participation in the activity does not diminish or detract from the engagement of the others. Thus, in the political community, one cannot be happy unless everyone else is happy, and one's happiness removes nothing from the happiness of others. Happiness is a common good because it could only be attained with the help of others and together with them. This does not imply, of course, that everyone participates equally in happiness, as there could be differences in degrees. For this reason, demographic markers concerning sex, age, civil status, and so forth, retain their significance. However, the main "gatekeeper" for full access to happiness, as we have seen, is the condition of citizenship in the political community.

Citizenship is the highest acknowledgment of human dignity and what guarantees an individual the full range of rights and freedoms in society. The sense behind all these rights and freedoms is, certainly, that they be exercised properly and responsibly in social participation. Little progress will be obtained if everyone uses them to be hooked on to pleasure machines for an endless dose of soma, as in Huxley's dystopian *Brave New World* (1995). The need for voluntary social participation – be it in politics or in religion – also explains the value of procedural utilities, which often exceeds that of outcome utilities for happiness. Social participation reinforces an internal locus of control which makes the exercise of politics and religion, to cite a couple of institutions, so inherently satisfying. And most important, it is through voluntary social participation that one is able to develop the whole panoply of virtues as distinctive human excellences.

HAVING, DOING, BECOMING

The absence of a robust account of the virtues is, arguably, the greatest weakness of modern happiness studies in its attempt to explain its subject matter. This comes about as the result of having largely neglected the tradition of philosophical inquiry, and in particular, Aristotelian virtue ethics. The recovery of Aristotelian virtue ethics serves to give a stronger foundation and greater integration or coherence to many of the findings of modern happiness research. It also helps to explain the causes of various difficulties or quandaries encountered. Indeed, the picture of happiness that has emerged is filled with paradoxes (Martin 2008). It lies not in the individual possession of material goods (money, pleasures), but in generous self-giving.

It is achieved not when one concedes absolute value to the freedom of choice, but when one learns realistically to accept limitations. And lastly, despite being the final end of human life, it seems to be best pursued indirectly, almost like a by-product of an "autotelic" activity.

Due to its neoclassical economic origins and background, modern happiness studies has always understood happiness in relation to consumption. Happiness has been commodified, transformed into a commodity that is produced, sold, and bought, ultimately, in order to be consumed (Makant 2010). Consumption, then, becomes the activity through which individuals are supposed to achieve happiness, and consumerism is the overall lifestyle this creates. In due course, a large part of modern happiness research has documented the dysfunctionalities modern consumerism has produced, such as radical individualism ("me first" in everything), the absolutization of the freedom of choice divorced from reason and commitments, and the deification of pleasure, among others.

Underlying these phenomena is a desire that has gone mad and self-destructive, because consumerism is not the desire of something, but the "desire of desire" above all (Makant 2010). Indeed, as Cavanaugh (2008: 35) pointedly remarks, "consumerism is not so much about having more as it is about having something else." And unfortunately, as everyone knows, there will always be something else to be had. By inserting individuals into an endless cycle of working, selling, and buying, only to work, sell, and buy even more, consumerism has fallen miserably short on its promise of happiness. And even worse, it has completely taken over the sense of identity, belonging, and meaning in the lives of many, for "consuming is what we do, and as such it is who we are" (Makant 2010: 293).

Virtues are what allow us to harness the power of desires such that they actually lead to happiness, while keeping their destructive potential in check. Far from being inimical to freedom, virtues require freedom. Education in the virtues – which is the primordial task for legislators (NE 1103b) – through proper habituation and education only makes sense within the context of freedom.

Freedom exists on three different levels. The first is physical freedom, which consists in an openness to or capacity for movement in accordance with one's nature. When human beings are bound or imprisoned, for example, they are deprived of this freedom. Next comes psychological freedom or freedom of choice. Whenever people choose, the determining factor is none other than their sovereign will. In consequence, people identify with their choices, assuming responsibility for them. The third level of freedom is moral freedom. Unlike the first two levels, which are "givens," forming part of the natural condition of human beings, moral freedom is the result of a struggle or a conquest. Physical freedom and psychological freedom are "negative freedoms"; freedoms from contrary physical forces and psychological determinants, respectively. Moral freedom, on the other hand, is a "positive freedom," a freedom for something superior and greater than one's natural condition. Moral freedom is achieved when one develops good habits or virtues.

In the same way that physical freedom corresponds to a certain "power," and psychological freedom, to a "power to choose," moral freedom builds upon both as a "power to choose the good": that is, a "power to choose that which perfects one's nature and being." Thanks to the virtues or good habits that constitute moral freedom, human beings are able to widen the scope of "natural freedoms," increasing and intensifying them. Virtuous habits enable people to perform more good actions and perform them better, not only from the objective viewpoint of the actions themselves, but also from their own subjective viewpoint, in terms of the agent's "moral skill," pleasure, or satisfaction. Most important, virtues allow individuals to create and take part in the common good of happiness or flourishing within the political community.

The consumerist model of happiness is built primarily upon having material things and doing with them whatever produces the greatest amount of pleasure for the individual self. This corrupts desire, exacerbating it instead of satisfying it. Happiness is not a commodity to be produced, sold, and bought. The virtue model goes beyond having and doing, and enters into the realm of becoming. It is based upon the rational use of freedom as the power to choose and do the good in a habitual manner. As we have seen, virtues not only improve the objective or external results of an individual's actions, but also perfect the individual subjectively or internally, making him a better person. Herein lies the superiority of the virtue model over the consumerist model. Happiness is not something one acquires or simply does, but something one becomes. Therefore, it is a matter of being the right sort of person by developing the proper virtues of character.

Perhaps we could sum up Aristotle's recipe for happiness (*eudaimonia*) in the following conditions. First, one needs to be born into the right institutions, including the family, intermediate groups, and the political community, something which to a large extent is, admittedly, a matter of luck. Otherwise, one should be able to collaborate with others in successfully transforming these institutional contexts into properly functioning ones. In second place – although equally necessary and important – comes a series of elements that depend more on the exercise of one's free agency, such as having enough, doing good, and becoming an excellent person by cultivating the virtues. Only then could one reasonably aspire to achieve happiness (*eudaimonia*), not as a right, but indirectly, as a gift or reward.

REFERENCES

Annas, J. 1993. *The morality of happiness*. New York/Oxford: Oxford University Press.

2011. *Intelligent virtue*. New York/Oxford: Oxford University Press.

Aquinas, T. 1988a. "Summa contra gentiles," in *St Thomas Aquinas on politics and ethics*, Sigmund, P. E. (trans. and ed.). New York: W. W. Norton.

1988b. "Summa theologiae," in *St Thomas Aquinas on politics and ethics*, Sigmund, P. E. (trans. and ed.). New York: W.W. Norton.

Aristotle 1978. *Aristotle's Categories and De interpretatione*, Ackrill, J. L. (trans. and notes). Oxford/New York: Clarendon Press.

1985. *Nicomachean ethics*. Irwin, T. (trans.). Indianapolis, IN: Hackett.

1988. *The politics*, Everson, S. (ed.). Cambridge: Cambridge University Press.

Bentham, J. 2000. *An introduction to the principles of morals and legislation*. Palo Alto, CA: Batoche.

Cavanaugh, W. 2008. *Being consumed: Economics and Christian desire*. Grand Rapids, MI: Eerdmans.

Hartman, E. 2013. *Virtue in business: Conversations with Aristotle*. Cambridge: Cambridge University Press.

Hinchliffe, G. 2004. "Work and human flourishing," *Educational Philosophy and Theory*, 36 (5): 535–547.

Hursthouse, R. 2013. "Virtue ethics," in Zalta, E. N. (ed.), *The Stanford encyclopedia of philosophy* (Fall 2013 edition), (http://plato.stanford.edu/archives/fall2013/entries/ethics-virtue/, accessed September 23, 2013).

Huxley, A. 1995. *Brave new world*. New York: Buccaneer.

Katz, L. D. 2014. "Pleasure," in Zalta, E. N. (ed.), *The Stanford encyclopedia of philosophy* (Spring 2014 edition), (http://plato.stanford.edu/archives/spr2014/entries/pleasure/, accessed February 27, 2014).

Kraut, R. 1979. "Two conceptions of happiness," *Philosophical Review*, 88 (2): 167–197.

2014. "Aristotle's ethics," in Zalta, E. N. (ed.), *The Stanford encyclopedia of philosophy* (Spring 2014 edition), (http://plato.stanford.edu/archives/spr2014/entries/aristotle-ethics/, accessed February 27, 2014).

La Mettrie, J. O. 1987. "L'anti-Sénèque," *Oeuvres philosophiques*. Paris: Fayard.

Makant, M. 2010. "The pursuit of happiness: The virtue of consumption and the consumption of virtue," *Dialog: A Journal of Theology*, 49 (4): 291–299.

Martin, M. W. 2008. "Paradoxes of happiness," *Journal of Happiness Studies*, 9: 171–184.

McMahon, D. 2006. *The pursuit of happiness: A history from the Greeks to the present*. London: Allen Lane.

Nagel, T. 1972. "Aristotle on 'Eudaimonia,'" *Phronesis*, 17: 252–259.

Pontifical Council for Justice and Peace 2004. *Compendium of the social doctrine of the Church*, Rome: Libreria Editrice Vaticana.

Shewring, W. H. 1996. "St. Perpetua: The Passion of Saints Perpetua and Felicity," in Halsall, P. (ed.), *Internet medieval source book* (www.fordham.edu/halsall/source/perpetua.asp, accessed April 17, 2014).

Sizer, L. 2010. "Good and good for you: An affect theory of happiness," *Philosophy and Phenomenological Research*, 80 (1): 133–163.

Skidelsky, E. 2009. "Capitalism and the good life," in Gregg, S. and Stoner, J. (eds.), *Profits, prudence and virtue: Essays in ethics, business and management*. Exeter: Imprint Academic, pp. 242–253.

Smith, T. W. 1995. "Aristotle on the conditions for and limits of the common good," *American Political Science Review*, 93 (3): 625–636.

Telfer, E. 1990. "The unity of the moral virtues in Aristotle's 'Nicomachean ethics'," *Proceedings of the Aristotelian Society*, 90 (1989–1990): 35–48.

Conclusion

Learning to be happy

Happiness does not depend so much on what you have, or on what you do, but on who you become. All of our efforts to try and find out what happiness is rest on the belief that it lies within one's power, at least partly, to achieve happiness. By the hand of Aristotle, and after having gone through most of the major findings of modern happiness research, we discover that cultivating virtue still is, by far, our best bet. Given the inescapable limitations of the human condition, developing virtue integrally in one's life and community, then, is the manner in which one learns to be happy.

Recognizing the validity of this original Aristotelian intuition regarding the role of virtue in happiness, however, should not blind us to many of Aristotle's prejudices which have now been thankfully overcome. The first refers to the unjustifiable political exclusion to which women, children, slaves, and non-Greeks in general were subjected. Another pertains to the very low regard that he had for work and all forms of productive activities, considering them to be beneath human dignity (at least, beneath what befits a proper Athenian gentleman). A third concerns his partiality toward an intellectual life and one dedicated to politics, against a life of business and commerce. Such unwarranted forms of discrimination would have sufficed to impede large swathes of humanity from even aspiring to have access to happiness.

At the same time, however, we cannot but acknowledge the profoundly anti-Aristotelian tilt in most of the premises of modern happiness studies. The very insistence on an objective, value-neutral way of quantifying happiness, pleasure, virtue, and moral worth would itself have been totally objectionable. A similar case could be made with regard to the outsized importance granted to money or income, sensible pleasures, and psychological satisfactions; not to mention work. Remember that the Aristotelian ideal consisted in being able to live comfortably without having to work oneself. Yet nevertheless, there's no denying that the study of welfare economics, behavioral economics, neuroeconomics, and positive, hedonic psychology have also generated a considerable number of valuable inputs to the theory of happiness which Aristotle, for one, could not have even imagined.

In the following paragraphs we shall dwell a bit more on these points, examining how virtue ethics could improve on them by preventing certain difficulties and responding to a number of particular questions they raise. As in the foregoing, our focus will be on helping business people and executives to practice the virtues within their specific circumstances, rather than on making any substantive contribution to the theoretical development of Aristotelian virtue ethics as such.

Oftentimes, the purposes of both entrepreneurs and managers are formulated in terms of welfare and happiness. Entrepreneurs are bent on satisfying customers or clients, for which they justly receive a reward in the form of profits. Managers, above all, are entrusted to look after the welfare of workers under their care, as these go about their job of producing the goods and services that society requires. It is more than reasonable, therefore, to try and measure happiness and satisfaction, if only as a benchmark for performance or how well one carries out a particular function. Yet as we have seen, this is an extremely difficult and complex task. It entails both objective and subjective indicators, individual and group factors, "hard" and "soft" methods, none of which are renounceable for the distinct information they provide. But most important, we come to the conclusion that neither the notion of happiness itself, nor its measurement, can be in fact value-neutral. That's the reason behind the need for a narrative, which provides the background or standard against which a person's life-goals are understood and tested. And although, to a large extent, all values are context-specific, nonetheless, we likewise come upon the realization that they are not all of equal worth.

Chapter 1, "Modern happiness studies and 'individual subjective wellbeing': you only get what you measure," furnishes business people with a variety of possible indicators, criteria, and strategies for measuring the satisfaction of targeted individuals or groups, be they consumers or employees. It also gives notice of the strengths and weaknesses of each particular method or technique, suggesting ways in which the former can be boosted and the latter overcome. Much has to do with attempting just the right degree of precision – no more, no less, than what happiness, satisfaction, or wellbeing itself allows – and acknowledging that it is a value-laden and evolving concept.

We need virtue as a compass or guiding light to navigate in what often degenerates into a morass of conflicting and even contradictory accounts of happiness. Without virtue we would be unable to tell the true happiness worth pursuing from the myriad of contenders which provide nothing more than aimless distractions. Identifying happiness, therefore, is an object of moral judgment rather than a matter of positive, empirical science. The only things we can measure are certain signs, manifestations, effects or consequences, but not happiness itself. In fact, there is nothing in our detection or measurement of these related and accompanying phenomena which indicates that they correspond to the ideal of happiness, except for the subject's personal judgment and belief. Virtue ensures that such judgment and belief are valid and truthful.

Surprisingly, money accounts for very little in personal happiness – much less than what most people imagine. Once you have enough to cover your basic needs, its marginal utility steadily decreases. Other factors usually associated with money, such as health, education, access to technology, democracy and a clean environment, may even have a stronger positive impact on happiness. Neither can the effects of one's hereditary dispositions or "genetic set-point" be discounted on the satisfaction and wellbeing experienced. Much of our happiness depends on our position relative to other members of the community. Due to our social nature, we cannot help but compare ourselves to those near us and to those like us. We are sensitive to inequalities – in particular, to the income and consumption gaps that distance us from each other. When severe, they could offend our sense of justice. Conspicuous consumption and contests for purely positional goods end up in zero-sum games in which everybody loses, despite perhaps a fleeting, short-term surge for whoever momentarily takes the lead. There are externalities involved, both positive and negative, in our rent-seeking and consumption behaviors which we can no longer afford to ignore.

In Chapter 2, "Happiness and income: how much happiness can money buy?" a manager begins to discover just how limited income could be as a motivator in the workplace. The bottom line is that you cannot bribe people into good behavior. Or better still, you can certainly try, but chances are that it won't work, except perhaps for the most insignificant of tasks; and even if it does, the effects most probably won't be enduring. For this reason it may be better to invest in other non-monetary forms of compensation, such as healthcare and leisure activities, training, greater participation in decision making, an agreeable corporate climate, help in achieving work–life balance, and so forth. Entrepreneurs need to count on a minimum subsistence level in society before they can engage in business ventures. Until then, it behooves local communities, welfare organizations, and states to assist people in obtaining the food, clothing, and shelter to which they have a right, in accordance with the principle of redistribution. Only after these basic needs are met could the market, in the sense of mutually beneficial free exchange, begin to function.

Knowledge regarding non-monetary motivators in consumption and satisfaction could be used to differentiate one's products in the marketplace. A lot has to do with intangible features that could enhance the consumer's experience of the product, such as providing greater information, offering a congenial customer service or assistance, suggesting exclusivity and a sense of community around the brand identity, and so forth. A shrewd marketing measure could even be the possibility of making a matching donation to a worthwhile philanthropic cause for every purchase, given the satisfaction consumers draw from helping others. In that case, doing good may also contribute to doing well in business.

Through the help of virtue, we are able to establish the particular optimal limit for each individual regarding income and other economic means conducive to happiness and flourishing. This is never an amount that can be fixed as an *a priori* through cold, scientific calculation exclusively. The degree of virtue one possesses (or lacks) in the end determines with how much (or how little) one is able to make do in order to thrive. What is important is that the order of intentionality or finality be safeguarded: it's money and income for the sake of wellbeing and flourishing, and not the other way around.

A closer look at desires and wants and their impact on happiness disabuses us of myths regarding the sovereignty of choices and the consumer. Although choices are indispensable to the exercise of freedom, more choices do not necessarily lead to greater utility or satisfaction. There are psychological limits to the number of choices human beings are able to process and find meaningful for actual decision making. Moreover, individuals do not always know what is best for them; nor do they unfailingly choose it. Preferences may not be reflected in decisions or choices; nor do these incontrovertibly capture what is objectively useful or good. For this reason, it becomes exigent to educate desires and wants, to orient freedom toward the good. This can be done through the help of experts in every given field, who can guide us through a carefully designed training process. In this effort, not only the "choice architecture" should be borne in mind, but also the individual's gradual progress in acquiring the requisite skills. Behind all this certainly lurks the danger of manipulation, just like in any other educational task, and so far, there is no effective safeguard against it, outside of moral integrity.

Chapter 3, "Choice, desire, and pleasure: is happiness getting what you want or wanting what you get?" alerts us to the presence of externalities, both positive and negative, in our decisions and behaviors. Despite our best efforts, we cannot live isolated from the rest, and whatever we do has repercussions on other people's happiness.

It is but fair that we face up to these responsibilities and acknowledge them as natural limits to our freedom. Inexorably, human beings
undergo a process of adaptation – more quickly to material objects
than to experiences or events – as a result of which a greater amount
or a more intense stimulus is needed in time, to generate just the same
degree of pleasure or satisfaction. Keeping this is mind should help
managers experiment with different ways of remunerating and moti-
vating workers, centering on the human significance of their offer
and not only on its monetary value. Such knowledge is also useful to
entrepreneurs in order to present enough variety and differentiation
in their products.

At the same time, entrepreneurs confront the inescapable challenge of educating consumers regarding the unique value-bundles
they propose. This requires careful thought concerning the number
of significant options they put out in the market, besides sensitivity
and respect for the dignity of consumers. Oftentimes, such educational objectives are not attained in a single attempt, requiring
instead a repeated, long-term relationship. Only a strong and genuine
commitment to the client or consumer's good generates loyalty in
reciprocation.

Virtue results from the proper education of choices and desires,
such that they are geared toward the human being's final end, which
is none other than happiness. All too often experience demonstrates
just how easily one's wants and desires run amok, so that they even
prove self-destructive. Virtue reins these passions in, ensuring that
both their force and direction are under adequate rational control.
The objective is not simply to squelch them, as we are always in need
of their vital force, but to orient them through the right channels,
such that they assist our higher goals: passion at the service of reason.

True happiness belongs to the entire human being composed
of body and soul, reason and free will, mind and brain. Furthermore,
it has to exist in the present, such that the mere memory or fantasy
of happiness will not do. For this reason, perhaps, happiness is
confused by many with pleasure and joyful feeling, which can only be

experienced in the now. However, it is not even actual pleasure, but its memory or prediction that influences us in our choices and decision making. Beyond the evanescence of joys and pleasures lies a more enduring and atemporal dimension of happiness as life-satisfaction and flow. Wanting to be steeped exclusively in positive emotions estranges one from real life, and there is much to be benefited and learned from negative emotions as well. But over and above these two levels is the normative ideal of happiness, as the voluntary fulfillment of one's human potential. This includes not only the successful result or outcome, but also the persevering struggle through the cultivation of the right habits to achieve worthwhile aims or goals. Mainly because of this, we are able to detect the falsehood behind promises of instant happiness through purely biotechnological means.

Chapter 4, "The biotechnology of happiness: not just a 'quick fix'," reminds us of the continuum that exists between anatomy, physiology, and psychology in human beings. It also underscores the importance of facing up to challenges and exerting effort to reach one's objectives, instead of just passively being afforded them, as if it were almost an entitlement. We seldom value what we haven't worked for. An attentive analysis of the rules governing experiences and valuation in decision making (duration neglect, peak-end rule, and violation of dominance) provides business people with insights into how best to sell their wares, touching on the "four Ps" (product, place, price, and promotion) of the "marketing mix." Many of these principles are counterintuitive and there are certain cognitive and perceptual illusions from which we cannot rid ourselves (prospection, subjectivity, realism, "presentism," and rationalization). Yet they are rules just the same, and bearing them in mind is certainly advantageous for whoever is engaged in entrepreneurial activities or interested in consumer behavior. At the same time, we realize the inevitability of evaluating competing, rival versions of happiness against some ethical standard.

Perhaps because pleasures can be so maddeningly absorbing, they emphasize just how much we need the virtues in order to experience them properly. For indeed, one could not be truly happy if the intensity and variety of pleasures were such that they were to over-come him to the point of losing himself; living in continuous ecstasy, as it were. Neither would one be satisfied if he were sunk in near abso-lute depression and apathy. Like in most other things, we'd also have to seek the "golden mean" of virtue amongst pleasures. This means taking delight in the noble things and within suitable circumstances, for the appropriate reasons and to the degree that is fitting; in short, exactly in the way that a virtuous person would.

The ambivalent attitude of human beings toward work piques curiosity about how employment actually affects happiness. Depend-ing on one's assumptions, such will be the policy promoted: *laissez-faire*, if one believes that unemployment is largely voluntary, and gov-ernment intervention, if one believes that it is not. The recent global economic crisis has heightened the need to discover the real score behind this issue, with its conflicting recommendations of providing a fiscal stimulus and promoting deficitary spending, on the one hand, and embracing austerity and enacting cut-backs, on the other. Be that as it may, the employed seem to be happier than the unemployed, who have to suffer both individual and social costs. There seems to be a fair amount of truth behind the "right to work" insofar as this is linked to human dignity. At the same time, we cannot be blind to work-associated stressors (some job-specific, others organization-specific, some objective and environmental, others subjective and personal) that diminish happiness, both in the professional domain and in life in general. In work as well as in leisure, happiness is more closely linked to intrinsic motivation (autonomy, mastery, and purpose) than to extrinsic motivation. And in certain kinds of activities, such as those which require even the most basic cognitive skills, introduc-ing extrinsic motivators destroys, rather than enhances, the effect of intrinsic motivators. Also, contrary to neoclassical economic predic-tions, we find that inflation exerts a much diminished influence on happiness compared to unemployment.

"Working on happiness" offers valuable insights not only to entrepreneurs but to politicians and other public policy makers as well, regarding the importance of creating employment and job opportunities. In fact, the creation of "decent work" may even be, arguably, the entrepreneur's single, most important contribution to social welfare and the common good. This consists in:

> work that expresses the essential dignity of every man and woman in the context of their particular society; work that is freely chosen, effectively associating workers, both men and women, with the development of their community; work that enables the worker to be respected and free from any form of discrimination; work that makes it possible for families to meet their need and provide schooling for their children, without the children themselves being forced into labor; work that permits the workers to organize themselves freely, and to make their voices heard; work that leaves enough room for rediscovering one's roots at a personal, familial and spiritual level; work that guarantees those who have retired a decent standard of living.
>
> (Benedict XVI, Caritas in veritate, 63)

Managers would do well to take note of the superiority of intrinsic motivation to extrinsic motivation, and the fact that, beyond the performance of rudimentary, mechanical tasks, extrinsic motivators drive out or corrupt intrinsic motivators. Inasmuch as inflation directly affects the purchasing power of income, it refers to an extrinsic motivator. On the whole, a safer, default option, then, is to suppose that employees actually like the work they're doing and that they're eager to improve. Hence, it's management's main responsibility to get out of the way. Managers should likewise pay attention to the different job and organizational features that affect workplace satisfaction, as well as the particular "chemistry" among them. From the perspective of happiness, work and leisure are not opposites; nor do they produce contrary effects. So long as intrinsic motivation is present, leisure, too, could be harnessed to favor work-satisfaction and performance.

Virtue becomes equally relevant to both work and leisure insofar as they allow for characterizations as *praxeis*: that is, as activities realized for their own sakes, and not for anything external or ulterior to them, such as their material products (their objective dimension). They will be able to contribute constitutively to genuine human flourishing or happiness to the precise extent that they provide individuals with a chance to develop knowledge, skills, habits, and virtues (their subjective dimension). Any kind of work or form of leisure will always be alienating or inhuman unless it acknowledges and upholds the superiority of the subjective dimension over the objective dimension. The experimental work in modern psychology regarding the difference between extrinsic and intrinsic motivations seems to verify this same notion.

Granted that the correct attitude to happiness is an active and not a passive one, it comes as no surprise that voluntary participation in institutions is key. This is guaranteed in democratic political regimes through the different rights and freedoms afforded citizens, which allow them not only to take greater ownership of deliberative outcomes, but also to capture procedural utilities. Similarly with religious institutions, voluntary participation leads to greater happiness, as evidenced by the higher levels of satisfaction experienced by adherents of "open-market" faiths compared to those of traditional, "monopolistic" churches. People like to have an internal locus of control that permits them to meaningfully exercise autonomy. This generates plenty of positive affect and improved mental health. In any case, good governance of institutions – be they political or religious – is not so much a matter of rule following (*poiesis*) as of personal virtue (*praxis*) (Sison 2008).

Chapter 6 on "Happiness, politics, and religion: now and at the hour of our death" confirms what most entrepreneurs know by instinct, that greater voluntary participation in communal affairs brings a heightened sense of self-worth and satisfaction. That could be the main reason why they have embarked on a business venture all by themselves, shunning the security and comfort of receiving a fixed salary from a big and established corporation. It is true that if a business start-up were to fail, they would have no one else to blame but themselves; but it is equally true that if it were to succeed, they would receive all the praise and congratulations. There's no denying that the entrepreneurial path requires more hard work and discipline; it's not for the faint-hearted and risk-averse.

Managers, on the other hand, could learn never to underestimate worker initiative. Instead, it ought to be cleverly harnessed to serve organizational goals. Channels for worker participation should be institutionalized and encouraged, therefore. Bottom-up makes more sense and is ultimately more effective than a top-down, command-and-control leadership style. For this, organizational structure should be flatter and more egalitarian than hierarchical and with great power-distances. The uniqueness and value of each worker's contribution to organizational objectives has to be acknowledged and celebrated.

Due to its origins in economics, modern happiness studies starts off with a conception of individual subjective wellbeing as a function of consumption. In this it follows the dominant neoclassical school that inquires into the basket of goods and services an individual ought to purchase – given limited resources – in order to achieve maximum satisfaction. Little by little, however, modern happiness studies has found itself having to part ways with neoclassical economics, upon discovering the myriad contradictions to which such a line of thinking has led. The commodification of happiness and the adoption of a consumerist lifestyle, together with its underlying triad of assumptions on radical individualism, the absolutization of choice, and the deification of pleasure, have proved to be utterly self-defeating. At this stage, inputs from various branches of empirical psychology have been very helpful, insofar as they have re-oriented the search for happiness from merely "having" to "doing" or the performance of socially meaningful activities. However, this, too, has turned out to be thoroughly insufficient, because of the conflicts and contradictions among the multitude of purportedly self-fulfilling activities that individuals have proposed.

Here is where Aristotelian politics, which integrates both economy and ethics, comes in. Happiness is identified as the supreme good and final end of human life, to be attained only within the context of the political community. Hence, it is the object of politics. Yet, given the condition of human beings as rational animals, happiness requires both external as well as internal goods; hence the need for economy and ethics, respectively. (Business, which refers to the production of external goods, is subordinated to economy.) Virtues are put forward as the internal good *par excellence*, the controlling factor thanks to which external goods are properly acquired and used, such that they effectively allow us to reach happiness or flourishing (*eudaimonia*). As an acquired "second nature," virtues empower us to become our best selves, through the habitual exercise of reason and freedom. Similarly, virtues also permit us to participate in all collective pursuits, be it in the realm of politics or religion, in the right way, enhancing the strengths of other individuals and remedying their deficiencies.

Knowing one's final end or purpose in life provides indispensable guidance to one's "lesser activities" in the discrete domains of family and the professions, for instance. Chapter 7 on "Aristotelian virtue ethics: the forgotten philosophical tradition on happiness" accomplishes precisely this. It lays out the "architecture of happiness" along the different realms of human activity, from the family through intermediate institutions all the way to the political community and civil society. It helps entrepreneurs and managers understand both the objective and subjective meanings or dimensions of their work, supplying a context for their actions. Above all, it speaks of the integrative power of virtue, that multi-track disposition that constitutes the vital link with authentic human flourishing. Elsewhere, virtue has been described as a form of capital, particularly "moral capital," insofar as it constitutes a resource that grows and accumulates in time through investments of work and money from which alternative uses can be drawn in the future (Sison 2003). Now we realize that virtue also represents the ultimate value proposition in business.

* * *

What do we need virtue for in happiness? Virtue allows us to distinguish genuine happiness from its counterfeits, and thus make sense of the various indicators and measures available. It helps us discern the limits to which material resources such as income may contribute to our own flourishing. With virtue we can choose which pleasures and satisfactions are truly worthwhile pursuing. Virtue also reminds us that who we become through our work is much more important and valuable than whatever we may produce. And finally, virtue teaches us that happiness is a common good that one can only attain in concert with all the other members of the political community. Happiness cannot be achieved alone or with one's back turned to others. One's own happiness depends on others just as much as every other individual's happiness depends on one.

REFERENCES

Benedict XVI 2009. *Caritas in veritate*, www.vatican.va/holy_father/benedict_xvi/encyclicals/documents/hf_ben-xvi_enc_20090629_caritas-in-veritate_en.html, accessed March 18, 2014.

Sison, A. J. G. 2003. *The moral capital of leaders: Why virtue matters*. Cheltenham, UK/Northampton, MA: Edward Elgar.

2008. *Corporate governance and ethics: An Aristotelian approach*. Cheltenham, UK/Northampton, MA: Edward Elgar.

Index